SUCCESS
UNLEASHED

Elevating Your Journey to Exceptional Success

Steven B. Bryant

Copyright © 2024 by Steven B. Bryant. All rights reserved.

Printed in the United States of America. Except as permitted under the United States Copyright Act of 1976, no part of this publication may be reproduced or distributed in any form or by any means, or stored in a database or retrieval system, without the prior written permission of the publisher or copyright holder. Additionally, this publication mentions trademarks and copyrights such as V2MOM, originally developed by Marc Benioff, the Four Quadrants, conceptualized by Stephen Covey, and the Wheel of Life, a widely recognized personal development tool. These are acknowledged herein as the property of their respective owners. If any copyrights have not been explicitly mentioned, they remain the property of their rightful holders.

ISBN: 978-0-9962409-3-2

Publisher ID: 05072024-01

Cover Image generated by OpenAI's ChatGPT

10 9 8 7 6 5 4 3 2 1

To my father, Cottery, in loving memory,

Thank you for being the exemplary role model I've always admired, for instilling in me the courage to embrace life's adventures, and for showing me that the strength to overcome is found in our love for others and the legacy we build and leave behind.

Table of Contents

Preface — xi
    The Genesis of the Book — xi
    Why Read This Book? — xii
    Harnessing the Power of AI — xiii
    About The Author — xiv
    Your Invitation to Success — xiv

Charting Your Success Journey — 1
    Defining Success — 2
    Let Your Imagination Soar — 3
    A Life in Balance — 7
    Vivid Details Make a Difference — 10
    Setting Goals: Your Roadmap to Success — 14
    Navigating Life's Twists and Turns — 17

Navigating the College Experience — 21
    Choosing the Right Path — 22
    Academic Excellence — 25
    Campus Involvement — 28
    Networking and Relationships — 30
    Internships and Practical Experience — 33
    Financial Management — 36
    Well-Being and Self-Care — 38
    Study Abroad and Global Exposure — 40
    Preparation for the Future — 42
    Reflection and Adaptation — 45
    Life Skills — 47
    Charting Your Course Beyond College — 50

Navigating Your Career — 53
    Understanding Your Passions and Skills — 54

Uncovering Your Career Passion	56
Exploring Career Options	60
Educational Pathways	62
Exploring Military Options	65
Building Your Personal Brand	67
Networking Strategies	70
Crafting Resumes and Cover Letters	73
Interview Preparation	76
Navigating Job Offers	78
Navigating Workplace Success	81
Navigating Career Advancement	84
Strategies for Navigating Career Setbacks	87
Mastering Work–Life Balance	90
Conclusion	92
Navigating Your Retirement	**95**
Late-Stage Career Planning	96
Financial Preparedness for Retirement	98
Healthcare Considerations	101
Lifestyle Vision for Retirement	104
Emotional and Psychological Preparation	107
Estate Planning	109
Social Connections and Community	112
Continual Learning and Growth	114
Retirement Transitions	116
Your Action Plan	118
Conclusion	121
The Power of Discipline and Habits	**123**
Understanding Discipline	124
The Science of Habits	125
Identifying Key Habits	128
Building New Habits	130
Breaking Bad Habits	132
Discipline in Practice	135
Rituals and Routines	137

Accountability and Tracking	140
Overcoming Challenges	142
Conclusion	145

Mastering Your Time for Maximum Impact — 147

The Value of Time	148
Time Audit: Mapping Your Minutes	149
Prioritization	151
Guardrails for Productivity and Well-being	153
Effective Planning: Charting a Course for Success	155
Delegation: Multiplying Your Success	157
Reclaiming Your Momentum	159
Harnessing Digital Tools for Success	161
Fine-Tuning Your Path to Success	163
Embarking on Your Journey to Next-Level Success	166

The Catalyst of Action — 167

The Power of Taking Action	168
Overcoming Inertia	170
The Action-Oriented Mindset	172
From Planning to Execution	174
Measuring and Adjusting Actions	176
Call to Action: Ignite Your Journey	180
Conclusion	182

Building Financial Resilience — 183

Understanding Financial Basics	184
Budgeting and Money Management	186
Emergency Fund and Safety Nets	188
Debt Management and Credit Health	191
Savings and Investment Basics	193
Income Diversification	196
Financial Planning for Major Life Events	198
Insurance and Protection	201
Navigating Financial Challenges	203
Building a Financial Legacy	205

Empower Your Financial Future	207
Conclusion: Financial Resilience and Legacy	210

Cultivating Meaningful Relationships — 211

The Role of Relationships in Success	212
Types of Relationships	214
Building New Relationships	216
Deepening Existing Relationships	218
Conflict Resolution	220
The Impact of Social Media	223
Letting Go of Toxic Relationships	225
Mentorship and Guidance	227
Community Engagement	229
Conclusion	231

Thriving: Health as Success Leverage — 233

Holistic Health Overview	234
Nutrition and Success	237
Physical Activity's Impact	239
Mental Health and Mindfulness	241
Sleep's Role in Success	243
Avoiding Burnout	246
Substance Use and Abuse	248
Regular Health Check-ups	250
Action Plan for Health	252
Conclusion	255

Beyond Obstacles: Turning Setbacks into Success — 257

Historical Successes Born from Failure	258
Analyzing Setbacks	259
The Role of Resilience	261
Learning and Growing from Challenges	263
Action Plans for Recovery	265
Maintaining Motivation	267
Harnessing Setbacks for Greater Success	270

Your Next Level – Reflecting and Moving Forward   **271**
   Reflection on the Journey   272
   Celebrating Achievements   273
   Assessing Unmet Goals: Pathways to Progress   274
   Growth and Transformation   276
   Setting New Horizons: Charting Your Ascent   279
   Building a Support System: Your Success Network   282
   Giving Back: Extending Your Success   285
   Final Words of Encouragement   287

Voices of Experience   **289**

Preface

As I reflect on the formative years of my life, standing on the precipice of adulthood, I'm reminded of a pivotal moment that significantly shaped my path. It was upon my high school graduation that I received a gift that would illuminate my journey forward – a book titled "*Successfully Yours*" by Stephen A. Brennen. This book was more than mere words on paper; it was a beacon of wisdom, a treasure trove of insights and encouragement, guiding me to invest in the most significant project of my life, which he called: "You, Inc." Decades have passed, yet my copy, with its yellowed pages and softened spine, remains a cherished source of guidance and inspiration.

The profound impact of "Successfully Yours" on my life is indelible, yet, the book has long been out of print. Despite this, the principles it espoused, the encouragement it provided, and the vision it inspired are timeless. Motivated by a desire to pass the torch of knowledge and inspiration to the next generation, I embarked on a journey akin to Brennen's, crafting this book with you—the dreamers and doers of today – in mind.

The Genesis of the Book

While the inception of this book can be traced back to my high school graduation, I now sit at the other end of life, soon ready to write new chapters ultimately leading to a fulfilling retirement. I often ask, *"If I could go back in time and provide advice to my younger self, what would I say?"* This book, in large part, is the answer to that question. Success Unleashed is a confluence of inspiration, personal evolution, and a profound commitment to sharing the wisdom of success with a new generation.

My journey with "Successfully Yours" planted the seed for this endeavor. It was a mentor in paper form, guiding me through the complexities of young adulthood and laying the foundation for my understanding of success; a foundation I hope this book now lays for you.

The vision for this book is to create a bridge between generations, to distill the essence of timeless success principles into a format that resonates with the aspirations and challenges of today's adults – young, mid-career, or transitioning into retirement. This vision is not just about replicating the past – such as simply recreating Brennen's book and messages – but about infusing it with contemporary insights, experiences, and the transformative potential of technology.

Why Read This Book?

In a world brimming with self-help literature and success manuals, you might wonder what sets this book apart and why it deserves a place on your reading list. The answer lies in its unique approach to weaving the timeless threads of success principles with the vibrant, dynamic fabric of contemporary life and technology.

This book offers a fresh perspective on success, tailored for the modern era yet grounded in timeless wisdom. It transcends the conventional one-size-fits-all approach, recognizing that success is as diverse as the individuals pursuing it. Whether you're a college student standing on the brink of adulthood, a young professional navigating the early stages of your career, or simply someone who seeks to infuse your life with greater purpose and achievement, this book speaks to you.

Unlike books that focus solely on financial success or career advancement, this guide takes a holistic view, addressing the multifaceted nature of personal and professional growth. It delves into essential life domains – health, relationships, financial literacy, time management, and more – offering a comprehensive blueprint for a balanced, fulfilling life.

This book is replete with actionable insights and practical strategies, moving beyond theoretical discussions to provide concrete steps you can take to actualize your goals. Each chapter is designed to not only inspire but also to equip you with the tools necessary to turn inspiration into action.

Consider this book a mentor that guides you through the complexities of modern life. Its pages are filled with the distilled wisdom of years of experience, research, and observation. It's designed to be a companion on your journey to success, offering encouragement, wisdom, and support every step of the way.

Harnessing the Power of AI

The process of bringing this book to fruition is a testament to the power of collaboration, making it a mosaic of perspectives that reflect the complexity of success in today's world. In an innovative twist, this book harnesses the capabilities of Artificial Intelligence (AI), blending human insight with machine intelligence to enrich the content. This collaboration ensures a depth and breadth of content that is both engaging and informative, offering a perspective that is at the cutting edge of today's technological possibilities.

The integration of generative AI has been instrumental in refining the content, ensuring a coherent and enriched narrative. This partnership with AI has brought about an unprecedented efficiency in the writing and editorial process, allowing for the transition from concept to publication in mere months instead of years.

However, it's essential to consider the use of AI with ethical consideration, especially in maintaining the authenticity and originality of content. In crafting this book, AI served as a tool to augment and enhance the material, never overshadowing the genuine contributions that form its core.

Steven's enthusiasm for Human–AI Collaboration is at the core of his innovative approach to problem-solving and creativity. He is a pioneer in leveraging state-of-the-art generative AI tools, like OpenAI's ChatGPT, to augment human capabilities. This book itself stands as a testament to the incredible potential of such collaborations, showcasing how AI can be used not only as a tool but as a co-author in the literary process.

About The Author

Steven Bryant's professional journey spans four decades, beginning with humble roles such as a computer ribbon re-inker and warehouse stockperson, culminating in senior leadership positions within leading financial services and consulting firms. Steven's academic journey includes a Master of Science in Computer Science from the Georgia Institute of Technology and a Master of Business Administration from the University of San Diego. This diverse experience has endowed Steven with a wealth of practical insights and a profound understanding of the corporate landscape where people, technology, and business intersect.

Additionally, Steven is deeply committed to education both as a lifelong learner and as an educator. As a faculty member in the College of Computing at the Georgia Institute of Technology, he plays a pivotal role in shaping the minds of over 3,000 students each year. He has a passion for teaching and translating complex concepts into accessible knowledge.

As a mentor, Steven has guided high school seniors transitioning to college, college seniors stepping into the workforce, and professionals ascending the career ladder. His mentorship is built on a foundation of empathy, encouragement, and strategic guidance, having influenced countless individuals who have gone on to become influential leaders and entrepreneurs.

Your Invitation to Success

This book is an invitation to embark on a journey of self-discovery and empowerment. It aims to ignite a spark within you, inspiring you to challenge yourself, to rise above the ordinary, and to embrace a life of fulfillment and success. Through these pages, you will be provided with tools to nurture your heart, enrich your mind, invigorate your body, and uplift your soul.

While we may explore these facets separately, remember that they are intricately woven together, each contributing to the symphony of "You."

Like Brennen's book, which remains an ongoing source of personal inspiration, this book concludes with a tapestry of voices and experiences, providing a broad spectrum of perspectives on success. It's not just a singular narrative but a chorus of insights from various individuals who have navigated their paths to achievement, offering a rich, multifaceted view of what success can look like.

In essence, this book is an invitation to explore the dimensions of success beyond conventional definitions, to embrace the potential within you and the opportunities afforded by the modern world. It is a beacon for those navigating the journey of life, seeking to achieve success in its myriad forms. It's a guide for those who dare to dream, to aspire, and to achieve—empowering you to write your own success story in the vibrant hues of your individuality and the dynamic context of the 21st century.

As you turn these pages, you are invited to embark on this journey with an open heart and a curious mind, ready to explore the landscapes of success that lie ahead. May this book help you find what it means to live a life of purpose, achievement, and fulfillment in an ever-changing world.

Chapter 1

Charting Your Success Journey

Embarking on the journey of success is much like setting sail on the vast ocean of possibilities. It requires not just a destination in mind but also a keen understanding of the vessel you command — yourself. This chapter is designed to be your compass and map, guiding you through the intricate process of defining what success truly means to you, setting your course with clear, achievable goals, and navigating through the inevitable storms and calm seas with resilience and adaptability.

Success, as you'll soon discover, is not a one-size-fits-all destination but a highly personal voyage that varies from one individual to another. It's about understanding where you stand today, envisioning where you want to be, and meticulously plotting the course to get there. This chapter will help you peel back the layers to uncover what truly resonates with your inner aspirations and values.

Through a blend of introspective exercises, practical advice, and inspiring success stories, we'll embark on a journey to set the foundations of a fulfilling and successful life. Whether you're navigating the challenges of college, the early stages of your career, or simply seeking a more directed path in life, the insights within these pages will empower you to take the helm of your destiny.

As you turn these pages, you'll be invited to craft a vivid vision for your future, one that encompasses all facets of a well-rounded life. From the heights of professional achievement to the depths of personal growth, every aspect of your vision will be explored and expanded upon. With each step, you'll be building a more detailed and actionable roadmap, equipped with the tools and resilience needed to overcome obstacles and adapt to the ever-changing landscapes of life.

So, take a deep breath and prepare to dive into the depths of your own potential. The journey to your version of success starts here, with the first step being a commitment to yourself to pursue a life of meaning, purpose, and joy.

Defining Success

Embarking on a journey toward a future filled with your dreams and aspirations begins with a solid foundation of self-awareness. Once you have a clear picture of where you stand today, the exciting part starts – sketching out a vibrant vision of your future. Think of this vision as your personal north star, illuminating the path to the life you dream of living. We'll explore the art of painting a future that's not only bright but also deeply connected to who you are and what you cherish. And don't worry, we'll introduce some handy tools and techniques to help you navigate each step.

Creating a vision is like painting on a vast canvas, where your hopes, dreams, and deepest desires come together in a beautiful mosaic of your future life. It's more than a to-do list of goals; it's a heartfelt narrative of the life you yearn for, filled with color, emotion, and texture. This vision becomes your source of energy and motivation, a guiding light that keeps you focused and resilient, especially when the going gets tough.

Dreaming Up Your Ideal Tomorrow

1. **Let Your Imagination Soar**: Kick things off by dreaming big. Imagine a world where anything is possible for you. What would you do if there were no barriers? What

career would you have if the amount you earn was unchanged, regardless of the job you performed? This limitless thinking is the key to uncovering what you truly desire. We'll introduce techniques like mind mapping and vision boards to help unlock your imagination and explore your deepest aspirations without constraints.
2. **A Life in Balance**: Craft a vision that covers all the important areas of your life, from your career and personal development to your relationships, health, and passions. Striving for balance ensures a life that's not just successful but also rich and fulfilling. To aid in this holistic approach, we'll guide you through the Wheel of Life exercise, a powerful tool for ensuring your vision encompasses a well-rounded and satisfying life. We also introduce the "Seven Whys?" questioning technique to uncover what motivates you.
3. **Vivid Details Make a Difference**: The more vivid and detailed your vision, the more magnetic it becomes. Don't just outline what you want to achieve; immerse yourself in the feelings, impacts, and personal growth that come with it. We'll explore techniques like the V2MOMA and detailed journaling to help you paint a detailed and compelling picture of your ideal future.

Ensuring your vision is deeply intertwined with your core values is crucial. True success is most rewarding when it reflects what truly matters to you. Your values lay the foundation for a vision that not only drives you forward but also brings genuine fulfillment and purpose to your achievements. We'll explore exercises to help you identify and integrate your core values into your vision, making sure your future aligns with what's genuinely important to you.

Let Your Imagination Soar

Embarking on the journey to your ideal future begins with a single, empowering step: allowing your imagination to soar. Picture a reality where the sky's the limit, where every dream is within reach, and obstacles are merely steppingstones. What paths would you explore if nothing stood in your way? This boundless exploration is the foundation upon which your true desires and deepest aspirations are built.

To navigate this expansive landscape of possibilities, we introduce two powerful techniques: mind mapping and vision boards. These tools are designed to unlock your creative potential and bring your dreams into sharper focus.

Mind Mapping: Your Imagination's Compass

Mind mapping is a dynamic tool that mirrors the radiant thinking of your brain, allowing ideas to flow freely in all directions. Here's how you can harness its power:

1. **Start with Your Core Dream**: At the center of your mind map, write down a statement of your core dream or aspiration. This is the seed from which all other ideas will sprout.
2. **Branch Out**: From this central idea, draw branches for different areas of your life that your dream touches upon—career, personal growth, relationships, hobbies, and health. Let each branch represent a broad category related to your vision.
3. **Explore Sub-branches**: From each main branch, extend sub-branches that represent specific goals, desires, or aspects within that category. Allow your thoughts to flow without judgment, capturing even the most whimsical ideas.
4. **Use Colors and Images**: Engage your right brain by adding colors, images, and symbols. This not only makes your mind map visually appealing but also enhances your emotional connection to the ideas it represents.
5. **Revisit and Expand**: Your mind map is a living document. Revisit it regularly to add new insights or refine existing ones. Over time, it will evolve into a comprehensive map of your aspirations.

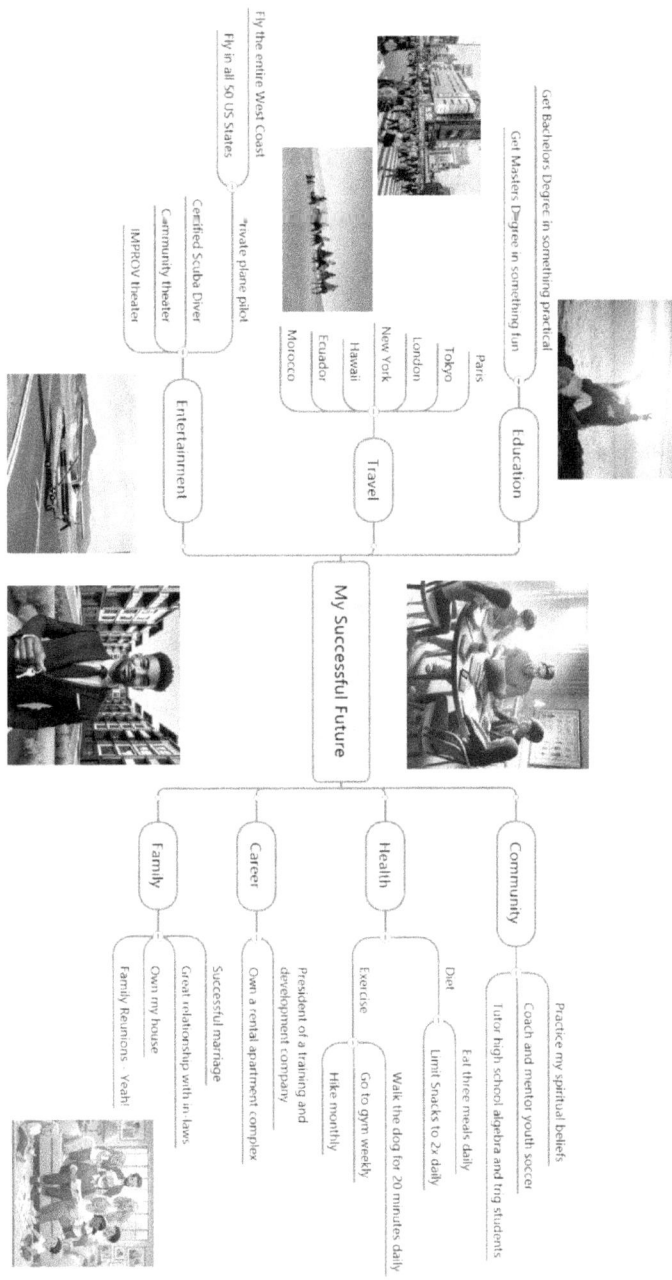

Example Mindmap

Vision Boards: Your Dreams in Pictures

A vision board is a tangible representation of your aspirations, crafted from images, quotes, and items that inspire and motivate you. Creating a vision board can turn abstract dreams into concrete visuals, making your goals feel closer and more attainable.

1. **Gather Inspiration**: Collect images that resonate with your dreams and goals. These can come from magazines, photographs, or online sources. Look for visuals that spark joy and excitement within you.
2. **Choose a Canvas**: Decide on the format of your vision board. This could be a physical board, like a corkboard or poster board, or a digital version using a platform like Pinterest.
3. **Arrange Your Vision**: Start placing your images and quotes on your board. There's no right or wrong way to do this—let your intuition guide the layout. Each piece should contribute to the overall feeling of achieving your dreams.
4. **Make It Visible**: Place your vision board somewhere you'll see it every day. This constant visual reminder can serve as daily inspiration, keeping your aspirations at the forefront of your mind.
5. **Update as You Grow**: As your journey unfolds, your dreams and goals might shift. Feel free to add, remove, or rearrange elements on your vision board to reflect your evolving vision.

Example Vision Board

By incorporating mind mapping and vision boards into your process, you're not just dreaming; you're actively designing a future that resonates with your deepest desires and aspirations. These tools don't just clarify your vision—they invite the universe to start conspiring in making your dreams a reality. So, let your imagination take flight and watch as the life you've always dreamed of begins to unfold before your eyes.

A Life in Balance

Achieving your dreams isn't just about hitting professional milestones or financial targets; it's about nurturing every aspect of your life to create a rich tapestry of experiences and relationships. A truly successful life is one that's well-rounded, fulfilling, and in harmony with your deepest values and passions.

To help you craft a vision that encapsulates this holistic approach, we introduce two invaluable tools: the Wheel of Life exercise and the "Seven Whys?" questioning technique.

The Wheel of Life Exercise

The Wheel of Life is a visual tool that helps you assess and reflect upon different areas of your life, ensuring a balanced approach to your vision. Here's how to create and use your Wheel of Life:

1. **Draw a Circle**: Begin by drawing a large circle on a piece of paper, dividing it into ten equal segments. You'll see a template on the next page. Each segment represents a different area of your life, such as career, personal growth, relationships, health, finances, leisure, environment, and spirituality or values.
2. **Assess Each Area**: For each segment, rate your current level of satisfaction on a scale of 1 to 10, where 1 is completely dissatisfied and 10 is fully satisfied. Mark your score within each segment.
3. **Connect the Dots**: Join the marks in each segment to create a new outer edge for your wheel. This visual representation will show you which areas of your life are flourishing, and which may need more attention.
4. **Reflect and Plan**: Look at the areas with lower scores and reflect on what changes or goals could improve your satisfaction in these areas. This reflection will guide you in setting more balanced and holistic goals for your vision.

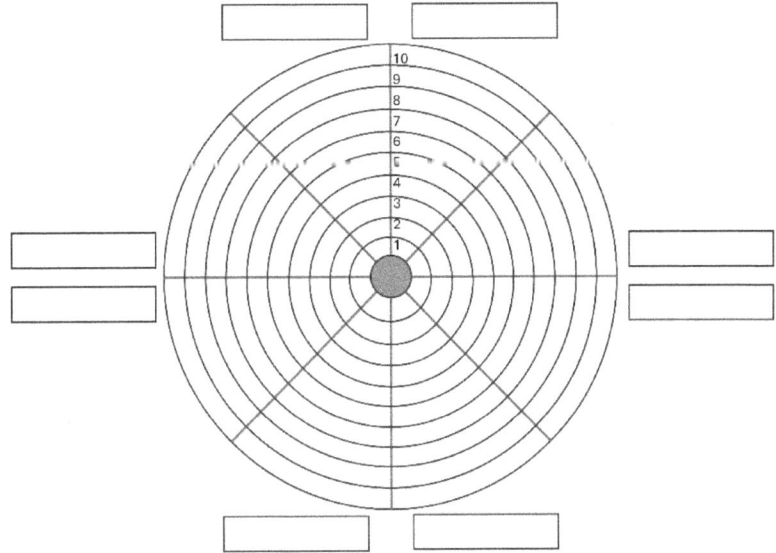

Wheel of Life Template

The "Seven Whys?" Questioning Technique

To ensure that your vision aligns deeply with your personal values and motivations, employ the "Seven Whys?" technique. This questioning process helps you drill down to the core reasons behind your goals, ensuring they resonate with what truly matters to you.

1. **Start with a Goal**: Begin with a statement of one of your goals or a part of your vision.
2. **Ask "Why?"**: Ask yourself, "Why is this important to me?" Write down your answer.
3. **Go Deeper**: Take the answer you've just written and ask "Why?" again. Repeat this process a total of seven times, each time using the last answer as the starting point for the next "Why?".
4. **Discover Your Core Why**: By the time you reach the seventh "Why?", you should arrive at a fundamental reason that is deeply meaningful and motivational to

you. This core "Why" reflects your underlying values and can be a powerful driver in pursuing your vision.

Using the Wheel of Life, you can visualize the balance (or lack thereof) in your current life, which helps in setting goals that encompass all areas of your well-being. The "Seven Whys?" technique then ensures that each goal within your vision is deeply rooted in your personal values and core motivations.

Together, these exercises offer a comprehensive approach to crafting a life vision that's not only ambitious and exciting but also balanced and deeply fulfilling. They encourage you to consider success not just in terms of career achievements or financial wealth, but as a harmonious blend of personal growth, relationships, health, and happiness.

Your self-assessment is not a one-time activity but an ongoing process. As you grow, achieve goals, and face new challenges, your strengths, vision, and underlying reasons "why" will evolve. Regularly revisiting your self-assessment ensures that your strategies and goals remain aligned with your current capabilities and aspirations.

Through thoughtful self-assessment, you gain the self-awareness necessary to navigate your path to success more effectively. Understanding your starting point allows you to chart a course that leverages your strengths, builds your weaknesses, and remains attractive and compelling, setting the stage for meaningful growth and achievement.

Vivid Details Make a Difference

In crafting your vision for the future, the devil truly is in the details. A vision that's rich in detail doesn't just outline what you want to achieve; it pulls you into a vivid tableau of your future life, complete with the emotions, sensations, and transformations that accompany your goals. This immersive approach turns your vision from a mere sketch into a compelling force, drawing you towards your ideal future with irresistible clarity and purpose. To help you infuse your vision with this level of detail, we delve into two powerful techniques: the V2MOMA framework and detailed journaling.

The V2MOMA Framework

The V2MOMA framework, adapted from Marc Benioff's V2MOM framework, is a structured approach that helps you articulate a clear and detailed vision by breaking it down into key components: Vision, Values, Methods, Obstacles, Measures, and Assets. Here's how to apply each element to your vision:

1. **Vision:** Define your goal in vivid detail. Instead of stating, "I want to be successful," paint a picture of what success looks like for you. Where are you? Who are you with? What are you doing? The more descriptive, the better it be in helping you to imagine the vision coming to life.
2. **Values:** Identify the core values driving your vision. How do these values manifest in your ideal future? Describe scenarios where your values come to life in your daily activities, relationships, and personal achievements.
3. **Methods:** Detail the high-level strategies and actions you'll employ to realize your vision. Describe these methods in action—imagine yourself executing your plan and overcoming challenges with skill and determination.
4. **Obstacles:** Anticipate potential challenges and visualize yourself navigating these hurdles. How do you feel? What resources do you draw upon? Illustrating these moments strengthens your resolve and prepares you for the road ahead.
5. **Measures:** Set clear benchmarks for success and envision reaching them. Picture the moment of achievement and the sense of accomplishment that comes with it. What does it look like? How do you celebrate?
6. **Assets:** Reflect on the strengths and resources you already possess that will aid your journey. Visualize yourself utilizing these assets to their fullest potential, enhancing your path to success.

> **V2MOMA for George Washington: Founding the United States**
>
> **Vision**
> - Establish a free, independent, and self-governing nation where democracy and liberty flourish.
>
> **Values**
> - Liberty
> - Democracy
> - Unity
> - Justice
> - Perseverance
>
> **Methods**
> - Lead the Continental Army to victory against British Forces.
> - Facilitate the drafting and ratification of the U.S. Constitution.
> - Set foundational precedents as the first President.
>
> **Obstacles**
> - Overcoming superior British military power.
> - Unifying diverse colonies with different interests.
> - Establish a stable post-war government.
>
> **Measures**
> - Successful independence from Britian.
> - Ratification of the U.S. Constitution.
> - Establishment of a functional federal government.
>
> **Assets**
> - Personal leadership, integrity, and public trust.
> - Experience from military service.
> - Support from key figures (e.g., Franklin, Jefferson, Hamilton).
> - Revolutionary spirit among the colonies.

Example V2MOMA

I'd like to share the inspiring journey of Siggi Wilzig. Wilzig's story stands as a compelling example of leveraging one's inherent assets, even when external resources seem nonexistent. He arrived in the United States after surviving the atrocities of Auschwitz with nothing but his resilience, tenacity, and a vision for a better future. These intangible assets became the cornerstone of his success.

Wilzig transformed his life from a penniless immigrant to a prominent business leader, presiding over two New York Stock Exchange-listed companies: The Trust Company of New Jersey, which he grew into a $4 billion company, and Wilshire Oil

Company of Texas. His trajectory from surviving one of history's darkest periods to achieving remarkable business success epitomizes the essence of the "Assets" component in V2MOMA – highlighting that our most significant resources are often the qualities and experiences we carry within us.

It's clear that the V2MOMA framework offers a flexible and deeply personal blueprint for sculpting your path to success. It's designed to align with your core values, utilize your existing strengths, and adapt to your unique vision. The beauty of V2MOMA lies in its versatility—whether captured in simple bullet points during a flash of insight or elaborately presented in a vision board teeming with colors and images, the essence of V2MOMA is in its intention and thoughtfulness.

Your V2MOMA can be as dynamic and evolving as you are, changing and growing with you as you journey towards your goals. It's a living document that not only serves as a daily reminder of your objectives but also inspires continuous reflection and adaptation. Embrace the V2MOMA approach that resonates with you, ensuring it becomes a valuable companion in your quest for achievement and personal growth.

Detailed Journaling

Detailed journaling takes the vividness of your vision a step further by immersing you in the narrative of your future self. Through regular journal entries, you can explore different facets of your ideal life in depth, reinforcing the emotional and sensory aspects of your vision. Here's how to get started:

1. **Daily Entries**: Dedicate time each day to journal about your future life. Each entry can focus on a different aspect of your vision, from career achievements and personal growth to leisure and relationships.
2. **Sensory Details**: Incorporate all five senses into your entries. What do you see, hear, taste, touch, and smell in your ideal future? The more sensory details you include, the more real and attainable your vision feels.
3. **Emotional Landscape**: Dive into the emotions associated with your vision. How do you feel when you achieve your goals? What are the emotional highs and

lows along the way? Capturing these emotions adds depth and authenticity to your vision.
4. **First-Person Narrative**: Write from the first-person perspective to enhance the personal connection to your vision. Use present-tense verbs to create a sense of immediacy and engagement.

By combining the structured approach of the V2MOMA framework with the immersive experience of detailed journaling, you'll create a vision that's not only clear and comprehensive but also deeply moving and motivational. This vivid and detailed vision becomes a living, breathing part of your everyday life, constantly guiding and inspiring you toward the future you desire.

Setting Goals: Your Roadmap to Success

With a clear understanding of your personal success criteria, the journey forward involves translating that vision into tangible, actionable goals. Think of goals as the signposts along your journey—they offer direction, spur motivation, and break down your overarching vision into achievable segments. This section will guide you through the art and science of effective goal setting, introducing proven techniques and strategies to ensure your goals are both inspiring and attainable.

The Art of Goal Setting

Goal setting is a delicate balance between daring to dream big and grounding those dreams. It's about setting goals that stretch your abilities without straying into the realm of the unattainable. The sweet spot lies in goals that are sufficiently challenging to excite you but realistic enough to be within your grasp, with clarity to guide your steps and significance to fuel your drive.

SMART Goals Framework

The SMART framework is a time-tested approach that brings structure and trackability to the goal-setting process. Here's how to apply it:

- **Specific:** Craft goals with precision and clarity. Instead of a vague aspiration like "I want to improve my health," specify "I aim to run a 5K in under 30 minutes within six months."
- **Measurable:** Attach quantifiable indicators to your goals. This could be numerical targets, deadlines, or other criteria that allow you to track your progress and know definitively when you've achieved your goal.
- **Achievable:** Set goals that are ambitious yet within the realm of possibility, considering your current capabilities and resources. If a goal seems too distant, break it down into smaller, more immediate objectives that build towards the ultimate aim.
- **Relevant:** Align your goals with your overarching life vision and values. This alignment ensures that each goal propels you not just towards a specific achievement, but towards a more fulfilling life.
- **Time-bound:** Establish a timeframe for each goal. Deadlines serve as powerful motivators, helping you prioritize tasks and celebrate milestones along the way.

Charting the Path to Success

Armed with a vision of your ideal future, the journey forward involves laying down a practical roadmap to bring that vision to life. This roadmap acts as your personal guidebook, detailing the steps, milestones, and strategies that will navigate you from where you are now to where you want to be. It's about transforming your grand vision into a series of manageable, actionable steps, ensuring a steady march towards your dreams.

Breaking Down the Vision

1. **Identify Key Milestones:** Begin by pinpointing significant achievements that signal substantial progress towards your vision. These are not just any achievements, but pivotal moments that edge you closer to your ultimate aspirations.
2. **Sequence Your Steps:** Arrange these milestones in a logical order, mindful of how some steps may need to precede others. This ordered list illuminates the path ahead, clarifying which tasks need your attention first.

Short-Term vs. Long-Term Goals

Distill each milestone into smaller, bite-sized goals achievable in the short term. These goals should embody the SMART criteria—specific, measurable, achievable, relevant, and time-bound—making them clear, concise, and actionable.

Actionable Steps

Dive deeper by breaking down each short-term goal into individual tasks or actions. These are the daily, weekly, or monthly efforts that, when combined, lead to the achievement of your short-term goals and, by extension, your milestones.

Resource Allocation

Determine the resources each task demands—be it time, money, skills, or support. Assess what you already have and identify what additional resources you need to gather or develop to support your journey.

Timeframes and Deadlines

Assign realistic deadlines to each task and goal. These deadlines foster a sense of urgency and structure your time effectively, propelling you forward with purpose and momentum.

Tools and Systems

Adopt tools and systems that keep your roadmap organized and within easy reach. Whether you prefer a digital tool for its reminders and progress tracking or a traditional planner for its tactile experience, choose a system that resonates with you and your planning style.

Staying Motivated

Keep the flame of motivation burning brightly by regularly reconnecting with your vision and the reasons behind your goals. Whether through a visible vision board or frequent revisits to your written vision statement, maintain a close bond with your aspirations.

Seeking Support

Remember, the journey is often more rewarding with companionship. Seek out mentors, friends, peers, or professionals who can offer guidance, encouragement, and a fresh perspective, enriching your journey with their insights and support.

Crafting your roadmap is more than just planning; it's about converting your vision into tangible steps that guide you toward your dreams. With thoughtful planning, unwavering commitment, and the willingness to adapt, this roadmap becomes the foundation upon which you'll build your success, one step at a time. Remember, the path to success is a marathon, filled with its own challenges and triumphs, and your roadmap is the compass that keeps you oriented towards your north star.

Navigating Life's Twists and Turns

In our pursuit of goals, we often encounter unexpected challenges and opportunities. The key to thriving amidst life's unpredictability lies in cultivating flexibility and adaptability, essential traits for sustainable success. This section offers actionable strategies to help you navigate change with resilience and poise.

Embracing Change

Change is a constant companion on our journey, appearing as new opportunities, shifting priorities, or unforeseen challenges. Accepting change as an integral part of life equips you with a mindset ready for adaptation.

Cultivating Flexibility

Flexibility is about adjusting your plans and perspectives in response to new information or circumstances. Here's how to cultivate it:

- **Stay Open-Minded:** Embrace new ideas and perspectives. This openness can unveil unforeseen paths and solutions.
- **Practice Letting Go:** Recognize when to hold firm and when to be flexible. Some aspects of your plan may need adjustment to align with new realities.

Enhancing Adaptability

Adaptability is your capacity to respond effectively to change, requiring both practical adjustments and shifts in mindset.

- **Proactive Learning:** Continually acquire new skills and knowledge to stay versatile and prepared for unexpected shifts.
- **Build Emotional Resilience:** Strengthen your ability to manage stress and bounce back from setbacks. Techniques like mindfulness and building a strong support network are invaluable.

Reflective Practice

Regular reflection helps maintain your course, ensuring your actions stay aligned with your evolving goals.

- **Set Regular Review Times**: Dedicate time weekly or monthly to assess your progress, the relevance of your strategies, and any necessary adjustments.
- **Embrace Learning from Setbacks**: View challenges as opportunities for growth. Each setback offers insights to refine your approach.

Staying True to Your Vision

While adapting, ensure your changes remain true to your overarching vision and values. These should be the compass guiding your adjustments, ensuring they contribute meaningfully to your ultimate objectives.

Action Steps for Navigating Change

1. **Openness Exercise**: Daily, practice considering alternative viewpoints or solutions to problems, big or small, to foster open-mindedness.
2. **Flexibility Journal**: Keep a weekly journal where you note instances where adjusting your approach led to better outcomes, reinforcing the value of flexibility.
3. **Skill Development Plan**: Identify and list new skills relevant to your goals and dedicate time each month to learning or improving these skills.
4. **Resilience Rituals**: Incorporate stress-reduction techniques into your daily routine, such as meditation, exercise, or journaling, to enhance emotional resilience.
5. **Vision Check-ins**: Monthly, review your vision and goals to ensure your adjustments align with your long-term aspirations.

Flexibility and adaptability empower you to steer through life's changes with wisdom and insight, making informed choices that keep you aligned with your goals. By integrating these practices into your life, you transform challenges into steppingstones towards your success, ensuring your journey is as rewarding as the destination.

Learning from Your Journey

View every experience as a learning opportunity. Journaling provides a tangible record of your journey, allowing you to revisit past challenges and successes and draw lessons from them. These insights become the building blocks for future strategies and decision-making.

The Role of Gratitude

Incorporate gratitude into your journaling practice by noting things you're thankful for each day. This habit cultivates a positive outlook, enhancing your resilience and overall well-being.

Taking the First Step

With these insights on reflection and journaling, you're equipped to capture the essence of your journey toward success. Start by choosing a journal that speaks to you and commit to a regular reflection schedule. This first step is pivotal in building a practice that nurtures your growth, resilience, and progression toward your goals.

Remember, the journey to success is a rich tapestry of experiences, each offering valuable lessons and insights. By committing to reflection and journaling, you ensure that no insight is lost, and every lesson is leveraged to propel you forward on your path to success.

Chapter 2

Navigating the College Experience

Embarking on your college journey is like diving into an ocean filled with endless possibilities, tough challenges, and experiences that'll change your life in ways you can't even imagine yet. This isn't just about acing exams or ticking off classes; it's a full-on adventure that's going to shape who you are, where you're headed, and how you see the world. As you dive deeper into this college adventure, you'll find that there's so much to learn and experience beyond the four walls of a classroom.

In this chapter, "Navigating the College Experience," we're here to give you the lowdown on how to make the most of these crucial years. Whether it's picking a major that fires you up, getting involved in campus life, or building a network that'll support you down the line, every move you make is a steppingstone to your future success.

We're going to talk about why nailing your grades matters, but we'll also show you why there's more to college than just hitting the books. You'll see how getting involved in clubs or teams can teach you real-world skills like leadership and teamwork. We'll also dive into the importance of making connections that can open doors for you long after you've turned your tassel at graduation.

But that's not all – we're also going to cover the nitty-gritty of managing internships, keeping your finances in check, and making sure you're looking after yourself amidst the chaos of deadlines and exams. The goal here isn't just to get through college but to thrive, building a well-rounded experience that sets you up for what comes next.

So, as you flip through these pages, think of this chapter as your college survival kit, packed with insights and strategies to guide you through. Get ready for one of the most thrilling, challenging, and rewarding rides of your life. Let's kick off this journey together, ready to tackle whatever comes next.

Choosing the Right Path

Starting your college journey is like embarking on an adventure across a vast sea of possibilities. The choices are endless, and finding the right path can be as thrilling as it is challenging. This section is designed to be your compass, helping you navigate these waters so that your academic decisions reflect your true aspirations, leverage your strengths, and adapt to the ever-changing landscape of opportunities.

Discovering Your Passion

The first step is to look inward. Ask yourself, what subjects or activities light a spark in you? What topics do you find yourself eagerly exploring in your free time?

> **Exercise: The Passion Map**
> - Draw a mind map with branches representing different areas of interest.
> - For each branch, jot down specific aspects that intrigue you.
> - Look for intersections between your interests and potential career paths.

Balancing Passion and Practicality

While following your passion is vital, considering the practical aspects of your chosen field is equally important. Utilize your college's career counseling services to explore various fields and understand their future prospects.

Embracing Academic Exploration

College offers a unique landscape for discovery. Here's how to make the most of it:

- **Diverse Coursework**: In your first year, enroll in a broad spectrum of classes. This not only broadens your horizon but might also reveal previously undiscovered interests.
- **Practical Research**: Look into job market trends, potential earnings, and employability in your areas of interest. Tools like the Bureau of Labor Statistics can offer valuable data.

Building Versatility

In today's world, being versatile is key. Consider a double major or a minor to expand your expertise and appeal:

- **Double Major**: Combining two fields of study can open up a wider range of career paths and enrich your educational experience.
- **Minor**: A minor can complement your major, adding depth and diversity to your primary field of study.

Exercise: Academic Crossroads
- List your top three majors or fields of interest.
- For each, outline potential career paths, pros and cons, and how they align with your personal values and goals.

Adapting to Change

It's important to remember that your initial choice doesn't have to be final. Interests can evolve, and it's okay to pivot:

- **Stay Open:** Be willing to reassess your path as you gain new experiences and insights. College isn't just about academic growth but personal development too.
- **Variety is Key:** Engage in extracurricular activities, internships, and part-time jobs. These experiences can provide valuable real-world insights and shape your future choices.

Navigating the journey to higher education, the author's path to college was marked by unexpected twists and the influence of his social circle and circumstances. Initially, his aspirations soared towards the skies as he dreamt of becoming a fighter pilot, unaware that this ambition required a college degree. This dream took a sharp turn when he learned of the potential hardships his father faced in the Navy, leading him to question his own future in the military. Prompted by the unsettling prospect of being at the mercy of such decisions, he turned to his peers, asking, "What are you doing after high school?" The common thread in their responses, "We're going to college," sparked a curiosity that led him to his high school guidance counselor, setting the course towards a local California State University.

While at university, the allure of a different path momentarily caught his attention as he explored the possibility of trade school at Colman College. Yet, a pivotal encounter with a counselor at Colman who advised him to remain in his Computer Science program at San Diego State University steered him back on his academic course. This journey underscored the importance of seeking advice and being open to guidance, highlighting how a single conversation can alter the trajectory of one's life. The author's educational path, intertwined with serendipity and the wisdom of others, not only shaped his career but also laid the foundation for the very creation of his book, emphasizing the profound impact of the decisions we make and the advice we take during our formative years.

Choosing your academic path is about intertwining your personal interests with strategic decisions about your future. By fostering a blend of exploration and focused learning, you'll equip yourself to carve out a journey that not only leads to professional success but also to personal fulfillment and growth. Remember, the college experience is as much about discovering who you are as it is about shaping who you will become.

Academic Excellence

Achieving academic excellence is more than just securing top grades; it's about mastering the skills and habits that will serve you well beyond your college years. This section outlines actionable steps and considerations to help you excel academically and transform challenges into opportunities for growth.

Adopting a Growth Mindset

1. **Embrace Challenges**: View each academic challenge as an opportunity to learn and grow. Remember, setbacks are not a reflection of your abilities but a natural part of the learning process.
2. **Learn from Criticism**: Constructive feedback is a valuable tool for improvement. Approach feedback with an open mind and a willingness to adapt.
3. **Persist**: Cultivate resilience by continuing to put forth effort even when faced with difficulties. Persistence is key to overcoming obstacles and achieving your goals.

Developing Effective Study Habits

1. **Identify Your Learning Style**: Determine whether you are a visual, auditory, or kinesthetic learner and tailor your study methods accordingly. This alignment can significantly enhance your learning efficiency.
2. **Active Learning Strategies**: Engage with the material actively by teaching concepts to others, applying knowledge in real-world contexts, and participating in group discussions.

3. **Regular Review:** Instead of cramming before exams, schedule regular review sessions to reinforce your learning and improve long-term retention.

Mastering Time Management

1. **Plan Your Schedule:** Use planners, digital calendars, or apps to organize your study sessions, assignments, and deadlines. A well-structured schedule can help you manage your time effectively.
2. **Prioritize Tasks:** Assess the urgency and importance of your tasks. Focus on high-priority items first and avoid distractions that detract from your academic goals.
3. **Learn to Say No:** It's crucial to recognize when commitments outside your academic responsibilities might hinder your progress and learn to decline them politely.

Leveraging Resources and Support

1. **Utilize Campus Resources:** Explore the support services offered by your institution, such as tutoring centers, libraries, and academic workshops. These resources can provide additional help and enrich your learning experience.
2. **Engage with Faculty:** Attend office hours and seek advice from your professors. Their expertise can offer deeper insights and clarify any uncertainties.
3. **Join Study Groups:** Collaborating with peers can provide new perspectives, divide workloads, and make studying more engaging.

Active Course Engagement

1. **Attend All Classes:** Consistent attendance is fundamental to understanding course material and staying up to date with assignments and discussions.

2. **Participate Actively:** Contribute to discussions and ask questions. Active participation enhances your learning and shows your commitment to your studies.

Balancing Your Course Load

1. **Be Realistic:** Choose a course load that challenges you but is manageable. Overloading can lead to stress and burnout, hindering your academic performance.
2. **Seek Balance:** Ensure your schedule allows for adequate study time, as well as relaxation and social activities. A balanced life contributes to both academic success and personal well-being.

Seeking Continuous Improvement

1. **Feedback for Growth:** Regularly seek and reflect on feedback from assignments and exams to identify areas for improvement.
2. **Set Incremental Goals:** Break down your academic objectives into smaller, achievable goals. This approach allows for continuous improvement and keeps you motivated.

Prioritizing Wellness and Self-Care

1. **Maintain a Healthy Lifestyle:** Ensure you're getting enough sleep, eating nutritious meals, and engaging in regular physical activity. Physical well-being significantly impacts cognitive function and academic performance.
2. **Manage Stress:** Incorporate stress-reduction techniques such as mindfulness, meditation, or hobbies into your routine. Managing stress is crucial for maintaining focus and motivation.

By implementing these strategies, you're not just working towards academic excellence; you're building a foundation of skills and habits that will support your personal and professional growth long after college. Remember, academic success is a journey that involves continuous learning, self-reflection, and personal development.

Campus Involvement

Diving into the vibrant life beyond the lecture halls can profoundly shape your college experience. This section will guide you through the benefits of campus involvement and provide actionable strategies to help you navigate and thrive in these opportunities.

Exploring Campus Activities

1. **Conduct a Campus Activity Audit:** Start by researching all the clubs, organizations, sports teams, and cultural societies your campus offers. Many colleges have an activities fair at the beginning of the term; make sure to attend.
2. **Align with Your Interests:** Identify clubs that match your current interests, whether it's a hobby, a sport, or an academic pursuit. Joining these groups can deepen your engagement with familiar passions.
3. **Embrace New Experiences:** Challenge yourself to join at least one organization outside your comfort zone. This could be anything from an international cultural group to an improv club, offering fresh perspectives and skills.

Developing Essential Soft Skills

1. **Participate Actively:** Don't just be a member in name. Attend meetings regularly, volunteer for events, and contribute ideas. Active involvement is key to developing leadership, teamwork, and communication skills.
2. **Seek Feedback:** Use your involvement as an opportunity to gain feedback on your soft skills from peers and leaders within the organization. Constructive criticism can be incredibly valuable for personal growth.

Building Your Network

1. **Engage with Peers and Leaders**: Make a conscious effort to connect with fellow members and organization leaders. These relationships can provide mentorship, support, and valuable networking opportunities.
2. **Alumni Connections**: Many campus organizations have strong alumni networks. Engage with these individuals for insights into career paths and potential job opportunities.

Making a Difference

1. **Join Cause-Based Groups**: If you're passionate about certain causes, seek out organizations that focus on community service, advocacy, or social issues. Contributing to these causes can be deeply rewarding and enhance your sense of purpose.

Balancing Involvement with Academics

1. **Prioritize Wisely**: While getting involved is important, your academics should come first. Use tools like planners or digital calendars to balance your academic workload with extracurricular activities.
2. **Learn to Say No**: It's okay to turn down opportunities if your schedule is already full. Overcommitment can lead to burnout and impact your academic performance.

Leveraging Leadership Opportunities

1. **Step Up to Lead**: Don't shy away from taking on leadership roles within organizations. These positions challenge you to develop strategic thinking, project management, and leadership skills.
2. **Document Your Leadership Journey**: Keep a record of your roles, responsibilities, and achievements within each organization. This documentation will be a valuable asset for your resume and future job applications.

Campus involvement is more than just an extracurricular checkbox; it's a multifaceted opportunity for growth, networking, and personal fulfillment. By strategically engaging in campus life, you can transform your college years into a dynamic period of exploration, development, and discovery.

Networking and Relationships

In the mosaic of your college journey, networking and nurturing meaningful relationships hold the keys to unlocking a world of personal and professional growth. This isn't just about adding contacts to your list; it's about weaving a network of genuine connections that can guide, inspire, and support you through college and beyond. Here, we examine actionable strategies for cultivating a network that can open doors to countless opportunities.

Embrace the Power of Genuine Connections

Networking transcends mere professional gain; it's rooted in forming authentic relationships anchored in shared interests, mutual respect, and reciprocal support. These connections become your compass, offering direction and insight as you navigate the intricate paths of your academic and career landscapes.

Cultivating Campus Connections

Your college campus is a fertile ground for sowing the seeds of your network. Here's how to start:

- **Engage with Peers**: Active participation in class discussions, group projects, and study groups can forge bonds that might evolve into significant professional relationships.
- **Join Clubs and Organizations**: Align your extracurricular involvement with your passions and interests. Leadership roles in these settings can amplify

your visibility and connect you with like-minded individuals.
- **Attend Campus Events**: Workshops, guest lectures, and social gatherings are not just educational; they're networking goldmines. Seize these opportunities to meet new people and exchange ideas.

Leveraging Faculty and Alumni Wisdom

Faculty and alumni are pillars of wisdom and experience, offering a bridge to the professional world.

- **Connect with Professors**: Office hours aren't just for academic queries; they're a chance to seek career advice, discuss industry trends, and potentially secure research positions or recommendations.
- **Tap into Alumni Networks**: Most colleges boast vibrant alumni networks eager to support current students. Attend alumni mixers, engage in mentorship programs, and don't shy away from reaching out to alumni in fields that intrigue you.

Gaining Experience Through Internships

Internships and part-time roles related to your field aren't just resume enhancers; they're networking hubs.

- **Seek Relevant Opportunities**: Whether through your college's career services, job fairs, or online platforms, find positions that align with your career aspirations.
- **Build Professional Relationships**: Treat every workday as a networking opportunity. From colleagues to supervisors, every interaction is a chance to learn and make a lasting impression.

Maximizing Networking Events and Workshops

Colleges often host events designed to connect students with professionals.

- **Prepare and Participate:** Before attending, research the companies and speakers. Prepare thoughtful questions to stand out and engage meaningfully with attendees.
- **Practice Your Pitch:** Develop a concise and compelling way to introduce yourself, highlighting your studies, interests, and career aspirations.

Cultivating an Online Professional Presence

In our interconnected world, your digital footprint can be as significant as your physical presence.

- **Optimize Your LinkedIn Profile:** Ensure your profile is complete, professional, and reflective of your career interests. Regularly update it with achievements, projects, and relevant activities.
- **Engage Thoughtfully Online:** Comment on industry articles, join relevant groups, and share your academic or project milestones. Authentic engagement can attract the attention of potential mentors and employers.

Soft Skills: The Networking Glue

Your ability to connect deeply with others often boils down to your soft skills.

- **Hone Your Communication:** Whether in writing or in conversation, clear and respectful communication forms the bedrock of strong relationships.
- **Active Listening:** Show genuine interest in others' thoughts and stories. Active listening can endear you to your connections and provide deep insights into their experiences and advice.

Nurturing and Sustaining Connections

The initial meeting is just the beginning; nurturing these relationships is where the real work lies.

- **Follow Up**: A thoughtful follow-up after a meeting underscores your interest and appreciation. A simple thank-you email can set the stage for ongoing communication.
- **Keep the Lines Open**: Regular updates about your progress, asking for advice, or sharing interesting articles can keep your connections warm and reciprocal.

The Cycle of Giving Back

As you advance in your journey, remember to extend the ladder to those climbing behind you.
- **Be a Mentor**: Offer guidance and support to younger students or peers. Your insights can light the way for someone else's journey.
- **Share Opportunities**: If you come across internships, scholarships, or job openings, share them within your network. Generosity fosters a culture of mutual support.

Networking and relationship-building during your college years is an investment in your future. By actively engaging with your peers, faculty, and professionals, and by nurturing these connections with intention and sincerity, you lay the groundwork for a thriving personal and professional life post-graduation. Remember, the strongest networks are built on the foundation of genuine relationships and shared growth.

Internships and Practical Experience

Gaining practical experience through internships, part-time jobs, volunteer work, or research projects is an integral part of the college experience. This section will guide you on how to navigate opportunities that not only complement your academic learning but also prepare you for the professional world.

The Value of Practical Experience

Practical experiences provide a real-world context to your academic studies, allowing you to apply theoretical knowledge in practical settings. They offer insights into the workings of industries related to your field of study, help you understand workplace dynamics, and refine your career goals based on firsthand experience.

Securing Internships

1. **Start Early**: Begin looking for internship opportunities early in your academic career. Many competitive internships have early application deadlines, and starting early gives you time to prepare and apply to multiple opportunities.

2. **Utilize Campus Resources**: Career services offices are a valuable resource for finding internships. They can provide access to job boards, networking events, and career fairs where you can meet potential employers.

3. **Online Platforms**: Websites like LinkedIn, Indeed, and specialized industry-specific job boards can be excellent sources for finding internships.

4. **Network**: Leverage your personal and professional networks to find internship opportunities. Professors, family, friends, and alumni can provide leads and recommendations.

Making the Most of Your Internship

1. **Set Clear Goals**: Identify what you want to achieve through your internship. Whether it's learning a specific skill, understanding an industry, or making professional connections, having clear goals will help you stay focused.

2. **Be Proactive:** Take initiative in your internship. Ask for more responsibilities, volunteer for projects, and seek opportunities to contribute meaningfully.

3. **Seek Feedback:** Regularly ask for feedback from your supervisor and colleagues. Constructive feedback can help you improve and grow professionally.

4. **Build Relationships:** Use your internship as an opportunity to build a professional network. Connect with colleagues, attend industry events, and maintain these relationships even after your internship ends.

Exploring Part-time Jobs and Volunteer Work

Part-time jobs and volunteer work can also provide valuable experiences that complement your academic and career goals. They can help you develop soft skills such as teamwork, communication, and time management, which are critical in any professional setting.

Engaging in Research Projects

For those in research-oriented fields, participating in research projects can offer deep insights into your area of study, develop critical thinking and analytical skills, and contribute to your academic profile. Reach out to professors who are conducting research in areas of your interest to explore opportunities for involvement.

Documenting Your Experiences

Keep a detailed record of your responsibilities, achievements, and the skills you develop through these practical experiences. This information will be invaluable when updating your resume and preparing for job interviews.

Reflecting and Learning

After each experience, take the time to reflect on what you learned, how it contributed to your personal and professional growth, and how it aligns with your career aspirations. This reflection will help you make informed decisions about your future career path.

Internships and practical experiences are more than just resume builders; they are opportunities to explore your interests, develop skills, and lay the groundwork for a successful career. By approaching these experiences with intentionality and reflection, you can significantly enhance your college experience and future employability.

Financial Management

Navigating financial management during your college years is pivotal for establishing a foundation for long-term financial health and independence. This section provides strategies and insights for effective financial management, emphasizing the importance of budgeting, understanding student loans, and embracing financial literacy.

Budgeting Basics

1. **Track Your Spending**: Begin by monitoring your expenses to understand where your money goes. Use apps or a simple spreadsheet to categorize your spending.

2. **Create a Budget**: Based on your tracking, create a realistic budget that covers your essentials (tuition, rent, groceries) and allocates amounts for savings and discretionary spending.

3. **Stick to Your Budget**: Discipline is key. Regularly review your spending against your budget and adjust as needed to stay on track.

Understanding Student Loans

1. **Educate Yourself**: Fully understand the terms of any student loans you take out, including interest rates, repayment terms, and any deferment or forgiveness options.

2. **Borrow Wisely**: Only borrow what you need, considering your potential earning power after graduation to ensure manageable repayments.

3. **Plan for Repayment**: Start thinking about your repayment strategy even before you graduate. Consider setting aside a portion of any part-time job income towards future loan payments.

Saving and Investing

1. **Emergency Fund**: Aim to save a small emergency fund, even if it's just a few hundred dollars, to cover unexpected expenses without needing to borrow.

2. **Consider Investing**: If you have some disposable income, consider basic investing options like a high-yield savings account or low-risk mutual funds to start growing your savings.

Credit Management

1. **Use Credit Wisely**: If you have a credit card, use it responsibly. Pay off your balance in full each month to avoid interest charges and build a good credit score.

2. **Understand Credit**: Learn how credit scores are calculated and the impact of your credit history on future financial opportunities, such as renting an apartment or buying a car.

Financial Literacy

1. **Educate Yourself:** Take advantage of resources on financial literacy. Many colleges offer workshops, and there are countless books, podcasts, and online resources available.
2. **Seek Advice:** Don't hesitate to seek advice from financial advisors or knowledgeable family members when making significant financial decisions.

Frugal Living

1. **Embrace Frugality:** Look for ways to cut unnecessary expenses. Use student discounts, buy used textbooks, and opt for cost-effective entertainment options.
2. **Side Hustles:** Consider part-time work or side hustles that can fit around your academic schedule to earn extra income.

Financial management during your college years is not just about making ends meet; it's about setting the stage for a financially secure future. By adopting sound financial habits now, you can mitigate stress and focus more on your academic and personal growth.

Well-Being and Self-Care

Prioritizing your well-being and self-care is crucial for maintaining balance, especially during the transformative college years. This section emphasizes the importance of holistic health, encompassing physical, mental, and emotional well-being, to ensure you thrive academically and personally.

Physical Health

1. **Nutrition:** Focus on a balanced diet rich in fruits, vegetables, lean proteins, and whole grains. Proper

nutrition fuels your body and mind, enhancing both physical health and cognitive function.

2. **Exercise**: Regular physical activity is vital. Aim for at least 30 minutes of moderate exercise most days of the week. Exercise not only improves physical health but also reduces stress and anxiety.

3. **Sleep**: Prioritize quality sleep. Aim for 7–9 hours per night to support cognitive function, mood regulation, and overall health.

Mental and Emotional Well-Being

1. **Stress Management**: Identify healthy stress-relief activities that work for you, such as mindfulness, meditation, yoga, or hobbies. Learning to manage stress effectively is key to maintaining mental and emotional balance.

2. **Seek Support**: Don't hesitate to seek support when needed. Utilize campus counseling services, support groups, or talk to trusted friends and family about your challenges. Recognize that you may need to proactively reach out for these services.

3. **Digital Detox**: Regularly unplug from digital devices and social media to reduce information overload and improve mental well-being.

Social Connections

1. **Foster Relationships**: Build and maintain strong relationships with friends, family, and peers. Social connections provide emotional support, enhance happiness, and can offer a sense of belonging.

2. **Set Boundaries**: Learn to set healthy boundaries in personal and academic life to maintain balance and prevent burnout.

Environmental Well-being

1. **Organized Space:** Maintain a clean and organized living and study space to reduce stress and enhance productivity.
2. **Nature Time:** Spend time in nature regularly. Exposure to natural environments can reduce stress, improve mood, and enhance creativity.

Well-being and self-care are not luxuries but necessities for a fulfilling college experience and life beyond. By adopting practices that nurture all aspects of your well-being, you're not only investing in your success as a student but also laying the groundwork for a healthy, balanced future.

Study Abroad and Global Exposure

Embracing opportunities for study abroad and global exposure can significantly enrich your college experience, offering unique educational and personal growth opportunities. This section explores the benefits of international study and how to make the most of these experiences.

Broadening Perspectives

Studying abroad allows you to immerse yourself in a different culture, broadening your perspectives and enhancing your understanding of global issues. It challenges you to adapt to new environments, fostering flexibility and resilience.

Academic Enrichment

Many study abroad programs offer courses and research opportunities not available at your home institution. This can complement your major with international perspectives, potentially giving you an edge in your field of study.

Language Skills

Immersing yourself in a country where a different language is spoken offers a valuable opportunity to develop or improve language skills. Language proficiency is not only personally rewarding but also highly valued in the global job market.

Personal Growth

Living and studying in a new country fosters independence and self-reliance. Navigating daily life, academics, and cultural differences in an unfamiliar environment can significantly boost your confidence and problem-solving skills.

Professional Advantages

Global exposure can enhance your resume, demonstrating to potential employers your adaptability, global awareness, and ability to thrive in diverse settings. The international networks you build can also provide valuable professional connections.

Making It Happen

1. **Research**: Start by researching study abroad options offered by your college. Consider factors such as the destination, duration, academic offerings, and how the program aligns with your degree requirements and career goals.

2. **Plan Financially**: Investigate scholarships, grants, and financial aid options for study abroad. Budget carefully to account for travel, living expenses, and any additional costs.

3. **Preparation**: Prepare for your study abroad experience by learning about your host country's culture, language, and customs. This cultural sensitivity will enrich your experience and help you adapt more quickly.

4. **Stay Engaged:** Fully immerse yourself in the experience. Engage with the local community, participate in cultural activities, and travel within the region to gain a deeper understanding of the area.

5. **Reflect and Share:** Upon returning, take the time to reflect on your experiences and how they've impacted you. Share your learnings and stories with your home institution and peers. This can inspire others and help you process your own growth.

Study abroad and global exposure opportunities are transformative elements of the college experience, offering unparalleled opportunities for personal and academic growth. By stepping out of your comfort zone and engaging with the world, you open doors to new possibilities, perspectives, and paths in both your personal and professional life.

Preparation for the Future

As you navigate through your college years, it's crucial to keep an eye on the horizon and actively prepare for your future. This section outlines strategies to ensure that your college experience not only enriches you academically and personally but also sets you up for success in your post-graduate life.

Career Planning

1. **Career Services:** Utilize your college's career services early and often. They can provide career counseling, resume workshops, interview preparation, and job search resources.

2. **Internships and Work Experience:** Seek internships and part-time jobs related to your field of study. These experiences provide valuable insights into your chosen career, build your resume, and can lead to job offers upon graduation.

3. **Networking:** Continue to build and nurture your professional network. Attend career fairs, alumni

events, and professional association meetings in your field of interest.

Skill Development

1. **Transferable Skills**: Focus on developing transferable skills such as communication, leadership, problem-solving, and digital literacy. These skills are highly valued by employers across various industries.

2. **Technical Skills**: Depending on your field, gaining proficiency in specific technical skills or software can give you a competitive edge. Look for opportunities to learn these skills through coursework, online tutorials, or certification programs.

Personal Branding

1. **Online Presence**: Cultivate a professional online presence, particularly on LinkedIn. Your profile should highlight your education, skills, experiences, and professional interests. Keep in mind that some employers will scan the internet to review posts and messages of potential candidates. So, be aware of the lasting impact of any messages you leave on sites like Facebook, Instagram, and X (former known as Twitter).

2. **Portfolio Development**: If applicable, create a portfolio showcasing your work, projects, and achievements. This can be particularly important for fields such as art, design, writing, and programming.

Lifelong Learning

1. **Continuing Education**: Stay curious and committed to lifelong learning. Whether through formal education, professional development courses, or self-directed learning, continuing to expand your knowledge and skills will serve you well throughout your career.

2. **Industry Trends**: Stay informed about trends and changes in your industry. This can help you adapt and remain relevant in a rapidly changing job market.

Financial Planning

1. **Budgeting and Saving**: Develop a post-graduation budget that accounts for student loan repayments, living expenses, and savings goals. Establishing good financial habits early can lead to greater financial stability.

2. **Retirement Planning**: It's never too early to start thinking about retirement savings. If your first job offers a retirement plan, take advantage of it, especially if there's an employer match.

3. **Funding College:** Did you know that the most reputale colleges will pay for your PhD tuition and a spipend for living expenses? So, rather than going into debt early in your educational career, consider attending an affordable college first and potentially returning later for more in-depth learning.

4. **Avoid Preditory Lending**: Be cautions of student loans and for-profit schools, espeically those that require you to assume loans for your education. Do your research to undertand how well regarded the graduates are and you likely income propsects after your are employed. For eample, you do not want to find yourself $200,000 in debt at a job that pays $50,000 a year.

Preparing for the future is an ongoing process that begins the moment you step onto campus and continues well beyond graduation. By taking proactive steps to plan your career, develop essential skills, and build a personal brand, you'll be well-equipped to transition smoothly from college to the next phase of your professional and personal life.

Reflection and Adaptation

The journey through college and towards personal and professional success is dynamic and ever-evolving. Reflection and adaptation are critical processes that enable continuous growth and learning. This section delves into the importance of self-reflection and the ability to adapt, ensuring that you remain aligned with your goals and responsive to new opportunities and challenges.

The Power of Reflection

Reflection involves looking back on your experiences, behaviors, and outcomes to gain insights and perspectives. It allows you to:

1. **Assess Progress**: Regularly evaluate your progress towards academic, personal, and professional goals. Recognize achievements and identify areas needing improvement.

2. **Understand Experiences**: Analyze both positive and challenging experiences to understand their impact on your growth. What lessons were learned? How have you changed?

3. **Clarify Values and Goals**: Reflection helps in reassessing and reaffirming your values and goals. It ensures that your actions remain aligned with what is truly important to you.

Embracing Adaptation

Adaptation is the ability to adjust your thoughts, efforts, and plans in response to new information, experiences, and changing circumstances. It involves:

1. **Being Open to Change**: Stay open to new ideas, opportunities, and ways of thinking. The willingness to change course when necessary is a strength, not a weakness.

2. **Resilience in the Face of Challenges:** View setbacks and failures as opportunities for learning and growth. Develop resilience by focusing on solutions rather than dwelling on problems.

3. **Innovative Thinking:** Encourage creativity and innovation in approaching tasks and solving problems. Sometimes, a fresh perspective can lead to breakthroughs.

Strategies for Effective Reflection and Adaptation

1. **Keep a Journal:** Maintain a journal to record your thoughts, experiences, and reflections. Writing can provide clarity and a tangible record of your journey.

2. **Seek Feedback:** Regularly seek feedback from peers, mentors, and professors. Constructive criticism can provide new perspectives and areas for improvement.

3. **Set Aside Reflection Time:** Dedicate regular time for reflection. This can be a quiet moment at the end of the day or a more structured weekly review.

4. **Practice Mindfulness:** Engage in mindfulness practices to enhance self-awareness. Mindfulness can improve your ability to respond thoughtfully to situations rather than reacting impulsively.

5. **Stay Informed:** Keep abreast of developments in your field of study and the broader world. Staying informed helps you adapt to changes and seize emerging opportunities.

6. **Embrace Lifelong Learning:** View education as a lifelong journey. Continuous learning keeps you adaptable and relevant in an ever-changing world.

Reflection and adaptation are not one-time tasks but ongoing processes that enrich your college experience and prepare you for a successful future. By regularly engaging in self-reflection and remaining flexible in the face of new challenges and opportunities, you equip yourself with the tools needed to navigate the complexities of life and career with confidence and resilience.

Life Skills

The college experience extends beyond academic achievement; it's a pivotal time for developing essential life skills that will serve you well throughout your personal and professional life. This section highlights key life skills to cultivate during your college years, ensuring you're well-prepared for the challenges and opportunities that lie ahead.

Time Management

Mastering time management is crucial for balancing academic responsibilities, extracurricular activities, social commitments, and self-care. Effective time management involves:

1. **Prioritization**: Learning to prioritize tasks based on urgency and importance ensures that you focus your efforts on what truly matters. Begin with a daily to-do list and circle the three things that must be completed that day to avoid something bad from occurring. Those are your priorities for the day. Simply make sure to complete those task.

2. **Planning**: Utilizing planners, calendars, or digital apps to schedule your tasks and commitments can help you stay organized and avoid last-minute stress.

3. **Efficiency**: Developing strategies to work efficiently, such as breaking tasks into smaller, manageable steps and eliminating distractions during focused work periods.

Communication Skills

Effective communication is key to building relationships, succeeding in collaborative projects, and articulating your ideas clearly. Enhance your communication skills by:

1. **Active Listening**: Practice active listening to fully understand others' perspectives, fostering mutual respect and collaboration. A common technique includes summarizing what you believe the other person said and meant before providing your response.
2. **Clarity and Conciseness**: Learn to express your ideas clearly and concisely, whether in writing or speaking, to ensure your message is understood.
3. **Non-Verbal Communication**: Be mindful of body language, eye contact, and tone, as these non-verbal cues can significantly impact how your message is received. Some find looking another in the eye challenging. To change this behavior, challenge yourself to look into the eyes of the next 100 people you speak with and make a bar chart of their eye color. While it can be fun to see the bar chart change over time, you are building and reinforcing the skill of looking others in the eye.

Critical Thinking and Problem-Solving

College challenges you to think critically, question assumptions, and solve complex problems. Strengthen these skills by:

1. **Analysis**: Practice breaking down complex information into its components to understand underlying principles and relationships.
2. **Evaluation**: Learn to assess the credibility of sources, arguments, and evidence, developing the ability to make informed judgments. Learn to separate the credibility of the source from the credibility of the content. A trusted source can say nonsensical things and an unknown source could provide an important insight.
3. **Creativity**: Encourage creative thinking to approach problems from multiple angles and develop innovative solutions.

Financial Literacy

Understanding personal finance, budgeting, saving, and investing is vital for long-term financial stability. Key aspects include:

1. **Budgeting**: Develop the habit of creating and sticking to a budget to manage your finances effectively.

2. **Saving and Investing**: Learn the basics of saving for future needs and the fundamentals of investing to grow your wealth over time.

3. **Credit Management**: Understand how credit works, the importance of a good credit score, and how to use credit responsibly. Using credit to purchase a home is often viewed as a sound financial practice, while using credit to finance your vacation is not.

Life skills acquired during your college years lay the foundation for a well-rounded, successful life. By actively developing these skills alongside your academic pursuits, you equip yourself with the tools necessary to navigate the complexities of life with confidence, competence, and resilience.

Category	Budgeted Amount	Actual Amount	Difference
Income			
- Salary			
- Other Income			
Total Income			
Expenses			
- Housing			
- Rent/Mortgage			
- Utilities			
- Transportation			
- Fuel			
- Maintenance			
- Food			
- Groceries			
- Dining Out			
- Healthcare			
- Insurance			
- Medical Bills			
- Entertainment			
- Savings & Investments			
- Miscellaneous			
Total Expenses			
Net (Income - Expenses)			

Sample Monthly Budget

Charting Your Course Beyond College

As you turn the pages of this book, embarking on or continuing your college journey, remember that the path to success is as unique as you are. College is not just a series of academic milestones but a holistic experience that shapes your character, hones your skills, and prepares you for the multifaceted challenges of life. Embrace each opportunity for learning, not just from textbooks and lectures but from the rich experiences and diverse individuals you'll encounter along the way.

Success transcends grades and accolades; it's about becoming a well-rounded individual equipped to contribute meaningfully to society. It's about cultivating resilience, embracing adaptability, and nurturing relationships that enrich your journey. The ultimate goal is not just to excel academically but to emerge from your college years as a thoughtful, skilled, and compassionate individual ready to take on the world's challenges.

As you chart your course beyond college, carry with you the lessons learned, the relationships forged, and the personal victories achieved. Let these experiences be your compass, guiding you through life's uncertainties with confidence and grace. Remember, the journey doesn't end with a diploma; it's a continuous path of growth, learning, and discovery.

In closing, you are encouraged to approach each day with curiosity, embrace each challenge with courage, and seize each opportunity with both hands. The world is vast, filled with endless possibilities waiting to be explored by those willing to venture forth. So go ahead, set sail on your journey with an open heart and an eager mind, ready to make your mark and achieve next-level success in every facet of life.

Chapter 3

Navigating Your Career

Embarking on a career journey is akin to setting sail on the vast ocean of opportunities, where each decision steers you towards new horizons. This chapter, "Navigating Your Career," is designed as your compass, guiding you through the complexities and challenges of building a fulfilling and successful career path. Whether you're standing at the threshold of your professional life or seeking to recalibrate your direction, the insights and strategies shared here aim to illuminate the way.

The journey to a rewarding career begins with a deep understanding of yourself—your passions, skills, and the unique value you bring to the professional world. It's about aligning your career with who you are and what you love, ensuring that your work not only brings you success but also fulfillment and joy.

As we delve into this chapter, we'll explore the myriad career options available to you and how to navigate the changing landscapes of industries. We'll discuss the importance of education, not just in its traditional form but as a lifelong pursuit that keeps you agile and relevant in a fast-paced world.

Your career is more than just a series of job titles; it's a reflection of your personal brand. We'll cover how to craft and curate this brand, making a lasting impression in your network and beyond. Speaking of networks, we'll unlock the power of connections, teaching you how to forge and nurture relationships that open doors to unforeseen opportunities.

The tactical aspects of career navigation — resumes, cover letters, interviews — are equally pivotal. Mastering these tools will set you apart in the job market, turning opportunities into offers. But it doesn't stop there; thriving in the workplace, advancing in your field, and facing setbacks with resilience are ongoing chapters in your career story.

This chapter is not just about climbing the professional ladder; it's about finding balance, ensuring that your career enriches your life as a whole. As you turn these pages, remember that your career path is uniquely yours to chart. With the right tools, mindset, and determination, you're set to navigate your way to a fulfilling and prosperous career. Welcome to the journey.

Understanding Your Passions and Skills

Embarking on a career journey begins with a deep dive into the essence of who you are: your passions and skills. This foundational step is not just about listing what you enjoy or what you're good at; it's about uncovering the core of your professional identity and aligning it with potential career paths. Here's how to embark on this insightful journey:

Unearthing Your Passions

Your passions are the activities that ignite your enthusiasm, the topics that you can talk about for hours without getting bored, and the pursuits that make you lose track of time. To identify these, reflect on the following:

- **Revisit Childhood Interests**: Often, our true passions can be traced back to our childhood. What activities or subjects captivated you as a child? Which of these still resonate with you?

- **Pay Attention to Your Curiosities**: Notice the topics or activities that pique your interest, even if they don't seem directly related to a career path. Curiosity can lead to passion.

- **Identify Your "Flow" Activities:** Consider the tasks or hobbies in which you experience "flow" – a state of deep focus and immersion. These are often indicators of underlying passions.

Assessing Your Skills

Skills are the competencies and abilities that you've developed through experience, education, and training. While some skills might be innate, most can be learned and honed over time. To assess your skills:

- **Inventory Your Skills:** Make a comprehensive list of your skills, including technical skills specific to certain tasks or industries, and soft skills like communication, problem-solving, and teamwork.

- **Seek Feedback:** Sometimes, others can see strengths we overlook in ourselves. Ask friends, family, and colleagues what skills they admire in you.

- **Analyze Your Achievements:** Look back at your achievements, both in educational settings and in any work or volunteer experiences. What skills were pivotal to these successes?

Bridging Passions and Skills

With a clearer understanding of your passions and skills, the next step is to explore how they intersect. This intersection is where your potential career paths begin to take shape.

- **Look for Patterns:** Identify themes or commonalities in your passions and skills. These patterns can point you toward industries or roles that align with both.

- **Research Careers:** Use your identified passions and skills as keywords in career exploration resources. Discover what professions value your unique combination.

- **Consider Side Projects or Hobbies:** Sometimes, a passion might not translate directly into a career but can complement your professional life as a hobby or side project, enriching your overall satisfaction and skill set.

This introspective process is not a one-time task but an ongoing journey of self-discovery and growth. As you evolve, so too will your interests and abilities. Regularly revisiting and reassessing your passions and skills will ensure that your career path remains aligned with the most authentic version of yourself, allowing for a fulfilling and successful professional life.

Uncovering Your Career Passion

Embarking on a career that resonates deeply with your interests and values is a key ingredient for long-term fulfillment and success. This section of the book is designed to guide you through a series of exercises aimed at uncovering your true career passions. These exercises blend introspection, practical experimentation, and reflection to help you navigate the vast landscape of career possibilities and pinpoint the path that aligns with your personal aspirations and strengths.

1. The 7 Whys Exploration

Dive deep into your career interests by asking yourself "Why?" seven times. This iterative questioning technique, introduced in chapter 1, helps peel back the layers of your initial responses, revealing the core motivations behind your career aspirations.

Steps:
- Begin with a broad statement of interest, like "I want to work with marine animals."
- Ask "Why?" and answer based on your initial statement.
- Repeat this question six more times, each time using your last answer as the base.
- Reflect on the underlying passion revealed through this process.

2. Skills and Enjoyment Mapping

Create a comprehensive list of your skills and a separate list of activities that bring you joy. Look for overlaps between these lists to identify potential career paths that harness both your capabilities and passions.

Steps:
- List down all your skills, including technical and soft skills.
- Make another list of activities and subjects that excite you.
- Identify intersections and consider careers that could incorporate these elements.

3. Vision Board Creation

Construct a vision board filled with images, quotes, and symbols that represent your ideal career and lifestyle. This visual tool serves as a constant source of inspiration and clarity about your career goals.

Steps:
- Gather magazines, printouts, and any other materials that inspire you.
- Focus on elements that you envision in your dream job and life, including work environment, achievements, and values.
- Arrange and secure these elements on a board in a way that resonates with you.

4. Informational Interviews

Engage in conversations with professionals in fields of interest to gain insights into various career paths. These discussions can offer valuable perspectives on daily responsibilities, job satisfaction, and potential challenges within the profession.

Steps:
- Identify individuals working in your areas of interest and reach out for informational interviews.
- Prepare thoughtful questions that look at their career paths, daily tasks, and advice for newcomers.
- Reflect on the insights gained and how they align with your interests and aspirations.

5. Journaling for Reflection

Maintain a journal to document your thoughts, experiences, and moments of job-related satisfaction or excitement. Regular entries and reflections can highlight consistent themes and passions.

Steps:
- Write daily or weekly about tasks, projects, or experiences that you found particularly engaging or fulfilling.
- Look for patterns in your entries that point to specific interests or industries.
- Use these insights to guide your career exploration and decision-making.

6. The Ideal Day Visualization

Imagine your perfect workday in vivid detail. Consider all aspects, from the moment you wake up to the end of your day, focusing on the work environment, tasks, interactions, and achievements.

Steps:
- Close your eyes and visualize a day in your ideal job, considering all senses and emotions.
- Write down the key elements of this visualization, noting what made the day ideal.
- Use these elements as a guide to evaluate potential career paths.

7. Online Personality and Career Assessments

Take advantage of reputable assessments designed to match your personality traits, strengths, and interests with suitable careers. These tools can provide a structured starting point for your exploration.

Steps:
- Complete one or more assessments, such as the Myers-Briggs Type Indicator (MBTI) or StengthFinders Test.
- Review your results and research careers that align with your identified personality type and interests.
- Consider how these suggestions fit with your personal vision and goals.

8. Professional Workshops and Courses

Enroll in workshops, courses, or classes related to potential career interests. This hands-on approach allows you to gain practical skills and insights into various fields.

Steps:
- Identify courses that align with your career interests, whether online or in your community.
- Engage fully in these learning experiences, applying yourself to projects and assignments.
- Reflect on your enjoyment and aptitude for the subject matter to guide your career decisions.

9. Mind Mapping Your Interests

Create a mind map with your career interest at the center and branch out with related roles, skills, industries, and values. This visual exploration can reveal unexpected connections and opportunities.

Steps:
- Start with a central idea related to your career interest.

- Branch out to include related aspects, roles, skills, and industries.
- Look for patterns and connections that might inform your career choice.

Exploring Career Options

Once you have a clear understanding of your passions and skills, the next step in charting your career path is to explore the vast landscape of career options available to you. This exploration is crucial in broadening your perspective and uncovering opportunities that resonate with your personal and professional aspirations. Here's how to embark on this explorative journey:

Diverse Industries and Roles

The modern job market is incredibly diverse, with myriad industries and roles to consider. From traditional fields like medicine, law, and education to emerging sectors such as renewable energy, digital marketing, and data science, the possibilities are endless. Start by:

- **Listing Industries of Interest**: Based on your passions and skills, list industries that intrigue you. Don't limit yourself at this stage; the goal is to cast a wide net.
- **Researching Roles**: Within each industry, research various roles and positions. Look into what these jobs entail, the skills they require, and the typical career progression paths.

Utilizing Resources for Research

Leverage a variety of resources to gather information about different career paths:

- **Online Platforms**: Websites like LinkedIn and online job boards can provide valuable insights into different careers, including day-to-day responsibilities, required qualifications, and real-world job experiences.

- **Informational Interviews**: Reach out to professionals in fields of interest for informational interviews. These conversations can provide firsthand insights into the realities of different roles and industries
- **Career Fairs and Networking Events**: Attend career fairs and networking events, both virtual and in-person. These can be excellent opportunities to learn about different sectors and make connections that could lead to job opportunities.

Experimenting and Gaining Experience

Hands-on experience is invaluable in understanding what a career truly involves:

- **Internships and Part-Time Jobs**: Seek internships or part-time positions in areas of interest. These experiences can provide a practical understanding of the industry and help you build a professional network.
- **Volunteering**: Volunteer opportunities, especially in non-profit organizations, can offer experiences relevant to your fields of interest and help develop transferable skills.
- **Side Projects**: Engage in side projects that align with your career interests. These can be particularly useful in creative fields or technology, where tangible projects can showcase your skills and passion.

Reflecting on Fit and Fulfillment

As you explore various career options, it's essential to reflect on how each aligns with your personal values, lifestyle aspirations, and definitions of success. Consider:

- **Work-Life Balance:** How does the career fit with your desired work-life balance?

- **Impact and Fulfillment:** Does the work resonate with your desire to make an impact or provide personal fulfillment?

- **Long-Term Viability:** Consider the long-term prospects of the industry and role, including growth potential, job security, and adaptability to future market changes.

Exploring career options is an iterative process that may evolve as you gain more experience and insights into your preferences and the job market. Keep an open mind and be prepared to pivot as you discover what truly excites and motivates you in your professional life.

Educational Pathways

Choosing the right educational pathway is a pivotal decision in your career journey, shaping not only your expertise and qualifications but also opening doors to various opportunities. This section will guide you through considering different educational avenues and how they align with your career aspirations.

Traditional Degree Programs

Traditional degree programs, whether they are associate's, bachelor's, master's, or doctoral degrees, provide a structured educational foundation in a specific field. Consider the following:

- **Field of Study:** Choose a major or area of study that aligns with your career interests and passions. Research potential career paths that stem from different majors. Be aware that some fields of study, while interesting, may have limited post-graduation career opportunities.

- **Institution Reputation:** The reputation of the institution in your chosen field can impact your career opportunities. However, remember that the individual's drive and skills also play a significant role in success.

- **Internships and Co-ops**: Look for programs that offer practical work experiences through internships or co-operative education, providing real-world experience and networking opportunities.

Vocational and Technical Training

Vocational and technical training programs are designed to prepare students for specific trades or careers, offering a more direct path to employment in fields like IT, healthcare, engineering, and skilled trades.

- **Certifications**: Many industries value specific certifications that demonstrate proficiency in certain skills or technologies. Research which certifications are most respected in your field of interest.

- **Apprenticeships**: Some careers, especially in trades, offer apprenticeships that combine on-the-job training with classroom instruction, providing a hands-on approach to learning and earning.

Online Learning and Self-Directed Study

The rise of online learning platforms has revolutionized access to education, allowing for self-paced, flexible learning that can complement traditional education or serve as a standalone method of skill acquisition.

- **MOOCs (Massive Open Online Courses)**: Platforms like Coursera, edX, and Udacity offer courses from institutions around the world in a vast array of subjects, many of which are free or low-cost.

- **Specializations and Microcredentials**: Some online platforms offer specialized programs or microcredentials in specific skill areas, allowing learners to gain targeted expertise relevant to their career goals.

- **Online Degrees:** Increasingly, institutions are recognizing online students as a complement to on-campus students, where both are expected to complete the same courses and exams to earn the same undergraduate or graduate degree.

Lifelong Learning

In today's rapidly changing job market, continuous learning is crucial. Embrace the concept of lifelong learning by:

- **Staying Current:** Keep up with the latest trends, technologies, and best practices in your field through webinars, workshops, and professional journals.
- **Expanding Horizons:** Don't limit learning to your immediate field of work. Explore interdisciplinary knowledge and skills that can enhance your adaptability and innovation.

Making Informed Decisions

When considering educational pathways, reflect on your career goals, learning preferences, and the financial and time investments required. Keep in mind:

- **ROI (Return on Investment):** Evaluate the potential return on investment of different educational options, considering tuition costs, potential debt, and the career opportunities they may unlock. For example, a student going into debt for a career with a starting pay of $50,000/year will have a much more challenging time repaying a student loan than a student with an earning potential of $125,000/year.
- **Personal Circumstances:** Consider your personal circumstances, including work and family

commitments, when choosing between full-time, part-time, or online learning options.

Choosing the right educational pathway is a deeply personal decision that depends on your career aspirations, learning style, and life circumstances. Regardless of the path you choose, the key is to remain engaged, curious, and committed to your growth and development.

Exploring Military Options

Joining the military is a significant educational and career pathway that offers unique training, benefits, and opportunities for personal and professional growth. This path not only serves as a powerful way to contribute to national service but also provides a robust platform for acquiring skills, education, and experience.

Military Training and Education

The military offers comprehensive training programs tailored to a wide range of specialties and careers. From technical and mechanical skills to leadership and strategic planning, the training provided equips service members with valuable, transferable skills for their military duties and future civilian careers.

Educational Benefits: The GI Bill

One of the most significant benefits of military service is the GI Bill, which provides substantial support for educational pursuits during or after service. It covers tuition, housing, and even supplies for college, making higher education more accessible and affordable for service members and veterans.

Career Progression in the Military

- **Officer Ranks:** Pursuing a career as a military officer typically requires a college degree. Officer training programs, like ROTC (Reserve Officers' Training Corps) or OCS (Officer Candidate School), offer pathways to earn a degree and enter service as a commissioned officer, leading to roles in management, engineering, healthcare, and other fields.

- **Senior Non-Commissioned Officer (NCO) Ranks**: Advancement into senior NCO ranks is increasingly competitive, with many candidates holding college degrees. The military encourages continued education and offers programs to assist service members in obtaining degrees, which can be crucial for career progression and post-military employment opportunities.

Advantages of Military Service

- **Skill Development**: Military service provides rigorous training and real-world experience in various fields, developing both technical and soft skills, such as leadership, teamwork, and problem-solving.
- **Networking and Mentorship**: The military is a community that fosters strong bonds, mentorship, and networking opportunities, valuable assets during and after service.
- **Financial Stability and Benefits**: In addition to educational benefits, military service offers financial stability, healthcare, and housing benefits, contributing to a secure foundation for personal and professional development.

Considering Military Service

When contemplating the military as an educational and career pathway, consider the following:

- **Commitment**: Military service requires a significant commitment of time and dedication. Reflect on your readiness to commit to the service term and the lifestyle

it entails. Recognize that service priorities are often determined by political leadership. So, it is important to be aware of the ways in which political leaders intend to utilize the armed forces during peacetime and during times of conflict.
- **Alignment with Goals**: Ensure that the career opportunities and training offered align with your long-term personal and professional goals.
- **Service and Sacrifice**: Military service is a noble commitment that involves serving the greater good, often requiring personal sacrifices. Consider your willingness and preparedness to make these commitments for the benefits of service and the opportunities it presents.

Joining the military can be a transformative experience, offering a unique blend of education, training, and personal development. For those drawn to the discipline, structure, and opportunities it provides, the military can be a pathway to achieving both immediate and long-term career and educational goals, all while serving the nation and contributing to a larger purpose.

Building Your Personal Brand

In today's interconnected world, building a personal brand has become essential for career advancement and success. Your personal brand is a unique combination of skills, experiences, and values that you present to the world, and it sets you apart from others in your field. Here's how you can build and maintain a strong personal brand:

Define Your Brand

Start by defining the core elements of your brand. Ask yourself:

- What are my unique strengths and skills?
- What values and passions drive my work?

- How do I want to be perceived by peers, mentors, and potential employers?

Use these answers to craft a personal brand statement that encapsulates who you are, what you offer, and what sets you apart.

Consistency Across Platforms

Ensure your brand is consistently represented across all platforms, from your resume to your social media profiles. This includes:

- **Professional Imagery**: Use a professional photo across your profiles to create a recognizable visual identity.

- **Unified Messaging**: Ensure your brand statement, bio, and professional achievements are coherent and consistent across platforms.

- **Content Alignment**: Share and create content that aligns with your brand and showcases your expertise in your field.

Leverage Social Media

Social media platforms are powerful tools for building and showcasing your personal brand:

- **LinkedIn**: Keep your profile up-to-date with your latest achievements, share industry-related content, and engage with your network through comments and posts.

- **Twitter/Instagram**: Use these platforms to share insights, join conversations about industry trends, and connect with thought leaders in your field.

- **Personal Blog or Website**: Consider creating a blog or a personal website where you can showcase your portfolio, share original content, and provide more in-depth information about your professional journey.

Networking and Thought Leadership

Building a personal brand is also about establishing yourself as a thought leader and valuable member of your professional community:

- **Engage in Industry Discussions**: Participate in forums, LinkedIn groups, or Twitter chats related to your industry to share your insights and engage with others.
- **Public Speaking**: Seek opportunities for public speaking at industry conferences, webinars, or local meetups to share your knowledge and increase your visibility.
- **Publishing Articles**: Write articles or blog posts on topics you are passionate about and that demonstrate your expertise. Consider publishing on platforms like LinkedIn, Medium, or industry-specific websites.

Continuous Learning and Adaptation

Your personal brand should evolve as you grow professionally. Stay informed about industry trends, continue developing new skills, and be open to reevaluating and adjusting your brand as needed. This could mean updating your brand statement, acquiring new certifications, or shifting your focus to new areas within your field.

Authenticity and Integrity

Above all, ensure your personal brand reflects your true self. Authenticity resonates with people and builds trust. Stay true to your values and be transparent about your journey, including the challenges you face and how you overcome them.

A compelling illustration of the importance of authenticity and integrity in building a personal brand comes from a job interview scenario. Consider the story of a candidate, whose response during an interview became a telling indicator of his lack of self-awareness and honesty.

During the interview, he was asked to describe a situation from his past projects that did not turn out positively, his role in that situation, and the eventual outcome. His response was striking: he claimed that he was so proficient in his work that his projects never faced any issues. This assertion, far from impressing the interviewers, raised red flags about his credibility and self-awareness. In the realm of complex and challenging projects, it's a given that problems arise; what's crucial is how one addresses and learns from these setbacks.

The candidate's inability to acknowledge any past difficulties or failures suggested a lack of honesty and integrity, traits that are fundamental to a strong personal brand and professional success. His response implied either a denial of typical project challenges or a lack of reflective insight into his own professional experiences. Consequently, this lack of transparency and humility resulted in him not advancing to the next stage of the interview process.

This example underscores the significance of embracing your imperfections and being open about the challenges you've faced. It demonstrates that authenticity and the ability to learn from past experiences are invaluable in building a personal brand that resonates with honesty and integrity.

Building a strong personal brand is an ongoing process that requires time, consistency, and authenticity. By carefully crafting and maintaining your personal brand, you open up new opportunities for professional growth and establish yourself as a distinguished individual in your industry. Remember, your personal brand is a reflection of your journey, including both triumphs and tribulations, and how you navigate these experiences defines your professional identity and reputation.

Networking Strategies

Networking is a pivotal element in building a successful career. It's about creating and nurturing professional relationships that can lead to opportunities, mentorship, and growth. Here are some effective strategies for developing a strong network:

Start with a Clear Objective

Before diving into networking, clarify your goals. Are you seeking job opportunities, looking for mentors, or aiming to learn more about your industry? Knowing your objectives will guide your networking efforts and help you connect with the right people.

Leverage LinkedIn

LinkedIn is an invaluable tool for professional networking. To make the most of it:

- **Optimize Your Profile**: Ensure your LinkedIn profile is complete, professional, and reflects your personal brand.

- **Connect Thoughtfully**: When connecting with someone new, include a personalized message explaining why you're interested in connecting.

- **Engage Regularly**: Share relevant content, comment on posts, and participate in discussions to stay visible and engaged with your network.

Attend Industry Events

Conferences, seminars, and workshops are great for meeting like-minded professionals. To network effectively at these events:

- **Prepare an Elevator Pitch**: Have a short, compelling introduction ready that summarizes who you are and what you do.

- **Be a Good Listener**: Show genuine interest in others. Ask questions and listen actively to their experiences and insights.

- **Follow Up**: After the event, reach out to the people you met with a personalized message. Mention something specific from your conversation to jog their memory.

Join Professional Associations

Becoming a member of professional associations related to your field can provide networking opportunities, access to industry insights, and professional development resources.

Utilize Alumni Networks

Your alma mater's alumni network can be a rich resource for connections. Many colleges and universities have online platforms or alumni groups where you can connect with former classmates and other alumni in your field.

Offer Value

Networking is a two-way street. Think about how you can offer value to your connections, whether it's sharing an interesting article, providing support, or offering your expertise on a subject.

Schedule Informational Interviews

Informational interviews are a great way to learn from people in your field and expand your network. Reach out to professionals whose careers interest you and ask if they'd be willing to share their experiences over a coffee chat or a virtual meeting.

Practice Good Networking Etiquette

- **Be Respectful of Time:** When reaching out for advice or a meeting, be mindful of the other person's time. Offer flexible options and keep the meeting concise.

- **Be Grateful:** Always express gratitude to those who offer you their time, advice, or assistance.

- **Reciprocate:** If someone helps you, think about how you can reciprocate in the future. Networking relationships should be mutually beneficial.

Nurture Your Network

Maintain your professional relationships over time. Regular check-ins, congratulatory messages for new achievements, and sharing relevant information can keep your connections strong and active.

Effective networking isn't about the quantity of connections you have but the quality of the relationships you build. By approaching networking with a strategic, respectful, and genuine mindset, you can create a valuable network that supports your career growth and development.

Crafting Resumes and Cover Letters

Your resume and cover letter are often your first points of contact with potential employers, acting as personal marketing tools that highlight your qualifications and fit for a role. Crafting compelling and tailored documents is crucial in making a strong first impression. Here's how to approach each:

Resumes: Your Professional Snapshot

A resume should succinctly outline your skills, experiences, and achievements, tailored to the job you're applying for. A good rule of thumb is to revise your resume for each job to which you apply. This customization can set your resume apart from those that do not reflect the specific needs for the role. Follow these guidelines to create an impactful resume:

- **Clear Format**: Use a clean, professional layout with clear headings, bullet points, and consistent formatting. Ensure it's easily readable by both humans and applicant tracking systems (ATS).

- **Tailored Content**: Customize your resume for each job application, emphasizing the experiences and skills most relevant to the job description.

- **Quantifiable Achievements**: Where possible, quantify your achievements with numbers or percentages to demonstrate the impact of your work.

- **Skills Section**: Include a mix of hard skills (technical abilities) and soft skills (interpersonal skills), relevant to the job.

- **Education and Certifications**: List your degrees, relevant coursework, and any certifications that enhance your candidacy.

- **Keywords**: Incorporate industry-specific keywords and phrases found in the job posting to ensure your resume aligns with what the employer is seeking and passes ATS filters.

Cover Letters: Your Personal Introduction

A cover letter provides an opportunity to narrate your professional story and express why you're a great fit for the position. Consider the following when writing your cover letter:

- **Personalized Address**: Whenever possible, address the letter to a specific person. If you can't find a name, "Dear Hiring Manager" is a suitable alternative.

- **Engaging Opening**: Start with a compelling opening line that grabs attention. Avoid generic openings like "I'm writing to apply for X position."

- **Connection to the Company**: Demonstrate your knowledge of and interest in the company. Mention specific aspects of the company or role that excite you and align with your career aspirations.

- **Relevant Experiences**: Highlight experiences and skills that directly relate to the job description. Use specific examples to illustrate how you've applied these skills in the past.

- **Your Value Proposition**: Explain how you can contribute to the company and what makes you uniquely qualified for the position.

- **Call to Action**: Conclude by thanking the reader for considering your application and express your interest in discussing your qualifications further in an interview.

- **Professional Tone**: Maintain a professional yet conversational tone throughout the letter. It should reflect your personality but also respect the formalities of the application process.

Final Tips for Both Documents

- **Proofread**: Ensure there are no spelling or grammatical errors. Consider having someone else review your documents for an additional perspective.

- **Contact Information**: Make sure your contact information is up-to-date and easily visible on both documents.

- **Consistency**: Your resume and cover letter should have a consistent design and tone, as they're often reviewed together.

- **Conciseness**: Be concise and direct in your language. Your resume should ideally be one page, especially early in your career, and your cover letter should not exceed one page.

Crafting effective resumes and cover letters takes time and attention to detail. By following these guidelines and continuously refining your documents, you'll improve your chances of making a memorable impression and advancing to the interview stage.

Interview Preparation

Preparing for an interview is crucial in making a positive and lasting impression on potential employers. It involves not just understanding the role and company but also being able to articulate your experiences, skills, and how you align with the company's goals and culture. Here's how to prepare effectively:

Research the Company

Deep knowledge of the company you're interviewing with shows your interest and dedication. Explore the following:

- **Company Website**: Understand the company's mission, values, products or services, and its customer base.
- **Recent News**: Stay updated on recent company news, industry trends, and any challenges they might be facing.
- **Culture and Values**: Learn about the company culture and values through their website, social media, and sites like Glassdoor.

Understand the Role

A thorough understanding of the job description helps you tailor your responses to show you're the perfect fit:

- **Job Responsibilities**: Be clear on what the role entails and think of examples from your past that demonstrate your ability to fulfill these responsibilities.
- **Required Skills and Qualifications**: Align your skills and experiences with those listed in the job description. Prepare to discuss how you've used these skills in past roles.

Practice Common Interview Questions

While you can't predict every question, practicing responses to common interview questions can help you articulate your thoughts clearly and confidently:

- **Tell me about yourself**: Craft a concise narrative that covers your professional background, relevant experiences, and why you're interested in the role.

- **Behavioral Questions**: Use the STAR method (Situation, Task, Action, Result) to answer questions that ask you to describe past work experiences and outcomes.

- **Why do you want to work here?**: Link your professional goals and values with what you've learned about the company.

- **What are your strengths and weaknesses?**: Be honest and strategic; discuss strengths that are relevant to the role and weaknesses that you're actively working to improve.

Prepare Questions for the Interviewer

Having questions for the interviewer shows your interest in the role and the company. Prepare thoughtful questions that reflect your research and genuine curiosity about the position and the organization.

Mock Interviews

Practice with mock interviews, either with friends, family, or through professional services. This can help ease nerves and improve your delivery.

Plan Your Attire

Choose an outfit that aligns with the company's culture but errs on the side of professionalism. Ensure your attire is clean, pressed, and makes you feel confident.

Logistics

- **Directions and Travel Time:** Know the interview location and how long it will take to get there. Plan to arrive 15 minutes early.

- **Documents:** Bring multiple copies of your resume, a list of references, and any other documents that might be relevant to the interview.

Night Before the Interview

- **Review Your Preparation:** Go over your notes, but don't cram. It's important to be rested and clear-headed.

- **Relax:** Set aside time to relax and get a good night's sleep. Being well-rested will help you be more alert and calm during the interview.

Interview preparation is about showcasing your best self and demonstrating your fit for the role and the company. By researching, practicing, and planning, you'll approach the interview with confidence and poise.

Navigating Job Offers

Receiving a job offer is an exciting milestone, but it's important to navigate this phase thoughtfully to ensure the opportunity aligns with your career goals and personal needs. Here's how to approach job offers with confidence and clarity:

Review the Offer Carefully

Take the time to thoroughly review the job offer, paying close attention to:

- **Salary**: Ensure the offered salary meets your expectations and aligns with industry standards for similar roles in your location.
- **Benefits**: Understand the full benefits package, including health insurance, retirement plans, paid time off, and any other perks like remote work options or professional development opportunities.
- **Job Responsibilities**: Review the job description to ensure you fully understand your expected duties and responsibilities.
- **Company Culture**: Reflect on your interactions with the company during the interview process and whether the company's culture and values align with your own.

Evaluate the Offer

Consider the offer in the context of your career aspirations, financial needs, and work–life balance preferences:

- **Career Growth**: Assess the potential for professional development and advancement within the company.
- **Work–Life Balance**: Consider how the role will fit into your personal life, including commute time, work hours, and flexibility.
- **Location**: If the job requires relocation, weigh the implications for your personal and professional life.

Negotiation

If aspects of the offer don't meet your expectations, it's often appropriate to negotiate:

- **Salary Negotiation**: If the offered salary is below your expectations, prepare to negotiate by researching salary data for similar roles and presenting your case based on your skills, experience, and market standards.
- **Benefits and Perks**: Beyond salary, consider negotiating for additional benefits like flexible working hours, professional development opportunities, or a signing bonus.

When negotiating, communicate clearly and professionally, expressing your enthusiasm for the role while explaining your rationale for the requested adjustments.

Seek Clarification

If any part of the offer is unclear, don't hesitate to ask for more information. It's important to fully understand the offer before making a decision.

Take Your Time

Most employers will give you a reasonable amount of time to consider an offer. Use this time to carefully evaluate the offer and consult with mentors, family, or peers if needed.

Responding to the Offer

When you're ready to respond to the offer:

- **Acceptance**: If you decide to accept the offer, do so in writing, confirming the terms of employment and expressing your gratitude and enthusiasm for the opportunity.
- **Declining**: If you decide the position isn't right for you, decline politely and professionally, expressing appreciation for the offer and the opportunity to interview.

- **Multiple Offers**: If you have multiple offers, consider each carefully. Communicate transparently with the employers, but avoid using one offer merely as leverage against another.

After Accepting

Once you've accepted an offer:

- **Resignation**: If you're currently employed, plan a respectful resignation from your current role, providing adequate notice and offering to help with the transition. While a common "myth" is that two-week's notice is required, this is not true. The amount of time is dependent on the role and position. Some in junior roles can leave rather quickly while those in more senior roles might provide several months' notice of their departure.

- **Preparation**: Begin preparing for your new role, including completing any required paperwork, and planning for your start date.

Navigating job offers is a crucial step in your career journey. By carefully reviewing, evaluating, and negotiating job offers, you can make informed decisions that align with your career goals and personal values.

Navigating Workplace Success

Thriving in the workplace involves more than just performing your job duties; it's about active engagement, continuous growth, and skillfully navigating the complexities of a professional environment. To help you excel and carve out a successful career path, consider these detailed strategies:

Understanding Company Culture

- **Observation and Adaptation**: Dedicate your initial days to observing the prevalent norms, communication styles,

and core values. Notice how decisions are made, how teams collaborate, and how achievements are celebrated. For example, you might observe in several zoom meetings how people use the "raise hand" feature before speaking, while in other organizations they simply interject or remail silent.
- **Integration**: Find ways to integrate these cultural insights into your daily work, ensuring your contributions resonate with the company's ethos.

Goal Setting with Precision

- **Collaboration with Management**: Collaborate with your supervisor to define specific, measurable goals that align with your team's objectives and the company's broader vision.
- **Periodic Reviews**: Regularly review these goals with your manager to assess progress, celebrate achievements, and recalibrate as needed.

Mastering Time Management

- **Prioritization**: Employ techniques like Stephen Covey's importance-urgency matrix to prioritize tasks based on urgency and importance. This approach groups tasks into four categories: Important and Urgent; Important and Not Urgent; Not Important and Urgent; and Not Important and Not Urgent. Focus on those tasks that are both important and urgent.
- **Productivity Tools**: Leverage digital tools for task management, and to enhance focus and efficiency.
- **Saying No**: Develop the skill of diplomatically declining non-essential tasks or commitments that don't align with your priorities.
- **Organizational Tools**: Leverage digital tools like Google Calendar or Microsoft Outlook for scheduling and task management to keep your professional and personal commitments organized.

Embracing Feedback and Growth

- **Proactive Feedback Seeking**: Regularly ask for feedback from your manager and peers. Frame your request around specific projects or skills to get actionable insights.
- **Development Plan**: Use the feedback to craft a personal development plan, identifying key areas for growth and actionable steps to improve.

Building Professional Relationships

- **Networking**: Engage in company events, professional associations, and informal gatherings to build your network.
- **Mentorship**: Seek mentorship opportunities within or outside your organization to gain insights and guidance.

Effective Communication

- **Clarity and Adaptation**: Tailor your communication to your audience, ensuring clarity and relevance. Practice active listening to enhance mutual understanding.
- **Conflict Resolution**: Develop strategies for constructive conflict resolution, focusing on clear communication and finding common ground.
- **Empathy and Understanding**: Approach conflicts with an aim to understand the other perspective, employing empathy and active listening.

Demonstrating Initiative

- **Opportunity Identification**: Stay alert to opportunities where you can add value beyond your defined role, suggesting improvements or volunteering for new projects.
- **Innovation**: Don't hesitate to present new ideas or innovations that could benefit your team or the company.

Teamwork and Collaboration

- **Contribution**: Actively contribute to team efforts, offering your skills and support to colleagues.
- **Recognition**: Acknowledge and celebrate the contributions and successes of your teammates, fostering a collaborative and supportive environment.

Commitment to Continuous Learning

- **Skill Enhancement**: Identify emerging skills in your field and pursue training or certifications to stay ahead.
- **Industry Engagement**: Engage with industry content, attend conferences, and participate in professional forums to keep abreast of trends and innovations.

By integrating these strategies into your professional life, you not only elevate your individual performance but also contribute positively to the workplace culture and your team's success. Workplace success is an ongoing journey of learning, adaptation, and contribution, with each step forward enriching your career and personal growth.

Navigating Career Advancement

Career advancement is more than climbing the corporate ladder; it's about broadening your skillset, responsibilities, and influence within your field. To elevate your career, a blend of strategic planning, proactive growth, and understanding the subtleties of workplace dynamics is essential. Below are comprehensive strategies enriched with specific steps and considerations to guide your career progression.

Setting Clear Career Milestones

1. **Define Your Ambitions**: Clearly articulate your long-term career objectives, including desired roles, skill mastery, and key achievements.

2. **Chart a Roadmap**: Break down your overarching goals into achievable milestones. Each milestone should represent a significant step towards your ultimate career aspirations.

Excelling in Your Current Role

1. **Surpass Expectations**: Consistently produce exceptional work, going beyond the basic requirements of your job to demonstrate your commitment and value. Remember, the best way to get promoted to the "next level" is to already be performing at that level.
2. **Seek Additional Responsibilities**: Volunteer for projects that allow you to showcase your strengths and acquire new competencies.

Continuous Skill Development

1. **Identify Industry Trends**: Stay abreast of emerging skills and technologies relevant to your field.
2. **Pursue Learning**: Engage in continuous education through courses, workshops, or certifications that enhance your professional value.

Leveraging Feedback and Mentorship

1. **Seek Constructive Feedback**: Regularly solicit feedback from supervisors and peers to identify growth opportunities.
2. **Find a Mentor**: Establish a mentorship relationship with a seasoned professional who can offer guidance, advice, and insights from their career journey.

Building a Professional Network

1. **Cultivate Relationships**: Actively network with individuals within and outside your organization to build a supportive professional circle.

2. **Engage in Industry Events**: Participate in conferences, seminars, and online forums to connect with like-minded professionals and thought leaders.

Demonstrating Leadership Qualities

1. **Show Initiative**: Proactively address challenges and propose solutions that contribute to your team's success.
2. **Lead by Example**: Volunteer for leadership roles in projects or committees, demonstrating your capability to manage and inspire.

Embracing New Opportunities

1. **Stay Open to Challenges**: Accept assignments that stretch your abilities, showcasing your adaptability and eagerness to grow.
2. **Communicate Your Interest**: Make known your willingness to take on new projects, especially those that align with your career trajectory.

Communicating Your Career Aspirations

1. **Articulate Your Goals**: Share your career aspirations with your manager and HR, expressing your desire for growth and advancement.
2. **Engage in Development Discussions**: Participate in career planning conversations, outlining your ambitions and exploring potential opportunities within the organization.

Mastering Internal Politics and Sponsorship

1. **Navigate Workplace Dynamics**: Develop an understanding of your organization's culture and power structures. Building strategic relationships can help you navigate internal politics effectively.

2. **Secure a Sponsor:** Identify and cultivate a relationship with a senior leader who can act as your advocate, opening doors to pivotal opportunities and providing essential support for your advancement.

Preparing for Transition

1. **Stay Market-Ready:** Keep your resume and professional portfolio current, reflecting your latest achievements and skills. You may wanat to keep a private, detailed multi-page resume the includes all of your accomplishments. You can then tailor this into a small, one-page resume, pulling the neceesary content from the detailed version.
2. **Evaluate Opportunities:** Be discerning about potential roles or transitions, ensuring they align with your career roadmap and personal values.

Career advancement is an ongoing process that demands dedication, strategic action, and a keen understanding of the broader professional landscape. By excelling in your role, committing to lifelong learning, effectively navigating workplace dynamics, and strategically planning your career path, you set the foundation for a rewarding and successful career journey.

Strategies for Navigating Career Setbacks

Career setbacks are not just obstacles; they are integral to the professional growth process, offering invaluable lessons and opportunities for development. The way you address these challenges can significantly enhance your resilience, adaptability, and success. Below is a comprehensive approach to effectively manage and learn from setbacks, complete with specific tools and techniques.

Acknowledge and Accept

The initial step in confronting a setback is to acknowledge its occurrence openly and without self-judgment. Recognize that setbacks are universal and an essential part of professional development. This acceptance paves the way for a constructive approach to overcoming the challenge.

Analyze the Situation

Understanding the factors that contributed to the setback is crucial. Employ techniques like the "Seven Whys" method to drill down to the underlying causes of the setback. Ask "Why?" repeatedly until you uncover the fundamental reason behind the setback.

Seek Support and Feedback

Building a support network is vital:

- **Mentorship**: Engage with a mentor who can offer wisdom, guidance, and an objective viewpoint.
- **Peer Support**: Discuss your experiences with trusted colleagues or peers who might have faced similar challenges.
- **Professional Coaching**: Consider working with a career coach who can provide personalized strategies and support to navigate your specific setback.

Reframe the Experience

Reframing your perspective on the setback can transform it from a negative experience into a catalyst for growth:

- **Learning Opportunities**: Identify the skills and knowledge you can gain from this experience.
- **Positive Reframing**: Practice positive reframing by identifying any potential benefits or opportunities that have emerged from this situation.

Develop a Plan of Action

Creating a clear action plan is essential for moving forward:

- **Skill Development**: Identify any skills or competencies you need to develop to overcome setbacks and plan for their acquisition.
- **Goal Setting**: Use the SMART goals framework to set specific, achievable objectives that will help you recover from the setback and advance your career.

Keep Things in Perspective

It's important to maintain a broader perspective:

- **Long-Term View**: Remind yourself of your long-term career goals and how this setback is just one step in your overall journey.
- **Success Journal**: Keep a record of your past successes and challenges you've overcome to remind yourself of your resilience and capabilities.

Stay Flexible

Adaptability is a key success factor in today's dynamic professional landscape. Be open to new paths or opportunities that may arise from this setback, which could lead to unexpected and fulfilling career developments.

Persistence

Persistence and determination are vital:

- **Resilience Practices**: Develop resilience by setting and working towards small, achievable goals, gradually building your confidence back up.
- **Feedback Loops**: Establish a system for regular feedback on your progress towards overcoming the setback and achieving your goals.

Navigating career setbacks effectively requires a blend of self-reflection, strategic planning, and emotional resilience. By adopting these strategies, you not only overcome challenges but also turn them into opportunities for significant professional and personal growth.

Mastering Work–Life Balance

In the quest for success, mastering the delicate art of work-life balance is crucial for sustaining well-being, productivity, and job satisfaction. As we navigate the demands of a fast-paced work environment, establishing equilibrium between our professional endeavors and personal fulfillment becomes paramount. This section offers actionable strategies and tools to help you cultivate a harmonious work-life balance.

Setting Clear Boundaries

- **Define Work Hours**: Clearly delineate your working hours and communicate these to your team and superiors. Stick to these hours except in cases of urgent deadlines.
- **Digital Detox**: Implement a "no work emails or calls" policy during personal time to mentally disconnect from work.
- **Physical Separation**: If working from home, designate a workspace that you can physically leave at the end of your workday to signal a shift from work to personal time.

Learning to Unplug

- **Tech-Free Zones**: Establish times and areas in your home where technology is off-limits to encourage disconnection from work.

- **Mindful Breaks**: Schedule short, regular breaks during your workday to step away from your desk and rejuvenate.

Making Time for Yourself

- **Schedule Personal Activities**: Just as you would a meeting, block off time in your calendar for personal activities and hobbies that enrich your life.
- **Self-Care Rituals**: Create daily self-care rituals that promote relaxation and well-being, whether it's a morning run, an evening reading session, or a weekly yoga class.

Delegate and Outsource

- **Professional Delegation**: Identify tasks at work that can be delegated to team members or colleagues to free up your bandwidth for higher-priority projects.
- **Personal Outsourcing**: Consider outsourcing time-consuming personal tasks like cleaning or errands to services that can help lighten your load.

Staying Active and Healthy

- **Exercise Plans**: Integrate regular physical activity into your schedule, whether it's a morning workout, a lunchtime walk, or a post-work exercise class.
- **Nutrition and Sleep**: Prioritize a balanced diet and sufficient sleep to maintain your physical and mental health, supporting better balance in life.
- **Mindfulness Apps**: Utilize apps like Calm for guided meditation sessions that fit into your busy schedule.

Regularly Reassess Your Balance

Set a regular schedule, perhaps monthly or quarterly, to assess your work-life balance and make necessary adjustments to your routines and commitments.

Seeking Support

Cultivate a support system of friends, family, and colleagues who understand your goals and can offer assistance or advice with navigating work-life balance challenges.

Crafting a sustainable work-life balance is an ongoing, dynamic process that requires continuous attention and adjustment. By implementing these strategies and leveraging the right tools, you can create a fulfilling and balanced life that supports both your professional aspirations and personal well-being.

Conclusion

Fostering a healthy work–life balance is not just about managing your time efficiently; it's about making intentional choices that reflect your priorities and values in both your professional and personal life. The journey towards balance is ongoing and personal, requiring continuous reflection and adjustment to align with your evolving goals and life circumstances.

Remember, achieving balance does not mean dividing your time equally between work and personal activities but finding a harmony that allows you to thrive in all areas of your life. This harmony looks different for everyone and can change over time based on career demands, personal interests, and life stages.

As you navigate your path toward work–life balance, be kind to yourself and recognize that perfection is not the goal. There will be times when work takes precedence and other times when personal needs are paramount. The key is to remain flexible, resilient, and mindful of your well-being.

Embrace the strategies outlined in this chapter as tools to help you navigate the challenges of balancing work and life. As you do, you'll not only enhance your well-being but also set the stage for sustained success and fulfillment in all aspects of your life.

Chapter 4

Navigating Your Retirement

As you approach the later stages of your career, the concept of retirement transitions from a distant thought to an impending reality. This chapter, "Navigating Your Retirement," is designed to guide you through the multifaceted journey of retirement planning, ensuring that your golden years are not just a time of rest, but a period of fulfillment, growth, and joy.

Retirement is more than just an end to a career; it's the beginning of a new chapter with its own set of opportunities and challenges. Whether you're decades away from retirement or just a few years from saying farewell to your full-time career, it's crucial to start planning now. This chapter will equip you with the tools and knowledge you need to prepare financially, emotionally, and socially for this significant life transition.

We'll delve into the essentials of late-stage career planning, focusing on how to solidify your financial foundation to support your desired retirement lifestyle. Understanding the intricacies of retirement accounts, investment strategies, and healthcare planning will be key to ensuring your financial security.

But retirement planning isn't solely about finances. We'll explore the emotional and psychological aspects of transitioning from a structured work life to the freedom of retirement. From maintaining a sense of purpose to nurturing social connections, we'll cover strategies to ensure your retirement is rich in activities and relationships that bring you joy and fulfillment.

Additionally, we'll touch on the importance of estate planning and making sure your legacy is secured in a manner that reflects your wishes. This chapter will also inspire you to view retirement as an opportunity for continual learning and personal growth, encouraging you to embrace new hobbies, interests, and even post-retirement career ventures.

Through practical advice, actionable strategies, and inspiring case studies, "Navigating Your Retirement" aims to prepare you for a smooth transition into retirement. Let this chapter be your roadmap as you chart a course towards a retirement that's as rewarding and vibrant as the career that preceded it.

Late-Stage Career Planning

As you edge closer to the horizon of retirement, late-stage career planning becomes a pivotal aspect of your journey. This phase is not just about counting down the days but actively preparing to ensure a seamless transition into retirement. Here's how you can strategically approach this crucial stage:

Assess Your Current Financial Status

Begin with a thorough assessment of your current financial landscape. This includes taking stock of all your assets, liabilities, savings, and investments. Understanding where you stand financially will give you a clear picture of how prepared you are for retirement and what steps you need to take to bolster your financial security.

- **Savings and Investments**: Review your retirement accounts, such as 401(k)s, IRAs, and any other investment accounts. Are they on track to meet your retirement goals?
- **Debt:** Aim to reduce or eliminate high-interest debts, including credit card debt, personal loans, and mortgages, to ease financial pressure in retirement.

Set Clear Retirement Goals

What does retirement look like for you? Do you envision a quiet life at home, extensive travel, or perhaps a part-time consultancy? Setting clear, realistic retirement goals will help you plan both financially and emotionally for this next phase.

- **Lifestyle Goals**: Consider the lifestyle you wish to maintain in retirement. Factor in travel, hobbies, and living arrangements.
- **Financial Goals**: Based on your desired lifestyle, calculate the financial resources you'll need. This includes daily living expenses, healthcare, and any additional activities or goals you have in mind.

Understand Your Timeline

Your timeline to retirement is a crucial factor in planning. If you're 5-10 years away, you might focus on aggressive savings and investment strategies. If retirement is imminent, your focus might shift towards asset preservation and fine-tuning your budget for retirement living.

- **Retirement Age**: Consider at what age you intend to retire and how that aligns with social security benefits and withdrawal rules for retirement accounts.
- **Career Endgame**: If you're considering a phased retirement or a transition into part-time work, start those conversations with your employer early.

Enhance Your Skills

Staying relevant in your field can open up opportunities for consultancy or part-time work in retirement, providing both financial and intellectual stimulation.

- **Professional Development**: Investing in your skills not only enriches your late-career phase but can also set you up for potential consulting roles or part-time opportunities in retirement.

- **Networking**: Maintain and expand your professional network. These connections can be invaluable for opportunities post-retirement.

Financial Safety Nets

As you approach retirement, ensuring you have adequate safety nets in place becomes paramount. This includes an emergency fund, insurance policies, and a plan for long-term care.

- **Emergency Fund**: Aim for an emergency fund that can cover 6–12 months of living expenses, especially as you transition out of full-time work.

- **Insurance**: Review your life, health, and long-term care insurance policies to ensure they're adequate for your needs in retirement.

Seeking Professional Advice

Consider consulting with a financial planner specializing in retirement planning. They can provide personalized advice based on your financial situation, retirement goals, and timeline.

Late-stage career planning is about making intentional decisions that align with your vision for retirement. By assessing your financial status, setting clear goals, understanding your timeline, enhancing your skills, and ensuring financial safety nets, you can pave a smooth road to retirement. Remember, the key to a successful transition is preparation, and the time to start is now.

Financial Preparedness for Retirement

Navigating the transition into retirement requires a solid financial strategy to ensure a comfortable and secure future. This section delves into essential financial considerations and practical steps to fortify your financial standing as you approach retirement. By adopting a proactive and informed approach to financial planning, you can pave the way for a stable and fulfilling retirement.

Assessing Your Financial Health

1. **Conduct a Financial Inventory**: Begin with a thorough assessment of your current financial situation, including savings, investments, debts, and potential retirement income sources like pensions, Social Security, or annuities.
2. **Net Worth Calculation**: Calculate your net worth by subtracting your liabilities from your assets. This snapshot provides a clear picture of your financial standing and helps in planning your next steps.

Retirement Savings Strategies

1. **Maximize Retirement Contributions**: Take full advantage of retirement accounts such as 401(k)s and IRAs. Familiarize yourself with the contribution limits, and if you're over 50, leverage catch-up contributions to increase your savings.
2. **Employer Match**: Ensure you're contributing enough to your 401(k) to get any employer match available, as this is essentially free money towards your retirement.

Investment Diversification

1. **Asset Allocation**: Diversify your investment portfolio across various asset classes to balance risk and return. A mix of stocks, bonds, and other investments can offer growth potential and income stability.
2. **Risk Assessment**: Regularly review your investment risk tolerance, especially as you get closer to retirement, to ensure your portfolio aligns with your current comfort level and retirement timeline.

Social Security Optimization

1. **Benefits Analysis:** Use online tools and resources to estimate your Social Security benefits based on different claiming ages to strategize the best time to claim benefits to maximize your income.
2. **Claiming Strategy:** Consider delaying Social Security benefits until after your full retirement age to increase your monthly benefit amount, if financially viable.

Crafting a Retirement Budget

1. **Expense Forecasting:** Create a detailed budget that includes all expected retirement expenses, from daily living costs to leisure and travel.
2. **Income Planning:** Match your projected expenses with your expected retirement income sources to identify any gaps or surpluses in your budget.

Healthcare in Retirement

1. **Medicare and Supplements:** Understand Medicare coverage and explore supplemental health insurance options to cover gaps, focusing on potential out-of-pocket costs for healthcare services.
2. **Long-Term Care Planning:** Consider the future possibility of long-term care and investigate insurance options to cover these potential costs.

Ongoing Financial Review

1. **Annual Check-ups:** Conduct annual financial reviews to adapt your plan to any changes in the financial landscape, personal life circumstances, or retirement goals, ensuring you remain on course.
2. **Professional Guidance:** Consider consulting with a financial advisor for personalized advice and strategies tailored to your unique situation and retirement objectives.

By prioritizing these financial preparedness steps, you'll be better equipped to navigate the complexities of retirement planning. This proactive approach not only secures your financial future but also grants you the peace of mind and freedom to enjoy your retirement years to the fullest.

Healthcare Considerations

As you transition into retirement, understanding and planning for your healthcare needs becomes increasingly important. This phase of life often brings about changes in health status and access to employer-sponsored healthcare, making it essential to have a well-thought-out healthcare strategy.

Medicare Enrollment

Medicare is a critical component of healthcare planning for most retirees. Familiarize yourself with the different parts of Medicare:

- **Part A** covers hospital insurance and is usually premium-free for most enrollees.
- **Part B** covers medical insurance and requires a monthly premium.
- **Part C** (Medicare Advantage Plans) offers an alternative to Original Medicare with different costs and coverage levels.
- **Part D** provides prescription drug coverage.

Enrollment windows and choices can be complex, so it's important to *research your options well in advance of your 65th birthday* to avoid penalties and ensure continuous coverage.

Supplemental Insurance (Medigap)

Consider purchasing a Medigap policy to cover costs not included in Original Medicare, such as copayments, coinsurance, and deductibles. Comparing plans and pricing from different insurers can help you find a policy that best suits your needs and budget.

Long-Term Care Insurance

With the rising costs of long-term care, including in-home care, assisted living, and nursing home care, having long-term care insurance can provide significant financial relief and peace of mind. Policies vary greatly in terms of coverage, eligibility, and premiums, so thorough research and possibly consulting with a financial advisor are recommended.

Health Savings Account (HSA)

If you have a high-deductible health plan before retirement, contributing to an HSA can be a wise move. Funds in an HSA can be used tax-free for qualified medical expenses.

Estimating Healthcare Costs

Estimate your healthcare costs in retirement by considering your current health status, family medical history, and potential future healthcare needs. Don't forget to account for out-of-pocket expenses, including premiums, deductibles, and costs not covered by Medicare or supplemental insurance.

Staying Healthy

Investing in your health through regular exercise, a balanced diet, and preventive care can pay dividends by potentially reducing healthcare costs in retirement. Consider wellness programs, community health resources, and other avenues to maintain and improve your health.

Legal Documents

Ensure you have the necessary legal documents in place, such as a healthcare power of attorney and a living will. These documents allow you to specify your wishes regarding medical treatment and appoint someone to make healthcare decisions on your behalf if you're unable to do so.

Actionable Steps for Healthcare Planning

1. **Medicare Mastery**: Begin by researching Medicare options 6-9 months before turning 65. Utilize resources like the official Medicare website, local seminars, and consulting with a Medicare specialist to understand your choices.
2. **Medicare Supplement Insurance (Medigap) Comparison**: Use online comparison tools and consult with insurance brokers to compare Medigap policies, focusing on coverage details and premium costs.
3. **Long-Term Care Assessment**: Schedule a meeting with a financial advisor to discuss long-term care insurance, considering your personal risk factors and financial capacity.
4. **Maximize HSA Contributions**: If eligible, maximize your HSA contributions before retirement, using online calculators to gauge tax benefits and potential growth.
5. **Healthcare Cost Calculator**: Utilize online healthcare cost calculators to project your retirement healthcare expenses, incorporating variables like health status and geographical location.
6. **Wellness Commitment**: Engage in a health and wellness program tailored for retirees, incorporating activities like fitness classes, nutrition workshops, and regular health screenings.
7. **Legal Preparations**: Consult with an attorney to draft or update your healthcare power of attorney and living will, ensuring your healthcare wishes are clearly documented.

By meticulously addressing these healthcare considerations, you can approach retirement with a robust plan that ensures you're well-prepared for the healthcare landscape in your golden years, allowing you to focus on enjoying this new chapter of life.

Lifestyle Vision for Retirement

Envisioning your retirement lifestyle is an exciting and crucial step in preparing for this new chapter of life. This section will guide you through contemplating and planning for how you want to spend your retirement years, ensuring they align with your personal aspirations and values.

Defining Your Ideal Retirement

Start by imagining your perfect day in retirement. Consider where you are, what you're doing, who you're with, and how you feel. This exercise can help clarify what matters most to you, whether it's leisure, adventure, family time, or personal development.

Location and Living Arrangements

Decide where you want to live during retirement. Some prefer staying in their current home for its familiarity and community ties, while others might dream of relocating to a retirement community, a new city, or even abroad. Consider factors such as climate, proximity to family and friends, cost of living, and access to healthcare and recreational activities.

Hobbies and Interests

Retirement is the perfect time to pursue hobbies and interests you may have put on hold. Whether it's gardening, painting, traveling, or learning a new instrument, think about the activities that bring you joy and fulfillment. Planning for these pursuits now ensures you have the resources and opportunities to engage in them fully once retired.

Social Connections

Maintaining and building social connections is vital for a fulfilling retirement. Consider how you'll stay in touch with friends, family, and former colleagues. Look into clubs, groups, or volunteer opportunities that align with your interests and provide social interaction.

Physical Activity and Health

A healthy lifestyle is key to enjoying your retirement years. Plan for regular physical activity that you enjoy, such as walking, cycling, yoga, or swimming. Staying active not only benefits your physical health but also your mental well-being.

Continued Learning and Growth

Lifelong learning keeps your mind sharp and can be incredibly rewarding. Think about subjects you'd like to explore or skills you want to develop. Community colleges, online courses, and local workshops offer a plethora of learning opportunities for retirees.

Part-Time Work or Volunteering

Some retirees find fulfillment in continuing to work part-time or engaging in volunteer work. This can provide a sense of purpose, extra income, and opportunities to use your skills and experience in meaningful ways. Reflect on whether this aligns with your retirement vision.

Travel

If travel is on your retirement wish list, consider the types of trips you'd like to take, from leisurely cruises to adventure travel or cultural immersion experiences. Planning and budgeting for travel early can make your dreams more attainable.

Adjusting Your Vision Over Time

Your vision for retirement may evolve as you approach and enter this phase of life. Regularly revisiting and adjusting your plans ensures that your retirement remains aligned with your current values and circumstances.

Bringing Your Vision to Life

- **Create a Retirement Vision Board**: A vision board can be a powerful tool for bringing your retirement dreams to life. This visual representation can serve as a daily reminder and motivation to achieve your desired retirement lifestyle. Compile images, quotes, and items that represent your retirement goals and aspirations.
- **Develop a Flexible Plan**: Recognize that your desires may shift over time. Stay open to revising your retirement plan as your interests or circumstances change.

Tools and Steps for Implementation

- **Financial Planning Software**: Use spreadsheets or online finanaical planning tools to map out your financial needs in retirement, ensuring you have the resources to support your desired lifestyle.
- **Lifestyle Design Workshops**: Participate in workshops or seminars focused on retirement planning that address both financial and lifestyle aspects.
- **Regular Check-ins**: Set aside time annually to review your retirement plan. Assess what's working, what's changed, and what adjustments are needed to stay aligned with your vision.

By thoughtfully considering each aspect of your desired retirement lifestyle and taking proactive steps to integrate your interests, relationships, and personal growth into your future, you can craft a retirement that is not only rewarding and enriching but also a true reflection of your life's aspirations. Remember, retirement is not an end but a new, exciting chapter full of possibilities and opportunities for fulfillment.

Emotional and Psychological Preparation

As you approach significant transitions in your career, such as retirement, understanding the emotional and psychological landscape of these changes is crucial. This section offers a deeper exploration of mental preparation strategies, ensuring you navigate career transitions with grace, well-being, and fulfillment.

Acknowledging the Emotional Spectrum

Transitions, especially retirement, evoke a wide range of emotions, from exhilaration at newfound freedom to apprehension about the unknown. Acknowledge and accept these emotions as natural responses to significant life changes. Tools like emotional journaling can help you articulate and process these feelings, providing clarity and easing the transition.

Redefining Purpose and Identity

With careers often tied to personal identity, transitioning can prompt a reevaluation of self. It's essential to explore new sources of purpose and meaning:

- **Engage in Reflective Practices**: Activities like meditation and mindfulness can help you connect with your core values and interests, guiding you toward fulfilling post-career roles.
- **Experiment with New Roles**: Consider volunteering, mentoring, or engaging in community leadership to find new avenues for contribution and purpose.

Cultivating a Supportive Community

The importance of a robust support network cannot be overstated during transitional phases:

- **Leverage Social Platforms**: Social meeting and networking tools can connect you with communities sharing similar interests or undergoing similar life changes.
- **Maintain Connections**: Regular catch-ups with peers, whether in person or via platforms like Zoom, can provide shared understanding and support.

Establishing a Fulfilling Routine

The sudden shift in daily structure post-retirement can be jarring. Creating a new routine is pivotal. Use a dialy calndar or electornic tools like Google Calendar or Microsoft Outlook to structure your day with activities that promote holistic well-being, from physical exercise to social engagements.

Keeping the Mind Engaged

Mental engagement remains vital for cognitive health:

- **Embrace Lifelong Learning**: Platforms like Coursera or Khan Academy offer courses to keep you intellectually stimulated.
- **Pursue Creative Outlets**: Creative expression through art, writing, or music can provide mental stimulation and emotional release.

Seeking Simplicity and Fulfillment

There's profound joy to be found in life's simpler moments. Regular mindfulness or gratitude practices can help you savor the everyday pleasures of life, enhancing overall fulfillment.

Prioritizing Mental Wellness

Be vigilant about your mental health, recognizing when to seek professional guidance. Utilize apps like Headspace for guided meditations or BetterHelp for online counseling, ensuring you have support when navigating emotional challenges.

Embracing Continuous Self-Discovery

View retirement or career transitions as opportunities for ongoing self-exploration. Dedicate time to personal projects or hobbies that have always intrigued you, fostering a sense of continuous growth and discovery.

Celebrating Your Journey

Remember to honor and celebrate the milestones you reach. Mark significant transitions with meaningful rituals or gatherings, acknowledging your achievements and the new chapters ahead.

Emotional and psychological readiness is about more than adjusting to a new daily rhythm; it's about wholeheartedly embracing the next chapter of your life with curiosity, resilience, and an openness to discovering new sources of joy and fulfillment. This holistic approach ensures that as you navigate your career's peaks and valleys, you do so with a foundation of mental and emotional strength, ready to explore the rich tapestry of experiences that await.

Estate Planning

Estate planning is a crucial aspect of retirement preparation, ensuring that your assets are managed and distributed according to your wishes after you pass away. It provides peace of mind, not just for you, but also for your loved ones, by clarifying your intentions and minimizing potential conflicts. This section outlines the key components of estate planning and how to approach this important task.

Understanding Estate Planning

Estate planning involves making decisions about who will receive your assets and handle your responsibilities after your death or incapacitation. It encompasses a range of documents and decisions, from wills and trusts to powers of attorney and healthcare directives.

Creating a Will

A will is a fundamental element of estate planning. It specifies how you want your assets to be distributed and can appoint guardians for minor children. Without a will, state laws determine the distribution of your assets, which might not align with your wishes.

Establishing Trusts

Trusts can be an effective tool for managing and protecting assets, both during your lifetime and after. They offer benefits such as avoiding probate, reducing estate taxes, and specifying conditions for asset distribution. Consider whether a revocable living trust, which can be altered during your lifetime, or an irrevocable trust, which cannot, is best suited to your needs.

Powers of Attorney

A durable power of attorney allows you to appoint someone to manage your financial affairs if you become incapacitated. This document is essential for ensuring that your finances are handled according to your preferences, even if you're unable to make decisions yourself.

Healthcare Directives

A healthcare directive, also known as a living will, outlines your wishes regarding medical treatment if you're unable to communicate them yourself. Additionally, appointing a healthcare proxy empowers someone to make medical decisions on your behalf.

Beneficiary Designations

Ensure that your retirement accounts, life insurance policies, and other assets with beneficiary designations are up to date. These designations often supersede instructions in wills, so it's important they reflect your current wishes.

Documenting Your Wishes

Keep all your estate planning documents in a secure, accessible location and inform your executor, family members, or other trusted individuals of their whereabouts. Consider also leaving detailed instructions about your digital assets, including social media accounts and digital files.

Professional Guidance

Estate planning can be complex, and laws vary by state. Seeking advice from an estate planning attorney can ensure your documents are legally sound and accurately reflect your intentions. Financial advisors and tax professionals can also offer valuable insights, especially when it comes to minimizing tax burdens and planning for asset distribution.

Regular Reviews and Updates

Life changes, such as marriage, divorce, the birth of children or grandchildren, and significant changes in assets, can affect your estate plans. Regularly review and update your documents to ensure they align with your current situation and wishes.

Estate planning is a profound expression of care for your loved ones, providing clarity and security during difficult times. By taking the time to establish a comprehensive estate plan, you safeguard your legacy and ensure your wishes are honored.

Social Connections and Community

Retirement offers a unique opportunity to enrich your social life and engage more deeply with your community. This phase of life can bring significant changes to your social network, especially as you transition away from the workplace. Cultivating and maintaining social connections is crucial for emotional well-being and can greatly enhance the quality of your retirement years. This section explores ways to build and sustain these important relationships.

Nurturing Existing Relationships

Retirement can affect your daily interactions, particularly with colleagues you're used to seeing regularly. Make an effort to maintain these connections by scheduling regular meet-ups, such as lunch dates or group activities. Similarly, staying in touch with friends and family members, and making these relationships a priority, can provide a strong support network and a sense of belonging.

Expanding Your Social Circle

Retirement is an ideal time to meet new people and expand your social circle. Engage in activities that interest you, such as joining clubs, taking classes, or volunteering. These settings not only provide social interaction but also the opportunity to connect with individuals who share your interests.

Leveraging Technology

Technology can be a powerful tool for staying connected, especially with friends and family who live far away. Utilize social media, video calls, and messaging apps to keep in touch. Online forums and social platforms can also introduce you to communities with shared interests, whether it's gardening, photography, or any other hobby.

Volunteering and Giving Back

Volunteering offers a way to contribute to your community while meeting others who value the same causes. Whether it's through local charities, schools, or community centers, giving your time can lead to fulfilling experiences and meaningful connections.

Participating in Community Events

Stay informed about local events and participate in community gatherings, festivals, and workshops. These events can be enjoyable ways to engage with your community and meet people from different walks of life.

Embracing New Roles

Retirement can provide the freedom to explore new roles, such as mentorship or advisory positions. Sharing your knowledge and experience with others can be incredibly rewarding and can help forge new relationships based on mutual respect and learning.

Staying Active in Group Activities

Consider joining or forming groups centered around physical activities you enjoy, such as walking clubs, dance classes, or sports teams. These activities offer the dual benefits of physical exercise and social interaction.

Seeking Social Opportunities in Living Arrangements

For those considering a move in retirement, look for living arrangements that offer built-in social opportunities, such as retirement communities or neighborhoods with active community centers. Senior centers and senior communities also offer outlets and activiteis for engaging with other seniors.

Balancing Solitude and Socializing

While social connections are important, it's also valuable to appreciate and embrace solitude. Balance your social activities with personal time, allowing for reflection, relaxation, and the pursuit of individual interests.

Cultivating Inter-Generational Connections

Engage with individuals of different ages, including younger family members or individuals from different generations within your community. These inter-generational interactions can provide fresh perspectives, mutual learning opportunities, and a deeper sense of community.

Building and maintaining social connections in retirement requires proactive effort but can lead to a richer, more fulfilling life. By diversifying your social activities, embracing technology, and contributing to your community, you can enjoy a vibrant social life that supports your well-being throughout your retirement years.

Continual Learning and Growth

Retirement opens up a new chapter for personal development and lifelong learning. Freed from the constraints of full-time work, you have the unique opportunity to explore new interests, deepen your knowledge, and even acquire new skills. This section delves into the importance of continual learning and growth in retirement and how they contribute to your overall well-being and sense of fulfillment.

Embracing a Growth Mindset

Adopting a growth mindset in retirement means viewing this period as an opportunity for expansion and exploration. It involves recognizing that your ability to learn and grow is not fixed but can be developed through dedication and effort. This mindset encourages curiosity, resilience, and a willingness to step out of your comfort zone.

Setting Learning Goals

Identify areas where you'd like to expand your knowledge or skills. These could be related to hobbies, academic interests, or practical life skills. Setting specific learning goals gives you direction and a sense of purpose, making the learning process more structured and rewarding.

Exploring Educational Opportunities

Many community colleges, universities, and online platforms offer courses tailored to retirees or older adults, covering a wide range of subjects from art and history to technology and languages. Take advantage of these resources to pursue formal or informal education in areas that intrigue you.

Leveraging Technology for Learning

Digital platforms provide endless opportunities for self-directed learning. Websites like Coursera, Udemy, Khan Academy, and TED Talks offer courses and lectures on virtually any topic imaginable. E-books, podcasts, and educational apps are also valuable tools for exploring new subjects at your own pace.

Joining Learning Communities

Look for local clubs or groups focused on learning and personal growth, such as book clubs, writing workshops, or discussion groups. These communities offer not only knowledge but also the chance to engage with like-minded individuals and expand your social network.

Turning Hobbies into Learning Experiences

Retirement is the perfect time to dive deeper into your hobbies or explore new ones. Whether it's gardening, photography, cooking, or painting, approach your hobbies with an intent to learn and master new techniques and concepts.

Volunteering as a Learning Experience

Volunteering can be a rewarding way to learn new skills and gain different perspectives. Many organizations and programs value the life experiences of retirees and can offer opportunities to learn about new fields, from conservation efforts to mentoring youth.

Continual learning and growth in retirement can lead to a richer, more satisfying life, filled with new challenges and discoveries. By actively pursuing personal development, you not only enhance your own life but also inspire those around you to embrace the joy of lifelong learning.

Retirement Transitions

The transition into retirement is a profound change that goes beyond the financial aspects, affecting your daily routines, social interactions, and sense of purpose. Successfully navigating this transition requires thoughtful planning and a willingness to adapt. This section offers guidance on how to manage and embrace the changes retirement brings, ensuring a smooth and fulfilling shift into this new life stage.

Gradual Transition

Consider a phased approach to retirement if possible. Gradually reducing your work hours or taking on part-time or consulting roles can ease the shift from full-time work to full retirement. This gradual transition can help you adjust to the changes in your schedule and identity while maintaining some structure and income.

Developing New Routines

The loss of work-related routines can leave a void in your daily life. Establish new routines that incorporate activities you enjoy and that contribute to your well-being, such as exercise, hobbies, volunteering, or social engagements. A structured yet flexible daily routine can provide a sense of normalcy and purpose.

Reassessing Your Identity

Work often forms a significant part of one's identity. Retirement offers an opportunity to explore and redefine who you are beyond your professional life. Reflect on your values, interests, and the roles you cherish, such as being a family member, friend, mentor, or community member, and embrace these aspects of your identity.

Staying Socially Connected

Maintain existing relationships and build new ones. Stay in touch with former colleagues, join clubs or groups related to your interests, and engage in community activities. Social connections are vital for emotional support and can provide a sense of belonging and community.

Embracing New Opportunities

View retirement as an opportunity to pursue passions and interests you may have set aside during your working years. Whether it's traveling, learning, volunteering, or starting a new hobby, retirement is your time to explore and engage in activities that bring you joy and fulfillment.

Maintaining Physical and Mental Health

Prioritize your physical and mental health through regular exercise, a balanced diet, and engaging in activities that stimulate your mind and foster creativity. Consider regular medical check-ups to stay on top of your health and prevent potential issues.

Seeking Support

Retirement can be an emotional rollercoaster. If you're struggling with the transition, don't hesitate to seek support from family, friends, or professionals. Counseling or retirement coaching can provide strategies to manage the changes and make the most of your retirement years.

Giving Back

Retirement can be an enriching time to give back to your community through volunteering or mentoring. Sharing your knowledge, skills, and time can be incredibly rewarding and can help you connect with others in meaningful ways.

Celebrating the Milestone

Recognize and celebrate the achievement of reaching retirement. This significant life milestone marks the culmination of years of hard work and dedication and the beginning of an exciting new chapter full of possibilities.

Navigating the transition into retirement is a personal journey that requires flexibility, planning, and a positive outlook. By embracing change, pursuing new interests, and staying connected with others, you can make your retirement years some of the most rewarding and fulfilling of your life.

Your Action Plan

As you approach the transition into retirement, creating a concrete action plan can help you navigate this significant life change with confidence and purpose. This section provides a step-by-step guide to developing your personalized retirement action plan, ensuring a smooth and fulfilling transition.

Reflect on Your Retirement Vision

- **Task 1:** Spend time reflecting on your vision for retirement. Consider what you want your daily life to look like, including activities, hobbies, and lifestyle. Write down your vision to clarify your goals.

Assess Your Financial Readiness

- **Task 2:** Conduct a thorough assessment of your financial situation. Review your savings, investments, debts, and potential retirement income sources. If necessary, consult a financial advisor to ensure you're on track to meet your financial needs in retirement.

Plan for Healthcare

- **Task 3:** Research your healthcare options, including Medicare and supplemental insurance. Calculate estimated healthcare costs and ensure you have a plan in place to cover these expenses.

Develop New Routines

- **Task 4:** Start thinking about how you'll structure your days in retirement. Plan for activities that promote physical health, mental stimulation, and social interaction. Consider drafting a sample weekly schedule as a starting point.

Expand Your Social Network

- **Task 5:** Identify ways to maintain existing relationships and build new ones. Look into clubs, groups, or volunteer opportunities that align with your interests. Make a list of organizations or activities you'd like to explore.

Embrace Lifelong Learning

- **Task 6**: Make a list of subjects or skills you're interested in pursuing. Research local classes, online courses, or workshops available in your areas of interest.

Prepare for Emotional Adjustments

- **Task 7**: Acknowledge and prepare for the emotional aspects of retirement. Consider journaling about your feelings or discussing your thoughts and concerns with friends, family, or a counselor.

Finalize Legal and Estate Matters

- **Task 8**: Ensure all your estate planning documents are up to date, including your will, trusts, power of attorney, and healthcare directives. Store these documents in a safe, accessible place and inform your executor or close family members of their location.

Set Short–Term and Long–Term Goals

- **Task 9**: Break down your retirement vision into achievable short-term and long-term goals. Assign realistic timelines and consider any steps or resources needed to accomplish these goals.

Schedule Regular Reviews

- **Task 10**: Set aside time for regular reviews of your retirement plan. Assess your progress toward your goals, and make adjustments as needed based on changes in your interests, financial situation, or other circumstances.

Celebrate Milestones

- **Task 11**: Recognize and celebrate milestones as you progress through your retirement transition. Acknowledging achievements, big or small, can provide motivation and a sense of accomplishment.

Creating and implementing an action plan is a dynamic process that can help you navigate the transition into retirement with intention and purpose. By taking proactive steps and regularly reviewing your plan, you can ensure that your retirement years are not only well-prepared for but also richly rewarding and aligned with your personal vision for this new chapter in life.

Conclusion

Navigating your retirement is a comprehensive journey that extends beyond mere financial planning to include emotional, social, and personal growth aspects. This chapter, "Navigating Your Retirement," has aimed to provide a holistic roadmap, equipping you with the knowledge and tools necessary for a fulfilling transition into this significant life phase. As we've explored, retirement is not the conclusion of active life but rather an exciting beginning, replete with opportunities for personal development, continued learning, and deepened social engagements.

In preparing for retirement, we've covered the importance of financial stability, the intricacies of healthcare planning, the joy of cultivating new and existing relationships, and the satisfaction of engaging in lifelong learning and community participation. The strategies and insights shared here are designed to help you approach retirement not just with readiness but with enthusiasm, viewing it as a vibrant period of life where growth and fulfillment continue to flourish.

As you move forward, remember that the quality of your retirement is in your hands. It's about making intentional choices, staying connected, and embracing the myriad opportunities that life continues to offer. Your retirement can be as dynamic and enriching as the career that preceded it, marked by exploration, achievement, and continuous learning.

May you navigate your retirement with confidence and joy, embarking on this new chapter with a heart full of anticipation for the adventures that lie ahead. Your journey through career and into retirement is a testament to your life's work and aspirations, setting the stage for a future that's not only secure but also abundant in happiness and satisfaction.

Chapter 5

The Power of Discipline and Habits

In the journey toward personal and professional success, discipline and habits emerge as the silent architects of our destinies. They are the unseen forces that shape our daily actions, sculpt our character, and, ultimately, determine the trajectory of our lives. This chapter, "The Power of Discipline and Habits," delves into the profound impact that structured behaviors and consistent practices can have on our ability to achieve our goals and realize our fullest potential.

Discipline is often misconceived as a form of restriction, a barrier to freedom. However, within these pages, we'll explore how discipline liberates us by creating a framework within which our creativity and productivity can flourish. It's the disciplined approach to our days that allows us to make the most of our time, energy, and talents, turning lofty aspirations into tangible achievements.

Habits, on the other hand, are the daily rituals that, piece by piece, build the mosaic of our lives. Whether we're conscious of it or not, our habitual actions carve deep grooves into the bedrock of our existence. By understanding the science of habit formation and harnessing it to our advantage, we can transform our lives in ways we've only imagined.

This chapter will guide you through the fundamentals of building a disciplined life and cultivating habits that serve your ambitions. From the psychological underpinnings of habit formation to practical strategies for embedding discipline into your daily routine, we'll cover the essential elements you need to elevate your life to the next level.

We'll also confront the challenges that come with altering long-standing behaviors and introduce you to tools and techniques for maintaining your newfound discipline and habits over the long haul. Through real-life examples and actionable advice, you'll learn how to create a life that reflects your highest ideals.

Embrace the journey ahead, for it is through the power of discipline and habits that your most significant successes will be forged. Let's begin.

Understanding Discipline

At its core, discipline is the practice of training oneself to act in accordance with specific rules or goals, often requiring the sacrifice of immediate pleasure or comfort for long-term gain. It is a skill that can be developed and honed over time, serving as the bedrock upon which the edifice of success is built. Discipline is what keeps us on track when distractions abound, ensuring we remain focused on our long-term objectives. To fully harness its power, we must first understand its true nature and the role it plays in our lives.

Ironically, discipline is a pathway to freedom, not a constraint upon it. By setting boundaries and standards for our behavior, we gain control over our impulses and reactions, which in turn, frees us from being at the mercy of fleeting desires or external pressures. This self-imposed structure creates a space where our true priorities can flourish, enabling us to live more intentional and fulfilling lives.

Success in any area of life, be it personal, academic, or professional, is rarely the result of random chance or innate talent alone. It is the outcome of consistent effort, resilience, and the disciplined pursuit of clearly defined goals. Discipline ensures that we make consistent progress towards these goals by doing what is necessary, even when we may not feel like it. It's the bridge between intention and accomplishment, turning aspiration into reality.

Developing discipline is akin to building muscle; it requires consistent effort and the right exercises. Start with small, manageable tasks that require discipline to complete. Over time, as you successfully meet these smaller challenges, your capacity for discipline will grow, allowing you to tackle more significant and more demanding tasks. It's about making a series of choices that align with your goals, even when they're the harder choices to make.

It's essential to approach the cultivation of discipline with self-compassion. There will be times when you falter, moments when your resolve wanes, and you succumb to temptation. Such instances are not failures but opportunities for learning and growth. Treat yourself with kindness, reflect on what led to the lapse, and use those insights to strengthen your discipline moving forward.

Discipline is not just a trait of the stoic or the austere; it is a quality that can be developed by anyone who wishes to take control of their life and steer it towards success. By understanding and embracing discipline, you equip yourself with a powerful tool to navigate the complexities of life and achieve your most cherished goals.

The Science of Habits

At the heart of every routine action lies a habit, a subconscious script that plays out behind the scenes of our daily lives. Understanding the science of habits is akin to unlocking a hidden control panel within ourselves, one that governs far more of our behavior than we might imagine. This section will delve into the neurological basis of habits, the structure that underpins them, and the profound implications they have for our personal development and success.

The Habit Loop

Central to the formation and execution of habits is a three-part process known as the "habit loop." A phrase devleoped by Charles Duhigg, this habit loop consists of a **cue**, a **routine**, and a **reward**. The cue triggers the habit, the routine is the behavior itself, and the reward is the benefit received from the behavior. Over time, this loop becomes increasingly automatic, transforming conscious actions into unconscious habits.

- **Cue:** A cue can be anything that acts as a signal to initiate the habitual behavior. It might be an emotional state, a specific time of day, a location, or the presence of certain people or objects. Recognizing these cues is the first step in understanding and modifying habits.

- **Routine:** This is the habit itself, the action you take automatically when triggered by the cue. Routines can be physical (going for a run), mental (recalling a comforting memory), or emotional (feeling a rush of excitement).

- **Reward:** The reward is what reinforces the habit loop. It's the benefit or pleasure derived from the routine, encouraging the behavior to recur. Rewards can vary widely, from the satisfaction of a craving to a sense of accomplishment or relief.

In the subfield of artificial intelligence, there's a concept remarkably similar to the habit loop known as reinforcement learning. This technique, which powers Large Language Models like OpenAI's ChatGPT or Google's Gemini, involves a similar loop structure. In reinforcement learning, a *cue* is represented as a *state*, essentially an observation of the surrounding environment. The *routine* is analogous to the selection of an optimal *action* in response to the current state and the execution of that *action*. Finally, the *reward* or feedback is received, evaluating the effectiveness of the action taken. This feedback helps to "reinforce" behaviors or actions that lead to positive outcomes, while reducing those that yield negative results.

Some rewards in reinforcement learning, akin to immediate feedback like swerving to avoid a car accident, are instant. Others, such as the outcome of a chess game, are realized after a sequence of actions over time. This delayed feedback mirrors the way long-term habits are formed and reinforced in humans.

By drawing parallels between the habit loop and the mechanism of reinforcement learning in AI, we can better appreciate the power of habit formation and the sophisticated nature of AI learning processes. Both systems rely on the consistent application of actions and feedback to refine and improve outcomes, highlighting the interconnectedness of human behavioral psychology and artificial intelligence.

The Role of the Brain

Neurologically, habits form in the basal ganglia, a part of the brain integral to the development of emotions, memories, and pattern recognition. When a behavior becomes a habit, the brain starts to expend less energy on it, allowing us to perform the routine without conscious thought. This efficiency is beneficial for freeing up mental resources but can be a double-edged sword when it comes to breaking bad habits.

Habit Formation

Habit formation is not an overnight process; it involves a gradual transition from effortful control to automaticity. Research suggests that the average time to form a habit is about 66 days, but this can vary significantly depending on the individual and the complexity of the behavior.

Changing Habits

Understanding the habit loop is crucial not just for recognizing how habits form but also for changing them. To modify a habit, one can keep the same cue and reward but change the routine that occurs as a result. This approach maintains the structure of the habit loop while altering its content, a strategy often more effective than trying to eliminate the loop altogether.

In essence, the science of habits reveals that our behaviors are more than just a series of choices; they are a complex interplay of cues, routines, and rewards deeply embedded in our neural pathways. By unraveling this intricate tapestry, we gain the power to reweave it, transforming our habits, our actions, and ultimately, our lives.

Identifying Key Habits

The journey toward personal excellence is paved with the bricks of small, daily habits. These habits, seemingly insignificant on their own, collectively form the foundation of our lives. To elevate ourselves to new heights of success, it's imperative to identify and cultivate key habits that propel us forward. This section explores the habits that are quintessential for anyone looking to enrich their life and achieve their fullest potential.

Habit of Early Rising

The early morning hours are a treasure trove of productivity and tranquility. Waking up early is a habit shared by many successful individuals, providing a head start to the day where one can focus on personal goals, exercise, or plan the day ahead without the distractions that come later.

Habit of Regular Exercise

Physical well-being is inextricably linked to mental and emotional health. Regular exercise not only strengthens the body but also enhances cognitive function and emotional resilience. Making exercise a habit ensures that it becomes a non-negotiable part of your routine, contributing to overall success and well-being.

Habit of Effective Time Management

Time is one of our most precious resources, and how we choose to spend it can significantly impact our success. The habit of effective time management involves prioritizing tasks, setting boundaries, and eliminating time-wasters, thereby ensuring that your actions align with your goals.

Habit of Mindfulness and Reflection

In the hustle and bustle of daily life, it's easy to lose sight of the bigger picture. The habit of mindfulness and reflection allows you to stay connected with your inner self, evaluate your progress, and make conscious adjustments to your path. This could be through meditation, journaling, or simply spending time in nature.

Habit of Networking and Relationship Building

Success is seldom a solo endeavor. The habit of networking and building meaningful relationships can open doors to opportunities, provide support during challenging times, and enrich your personal and professional life.

Habit of Financial Discipline

Financial stability is a cornerstone of a secure and prosperous life. The habit of financial discipline involves budgeting, saving, investing, and mindful spending. This habit ensures that you are working towards financial freedom and security.

Integrating Key Habits

Identifying these key habits is just the beginning. The next step is to integrate them into your daily life. Start small, focusing on one habit at a time, and gradually build upon your successes. Remember, consistency is key. It's not the intensity of your actions but the regularity that leads to lasting change.

As you embark on this journey of habit cultivation, be patient with yourself. Habits take time to form, and there will be setbacks. However, with persistence and dedication, these key habits will become second nature, propelling you towards a life of success and fulfillment.

Building New Habits

Embarking on the journey of building new habits is akin to planting seeds for a future garden of success. It requires preparation, care, and patience, but the rewards are bountiful. This section outlines a step-by-step guide to developing new, positive habits that can transform your life.

Start Small

The key to forming new habits is to start small. Choose one habit you wish to develop and break it down into the smallest possible action. For instance, if your goal is to read more, start with a page a day. This approach reduces the resistance to starting and helps to build momentum.

Anchor Your New Habit

An effective strategy for habit formation is to anchor the new habit to an existing one. This means performing the new habit immediately before or after a well-established habit. For example, if you brush your teeth every night without fail, consider meditating for a few minutes right after as your new habit.

Be Consistent

Consistency is the bedrock of habit formation. Perform your new habit at the same time and in the same place every day to strengthen the association in your mind. Consistency over time reinforces the habit loop, making the behavior more automatic.

Use Reminders

In the early stages of forming a new habit, external reminders can be incredibly helpful. These can be physical notes placed in strategic locations, digital reminders on your phone, or even alarms. The goal is to keep your new habit at the forefront of your mind until it becomes ingrained.

Reward Yourself

Incorporating immediate rewards after completing your new habit can significantly enhance habit formation. Rewards reinforce the habit loop by creating a positive association with the behavior. Choose rewards that are healthy and align with your long-term goals.

Track Your Progress

Keeping a habit tracker can be a powerful motivator. Marking off each day you successfully perform your new habit provides visual proof of your progress and can encourage you to keep going. It also helps you identify patterns or obstacles that may be hindering your progress.

Be Patient and Flexible

Building a new habit is a process that requires patience. Don't be discouraged by setbacks or days when you falter. What matters is getting back on track as quickly as possible. Be flexible in your approach and willing to adjust your strategies as you learn what works best for you.

Build on Small Wins

As your new habit starts to take hold, gradually increase the complexity or duration of the behavior. Building on small wins maintains momentum and prevents complacency. For example, if your new habit is to exercise, gradually increase the intensity or duration of your workouts as you become more accustomed to the routine.

Cultivate a Supportive Environment

Your environment plays a significant role in habit formation. Make your surroundings conducive to your new habit by removing temptations and obstacles. Surround yourself with people who support your goals and consider joining groups with similar interests to reinforce your new behavior.

Reflect and Adjust

Regular reflection on your habit-building journey allows you to assess what's working and what isn't. Take the time to celebrate your successes, no matter how small, and consider making adjustments to your approach if progress stalls.

Building new habits is a transformative process that reshapes not just your daily actions but your identity itself. As you repeat these positive behaviors, they begin to weave into the fabric of who you are, leading you toward the life you aspire to live. Remember, every great achievement starts with the decision to try.

Breaking Bad Habits

Transforming our lives often means confronting and breaking the bad habits that hold us back. These entrenched patterns of behavior can be stubborn obstacles on the path to success, but with the right approach, they can be dismantled. This section provides a strategic framework for understanding and overcoming undesirable habits.

Recognize the Habit Loop

The first step in breaking a bad habit is to recognize its components: the cue, the routine, and the reward. Identify what triggers the habit (cue), the behavior itself (routine), and the benefit you perceive from the behavior (reward). Understanding this loop is crucial to dismantling the habit.

Replace, Don't Erase

Attempting to simply stop a bad habit without a replacement strategy can lead to failure. Instead, focus on replacing the undesired behavior with a positive one that fulfills a similar need. For instance, if stress triggers a smoking habit, consider replacing smoking with deep breathing exercises or a short walk to manage stress.

Change Your Environment

Your environment can significantly influence your habits. Alter your surroundings to make bad habits more difficult to engage in and good habits easier. If you're trying to reduce screen time, for example, keep your devices in another room during family or personal time.

Leverage Negative Reinforcement

While positive reinforcement is effective for building new habits, negative reinforcement can be useful for breaking bad ones. This could involve setting up a consequence for engaging in the bad habit, such as putting money into a jar every time the habit occurs, which will be donated to a cause you don't support. An example would be donating to an opposing political candidate.

Use Mindfulness Techniques

Mindfulness can help break the automatic response that characterizes bad habits. By becoming more aware of your triggers and your behavior, you can create a pause between the cue and your routine, giving you the opportunity to choose a different response.

Seek Support

Breaking habits can be challenging, and support from friends, family, or a professional can provide motivation and accountability. Consider joining a support group of individuals facing similar challenges.

Visualize Success

Visualization is a powerful tool for breaking bad habits. Regularly imagine yourself successfully resisting the temptation and engaging in a healthier behavior instead. This mental rehearsal can strengthen your resolve when faced with real-world cues.

Track Your Progress

Keeping a log of your successes and setbacks can provide valuable insights into your habit-breaking journey. Celebrate your victories, no matter how small, and analyze your setbacks to adjust your strategy as needed.

Be Patient and Persistent

Breaking a bad habit is a process that requires time and persistence. Expect setbacks and understand that they are part of the journey. Each attempt is a step towards permanently breaking the habit.

Cultivate Self-Compassion

Approach habit breaking with self-compassion. Recognize that everyone has bad habits and that changing them doesn't happen overnight. Treat yourself with kindness and understanding, especially during challenging times.

Breaking bad habits is not just about stopping a behavior; it's about transforming your lifestyle and mindset to pave the way for lasting change. By systematically tackling the components of your bad habits and replacing them with positive alternatives, you create a foundation for a healthier, more successful life.

Discipline in Practice

Implementing discipline into your daily life is the bridge between setting goals and achieving them. It's the practice of consistently choosing actions that align with your aspirations, even when it's challenging or inconvenient. This section offers actionable strategies to cultivate discipline and integrate it into your daily routines, turning aspirations into achievements.

Establish Clear Priorities

Discipline begins with clarity. Define your priorities based on your goals and values. Knowing what is most important to you helps in making decisions that align with your objectives, even when faced with distractions or temptations.

Create Structured Routines

Structured routines provide a framework for disciplined action. Establishing a daily or weekly schedule that includes time for work, exercise, relaxation, and personal growth can help ensure that you're consistently moving toward your goals.

Set Boundaries

To maintain discipline, it's crucial to set boundaries around your time and energy. Learn to say no to non-essential tasks and distractions that don't align with your priorities. Protecting your focus is essential for disciplined progress.

Use Time-Blocking

Time-blocking is a technique where you allocate specific blocks of time for different activities or tasks. This helps in dedicating focused time to high-priority tasks, making it easier to stay disciplined and avoid multitasking, which can dilute your efforts.

Break Tasks into Smaller Steps

Large tasks can be overwhelming and may lead to procrastination. Break them into smaller, manageable steps. This makes it easier to start and maintain momentum, fostering a disciplined approach to tackling challenges.

Eliminate Distractions

Identify and eliminate or minimize distractions in your environment. This may involve decluttering your workspace, using apps to block distracting websites, or setting specific times to check emails and messages.

Practice Self-Control

Discipline is fundamentally about self-control. Strengthen this skill by challenging yourself in small ways daily, such as delaying gratification, resisting temptations, or sticking to your planned schedule even when you don't feel like it.

Develop Resilience

Discipline requires resilience, the ability to bounce back from setbacks and continue moving forward. Cultivate a resilient mindset by viewing challenges as opportunities to learn and grow, rather than insurmountable obstacles.

Celebrate Progress

Acknowledging and celebrating your progress, no matter how small, can reinforce disciplined behavior. Set milestones within your larger goals and celebrate when you reach them to maintain motivation.

Reflect and Adjust

Regular reflection on your disciplined practices allows you to assess what's working and what isn't. Be prepared to adjust your strategies, routines, and priorities as you gain insights into your own behavior and as your goals evolve.

Seek Accountability

Having an accountability partner or group can significantly enhance your discipline. Sharing your goals and progress with others can provide external motivation and support, making it easier to stay on track.

Incorporating discipline into your daily life is about more than just willpower; it's about creating systems and environments that support your goals. By practicing these strategies, you can transform discipline from a concept into a tangible set of actions that lead you closer to your desired outcomes, day by day.

Rituals and Routines

Rituals and routines are the scaffolding of a disciplined life, providing structure and predictability amidst the chaos of daily living. They transform lofty aspirations into tangible actions, embedding success into the fabric of everyday life. This section explores the significance of establishing rituals and routines and how they can be leveraged to enhance discipline, productivity, and overall well-being.

The Power of Rituals

Rituals are intentional practices that hold personal significance, transforming ordinary tasks into meaningful experiences. They can be as simple as a morning cup of tea savored in silence, or as elaborate as a pre-performance routine for athletes and artists. Rituals lend a sense of purpose and reverence to our actions, making them more impactful and less susceptible to procrastination.

Crafting Morning Routines

The way you start your day often sets the tone for the hours that follow. A solid morning routine might include exercise, meditation, journaling, or reading — activities that center and prepare you for the day ahead. By prioritizing these actions first thing in the morning, you ensure that they don't get overshadowed by the day's demands.

Establishing Work Routines

Work routines are essential for maintaining focus and productivity throughout your professional or academic endeavors. This could involve designated times for deep work, regular breaks to refresh the mind, and specific rituals to signal the start and end of the workday, helping to maintain a healthy work–life balance.

Evening Routines for Better Sleep

Just as a morning routine kickstarts your day, an evening routine can set the stage for restorative sleep. Activities that promote relaxation, such as reading, gentle yoga, or a skincare regimen, can signal to your body that it's time to wind down, enhancing the quality of your rest.

Building Habits into Routines

Integrating new habits into your established routines increases the likelihood that they'll stick. Anchor new habits to existing ones, creating a chain of behaviors that naturally flow from one to the next. For example, if you're building a habit of gratitude, consider writing in a gratitude journal immediately after your morning coffee.

Flexibility Within Structure

While routines provide structure, it's important to remain flexible. Life is unpredictable, and rigid adherence to routines can lead to stress when interruptions occur. Allow for adjustments and have contingency plans to maintain your core practices even when circumstances change.

The Ritual of Reflection

Incorporate regular reflection into your routines to assess your progress, celebrate successes, and identify areas for improvement. This could be a weekly review of goals and achievements or a nightly recap of what went well and what could be better.

Shared Routines

Routines shared with family members or colleagues can strengthen relationships and create a collective sense of purpose and achievement. Whether it's a family dinner ritual or a team huddle at work, shared routines foster community and mutual support.

Rituals for Transition

Use rituals to mark significant transitions, whether it's moving from work to relaxation, changing tasks, or shifting between roles (such as from professional to parent). These rituals can be simple, like changing clothes or taking a few deep breaths, but they help mentally and emotionally prepare you for the next phase of your day.

Celebratory Rituals

Create rituals around celebrating achievements, no matter how small. These could be personal treats, sharing successes with loved ones, or simply taking a moment to acknowledge your hard work. Celebration reinforces the value of your efforts and motivates continued discipline.

Rituals and routines are not about constraining freedom; they're about creating a framework within which freedom can flourish. By carefully designing and adhering to these structures, you pave a smooth path toward your goals, making success not just a possibility but an inevitable outcome of your daily practices.

Accountability and Tracking

In the pursuit of personal growth and success, the journey can be as significant as the destination. To navigate this path effectively, two critical tools come to the fore: accountability and tracking. These mechanisms not only illuminate your progress but also ensure that you remain steadfast in your commitment to your goals. This section delves into the importance of these tools and offers strategies to integrate them into your success journey.

The Role of Accountability

Accountability acts as a compass, guiding you back to your path whenever you stray. It involves taking responsibility for your actions and their outcomes, and it can be significantly enhanced by involving others in your journey.

- **Personal Accountability**: Start with a commitment to yourself. Set clear intentions and remind yourself regularly of the reasons behind your goals. Keeping a personal journal or a vision board can serve as a daily reminder of your commitments.

- **Accountability Partners**: Share your goals with a trusted friend, family member, or mentor who can offer support and encouragement. Choose someone who is not afraid to challenge you and provide honest feedback.

- **Groups and Communities**: Joining a group with similar interests or goals can provide a collective sense of accountability. Whether it's a fitness class, a book club, or an online forum, being part of a community fosters a shared commitment to progress.

The Power of Tracking

Tracking your progress is like mapping your journey, marking where you started, how far you've come, and how close you are to your destination. It transforms intangible efforts into tangible achievements.

- **Habit Trackers**: Utilize habit trackers to record your daily adherence to the habits you're trying to build. This could be a physical journal, a spreadsheet, or a mobile app designed for habit tracking.

- **Progress Logs**: Keep a log of your progress towards larger goals. This could include milestones reached, skills acquired, or improvements in performance. Reflecting on this log can boost motivation and provide insight into effective strategies and areas needing adjustment.

- **Visual Metrics**: Create visual representations of your progress, such as charts or graphs, to provide a clear picture of your journey. Visual metrics can be particularly motivating, as they offer a concrete representation of your hard work and achievements.

Setting Up Regular Reviews

Establish a routine for regular review sessions—daily, weekly, or monthly—to evaluate your progress. Use these sessions to:

- Reflect on successes and challenges.

- Adjust goals and strategies as needed.

- Celebrate achievements, no matter how small.

- Plan for the upcoming period with renewed focus.

Embracing Technology

Leverage technology to aid in accountability and tracking. Numerous apps and software are designed to track habits, goals, and time, offering reminders and insights to keep you aligned with your objectives.

Learning from Data

Use the data from your tracking efforts to learn and adapt. Identify patterns, understand what works, and recognize where there's room for improvement. This data-driven approach can significantly enhance your strategy for success.

Transparency and Openness

Be transparent with yourself and your accountability partners about your progress and challenges. Openness fosters a supportive environment conducive to growth and learning.

Accountability and tracking are not merely administrative tasks; they are integral components of a successful journey. They provide clarity, motivation, and a framework for continuous improvement. By holding yourself accountable and meticulously tracking your progress, you turn the abstract concept of success into a concrete, achievable reality.

Overcoming Challenges

Embarking on a journey to instill discipline and cultivate positive habits is often met with a spectrum of challenges. These hurdles, both internal and external, can test your resolve and hinder your progress. However, facing and overcoming these challenges is an integral part of personal growth. This section offers strategies to navigate and surmount obstacles, ensuring that they become stepping stones rather than stumbling blocks on your path to success.

Identifying the Root Causes

The first step in overcoming challenges is to identify their root causes. Is procrastination stemming from fear of failure, or is a lack of discipline due to unclear goals? Understanding the underlying reasons for your obstacles allows you to address them more effectively.

Setting Realistic Expectations

One common challenge is setting goals that are overly ambitious or unrealistic, leading to frustration and burnout. Break your larger goals into smaller, manageable tasks, and set realistic timelines. Celebrate small victories to maintain motivation.

Building a Support System

Having a robust support system can significantly ease the journey. Surround yourself with people who encourage and believe in you. Seek mentors who have navigated similar paths and can offer guidance and advice.

Embracing Adaptability

Rigidity can often amplify challenges. Cultivate adaptability by being open to changing your methods, timelines, or even goals as you encounter new information or obstacles. Flexibility can turn potential setbacks into opportunities for learning and growth.

Leveraging Failure as Feedback

Every failure carries valuable lessons. Instead of viewing setbacks as defeats, see them as feedback. Analyze what went wrong and why, and use these insights to refine your approach. This perspective shift can transform challenges into catalysts for improvement.

Prioritizing Self-Care

Neglecting self-care can undermine your discipline and resilience. Ensure that you're getting enough rest, engaging in physical activity, and taking time to relax and recharge. A well-cared-for body and mind are better equipped to handle challenges.

Developing Problem-Solving Skills

Enhance your problem-solving skills by approaching challenges with a solution-oriented mindset. Break down problems into smaller components, explore various solutions, and be willing to experiment until you find what works best.

Managing Stress Effectively

Stress can magnify challenges and impede your ability to think clearly and act decisively. Develop stress management techniques such as mindfulness, meditation, or deep breathing exercises to maintain your composure in the face of obstacles.

Staying Focused on Your 'Why'

When challenges arise, remind yourself of the reasons behind your goals. Reconnecting with your 'why' can reignite your motivation and provide the strength to persevere through difficult times.

Celebrating Progress, Not Just Perfection

Focusing solely on the end goal can make challenges seem insurmountable. Instead, celebrate the progress you make along the way, no matter how small. This helps build momentum and keeps you motivated through the ups and downs.

Seeking Professional Help When Needed

Some challenges may require professional assistance, whether it's a coach for personal development, a financial advisor for money management, or a therapist for mental health support. Recognizing when you need help and seeking it out is a sign of strength, not weakness.

Challenges are an inevitable part of any worthwhile endeavor. By employing these strategies, you can build the resilience and resourcefulness needed to overcome obstacles, ensuring that each challenge becomes a steppingstone closer to your ultimate goals.

Conclusion

The path to embedding discipline and positive habits into our lives is undeniably strewn with challenges. Each obstacle we encounter tests our resolve, patience, and adaptability. Yet, it is through these very challenges that the essence of personal growth and resilience is forged. This chapter has not only illuminated the common hurdles one might face on this journey but has also provided a toolkit of strategies to navigate and overcome them.

Embracing discipline and nurturing positive habits is more than a mere exercise in self-improvement; it is a profound commitment to crafting the life you envision for yourself. The journey is iterative, a continuous cycle of setting goals, facing challenges, learning, and growing. It demands patience, persistence, and a willingness to learn from every stumble.

Remember, the challenges you face are not roadblocks; they are opportunities to deepen your understanding of yourself, to refine your strategies, and to strengthen your resolve. Overcoming these obstacles is not just about employing the right techniques; it's about cultivating a mindset that views each challenge as a steppingstone towards your greater vision.

As you move forward, armed with the insights and strategies from this chapter, hold onto the understanding that the discipline you cultivate and the habits you form are the building blocks of your future success. They are the silent, steadfast companions on your journey to achieving your goals and realizing your potential.

Let this chapter serve as a reminder that while the road may be fraught with challenges, your capacity for resilience, adaptation, and growth is boundless. With each challenge overcome, you are not just moving closer to your goals; you are transforming into a more disciplined, determined, and resilient version of yourself. This is the true essence of success.

So, as you close this chapter and prepare to face the challenges that lie ahead, do so with the confidence that you are equipped not just to face them, but to rise above them. Your journey of discipline and habit formation is a testament to your commitment to personal excellence—a commitment that will illuminate your path to success, no matter the obstacles that arise.

Chapter 6

Mastering Your Time for Maximum Impact

Welcome to "Mastering Your Time for Maximum Impact," a chapter dedicated to one of the most valuable assets in your journey to success: time. In a world where distractions abound and demands on our attention are constant, mastering the art of time management is not just a skill—it's a necessity for anyone aspiring to achieve their goals and realize their full potential.

Time, unlike money, is a non-renewable resource. Once spent, it can never be regained, which makes how we choose to spend our time one of the most critical decisions we make daily. Yet, many of us find ourselves at the mercy of time, always feeling like there's never enough of it to accomplish everything we want. The good news? It's possible to take control of your time and use it in a way that propels you forward, rather than holds you back.

This chapter is designed to transform your relationship with time. Whether you're a student juggling academics and extracurriculars, a young professional striving to make your mark, or simply someone who wants to make more room for what truly matters, the principles and practices outlined here will serve as your guide. You'll learn not only to manage your time more effectively but to master it, ensuring that every hour you spend aligns with your deepest values and highest aspirations.

We'll start by exploring the intrinsic value of time and why mastering it is essential for success. From there, we'll dive into practical strategies for conducting a time audit, allowing you to see where your time is currently going and where adjustments can be made. You'll discover various prioritization techniques to help you focus on what truly matters, and we'll tackle the art of setting boundaries to protect your most precious resource.

Planning will take center stage as we discuss how to map out your days, weeks, and months for maximum productivity and fulfillment. We'll also explore the power of habits and routines in automating success, and the importance of delegation and outsourcing in multiplying your time.

Of course, no discussion on time management would be complete without addressing the elephant in the room: procrastination. We'll provide you with tools to combat this common adversary and ensure that it doesn't derail your progress. Additionally, we'll look at how technology can serve as both a friend and foe in managing your time, offering insights into making it work in your favor.

As you embark on this chapter, remember that mastering your time is about more than just getting things done. It's about creating a life that is rich, fulfilling, and aligned with your vision of success. It's about making space for the pursuits that light you up and the people who matter most. So, let's turn the page and begin the journey to mastering your time for maximum impact.

The Value of Time

Time, often said to be our most precious resource, is the one commodity we all have in equal measure yet often squander without a second thought. Unlike money, lost time cannot be earned back. Each moment presents an opportunity, a choice on how we spend it, and these choices cumulatively shape the trajectory of our lives. Understanding the intrinsic value of time is the first step towards mastering it for maximum impact.

In our fast-paced world, it's easy to fall into the trap of equating busyness with productivity. However, being busy does not necessarily mean being effective. The key lies in making conscious decisions about how we allocate our time, ensuring that our activities align with our broader goals and values. This discernment transforms time from a fleeting enemy to a powerful ally in our quest for success.

Consider the concept of 'opportunity cost' from economics, which refers to the potential benefits an individual misses out on when choosing one alternative over another. Every hour spent on a task is an hour not spent on countless other possible activities. This makes it crucial to choose wisely, focusing on actions that yield the highest return on investment in terms of personal and professional growth.

The impact of effective time management extends beyond achieving career milestones or academic success; it also enhances our well-being. By making room for activities that nourish us physically, mentally, and emotionally, we cultivate a balanced life, ripe with fulfillment and joy.

As we delve into the strategies and practices that can help harness the power of time, keep in mind that the goal is not to fill every moment with activity. Instead, it's about making each moment count, ensuring that our time is spent in ways that bring us closer to the life we aspire to lead. In the pages that follow, we'll explore how to audit your time, prioritize tasks, set boundaries, and employ techniques that amplify your productivity, enabling you to master your time for maximum impact.

Time Audit: Mapping Your Minutes

Embarking on a time audit is akin to a financial audit; it's about taking stock of where your time is currently invested to understand how it aligns—or doesn't—with your priorities and goals. This exercise can be eye-opening, revealing the discrepancies between how you intend to use your time and how you actually do. Let's delve into how you can conduct an effective time audit and interpret its findings to enhance your life's trajectory.

Starting Your Audit

1. **Choose Your Tracking Tool**: Opt for a method that suits your lifestyle, whether it's a simple pen and paper, a

spreadsheet, or a time-tracking app. The key is consistency and ease of use.

2. **Define Categories:** Before you begin, categorize your activities. Common categories include work/study, sleep, meals, commute, leisure, exercise, and socializing. Feel free to customize these to fit your life.

3. **Log Your Activities:** For one week, diligently record how you spend your time. Be as detailed as possible, noting the start and end times of each activity. The granularity of your logging is crucial for an accurate analysis.

Analyzing Your Audit

Once you've completed a week of tracking, it's time to analyze the data:

1. **Calculate Totals:** Tally the time spent in each category. This will give you a macro view of where your hours are going.

2. **Identify Surprises:** Compare your expectations against reality. You might find you're spending more time on social media than you thought or less on activities that align with your goals.

3. **Highlight Discrepancies:** Pinpoint areas where your time usage conflicts with your priorities. For instance, if advancing in your career is a goal but you're spending minimal time on professional development, there's a misalignment.

4. **Note Productive Peaks:** Pay attention to when you're most productive. Are you a morning person or a night owl? Aligning challenging tasks with your peak productivity times can enhance efficiency.

Leveraging Your Audit Findings

With your audit insights in hand, you can start making informed adjustments:

1. **Reallocate Time**: Shift time from low-priority areas to activities that contribute to your goals. For example, reduce idle browsing to make room for a skill-enhancing course.

2. **Set Boundaries**: If certain activities are bleeding into your productive time, set stricter boundaries. This might mean designating specific times for email or social media.

3. **Optimize Routines**: Align your daily routines with your productivity peaks. Schedule demanding tasks during your high-energy windows and low-energy tasks when you're less alert.

4. **Plan for Leisure**: Don't overlook the importance of rest and relaxation. Ensure your audit leads to a balanced schedule that includes time for rejuvenation.

A time audit is not a one-off exercise but a tool for continuous improvement. Regular audits can help you adapt to life's changing demands and ensure your time aligns with your evolving priorities and goals. By mastering the art of the time audit, you empower yourself to take control of your most precious resource, paving the way for greater success and fulfillment.

Prioritization

Mastering prioritization is akin to navigating a complex labyrinth; it requires a keen sense of direction to reach the end goal efficiently. In a world brimming with distractions and endless to-do lists, adopting effective prioritization techniques is crucial for maximizing impact and steering your success journey. Let's explore some methodologies, including the intuitive red-yellow-green method, to elevate your task management game.

The Pareto Principle (80/20 Rule)

The Pareto Principle posits that roughly 80% of effects come from 20% of causes. Applied to time management, this suggests that a small portion of your tasks (the vital few) will account for the majority of your results. Identifying these high-impact activities allows you to allocate your resources more effectively, ensuring that your efforts yield the greatest returns.

The Red-Yellow-Green Method

The red-yellow-green method brings a simple, visual element to task prioritization, much like a traffic light system:

- **Red Tasks:** These are your critical tasks that require immediate attention—think of them as stop signs demanding a halt to all other activities until these are addressed.

- **Yellow Tasks:** These tasks are important but not urgent. They are like caution lights, signaling the need to proceed with care and prepare for action, but without the immediate pressure of red tasks.

- **Green Tasks:** Green tasks are routine or low-priority items that can be tackled once the more critical tasks are under control. They represent the "go" for engaging in tasks that maintain your workflow but don't necessarily drive significant progress.

This color-coded system offers a straightforward way to visually categorize and tackle your tasks, making it easier to decide at a glance what requires your focus next. The key is to ensure that your red tasks are completed first.

Implementation Tips

- **Daily Review:** At the start of each day, categorize your tasks using your chosen prioritization method. This will give you a clear action plan and help prevent decision fatigue.

- **Flexibility**: Be prepared to re-evaluate your priorities as new tasks emerge. The dynamic nature of work and life means that what was a 'green' task one day could become a 'red' task the next
- **Limit Red Tasks**: Aim to keep the number of red tasks manageable. Too many urgent tasks can lead to burnout and reduce the quality of your work.

By integrating these prioritization techniques into your daily routine, you'll enhance your ability to distinguish between what truly demands your attention and what can wait. This not only boosts your productivity but also ensures that your efforts are aligned with your overarching goals, paving the way for next-level success.

Guardrails for Productivity and Well-being

In the pursuit of success, setting boundaries is not just beneficial; it's essential. Boundaries act as guardrails, helping you navigate through the myriad demands of daily life without veering off your path to achievement and personal fulfillment. Let's explore how establishing clear boundaries can bolster your productivity and safeguard your well-being.

Boundaries define the limits of what we find acceptable and unacceptable, allowing us to maintain focus on our priorities and protect our energy. In the absence of boundaries, it's easy to become overwhelmed, leading to burnout and a decrease in both productivity and quality of life.

Identifying Areas for Boundaries

1. **Work-Life Balance**: Establish clear distinctions between work and personal time. This might mean setting specific work hours and sticking to them, ensuring you have time to recharge and enjoy personal interests.

2. **Digital Detox**: Set boundaries around your digital device usage, particularly social media and email, to prevent constant notifications from fragmenting your attention and disrupting your focus.

3. **Saying No**: Learn to decline requests that don't align with your priorities or that overextend your capacity. Saying no is not a sign of weakness but a strategic choice to ensure you can say yes to what truly matters.

Implementing Boundaries

1. **Communicate Clearly**: Be open and clear about your boundaries with colleagues, friends, and family. For instance, if you're unavailable for work calls after a certain hour, communicate this proactively.

2. **Use Tools and Technology**: Leverage tools like email auto-responders or app blockers to enforce your boundaries digitally, signaling to others when you're not available and preventing distractions.

3. **Create Physical Spaces**: Designate specific areas for work and relaxation in your environment. Having a physical separation can reinforce the psychological boundaries between different aspects of your life.

Maintaining Boundaries

Setting boundaries is one thing; maintaining them is another. Regularly assess how well your boundaries are being respected and whether they're still serving your needs. Be prepared to adjust as necessary, and remember that it's okay to reinforce your boundaries if they're being challenged.

The Benefits of Boundaries

1. **Enhanced Focus**: By limiting interruptions and non-essential tasks, boundaries help you maintain focus on

what's truly important, increasing your efficiency and effectiveness.

2. **Increased Energy**: Boundaries prevent overcommitment and energy depletion, ensuring you have the vitality to pursue your goals with vigor.

3. **Improved ell-being**: Clear boundaries contribute to a more balanced life, reducing stress and increasing satisfaction across both personal and professional domains.

In essence, boundaries are not about isolation but about intentional engagement. They enable you to engage more fully with your work, your relationships, and your passions, by protecting your time, energy, and emotional well-being. As you navigate your path to success, remember that the boundaries you set are the framework within which your best self can emerge and thrive.

Effective Planning: Charting a Course for Success

Effective planning is the compass that guides you through the landscape of your ambitions, transforming visions into actionable steps. It's about more than just listing tasks; it's about strategically organizing your efforts to ensure progress towards your goals. This section delves into the principles of effective planning, offering a roadmap to turn your aspirations into achievements.

Understanding the Planning Process

1. **Big Picture Vision**: Start with a clear understanding of your long-term goals. What do you aspire to achieve in the various facets of your life? This vision will serve as the foundation of your planning process.

2. **Break It Down**: Decompose your overarching goals into smaller, manageable objectives. This step is crucial for making your goals feel attainable and for identifying the immediate actions required to move forward.

3. **Prioritize:** Assess the relative importance and urgency of your objectives. Use prioritization techniques to determine which goals should be addressed first and allocate your resources accordingly.

Creating Your Plan

1. **Set Milestones:** Establish key milestones along your journey to each goal. Milestones are checkpoints that help you gauge progress and stay motivated.

2. **Action Steps:** For each milestone, outline the specific tasks required to reach it. These should be clear, actionable steps that move you closer to your goals.

3. **Allocate Time:** Assign realistic time frames to each task and milestone. Consider your other commitments and be mindful of over-scheduling, which can lead to burnout.

4. **Flexibility:** Build flexibility into your plan. While it's important to stay focused, being too rigid can make it difficult to adapt to unforeseen challenges or opportunities.

Tools and Techniques for Effective Planning

1. **Planners and Calendars:** Utilize physical or digital planners to organize and visualize your tasks and deadlines. This can include daily to-do lists, weekly planners, or monthly calendars.

2. **Time Blocking:** Dedicate specific blocks of time to work on particular tasks or categories of work. This technique helps minimize multitasking and ensures focused effort on key activities.

Review and Adjust

An effective plan is not set in stone; it's a living document that evolves. Regularly review your plan to assess progress, celebrate achievements, and adjust course as necessary. This might involve revisiting your goals, re-prioritizing tasks, or modifying timelines based on what you've learned about your capacity and the challenges you've encountered.

Delegation: Multiplying Your Success

In the quest for next-level success, understanding the art of delegation and outsourcing is akin to discovering a force multiplier for your efforts. As you navigate the complexities of life and work, recognizing tasks that can be shared or assigned to others frees up your invaluable time and energy, allowing you to focus on areas where you can make the most significant impact.

The Strategic Value of Delegation

1. **Leveraging Expertise**: Delegating tasks to individuals with specialized skills or knowledge can lead to better outcomes. This not only enhances the quality of the work but also provides a learning opportunity for team members.

2. **Capacity Expansion**: Delegation increases your capacity to take on new opportunities. By entrusting tasks to others, you can manage a broader scope of responsibilities without compromising on quality or well-being.

3. **Empowerment and Development**: Effective delegation serves as a tool for empowering others, fostering a sense of trust and investment in shared goals. It aids in the development of future leaders by providing them with opportunities to demonstrate and enhance their capabilities.

Navigating the Delegation Process

1. **Identify Delegable Tasks**: Start by identifying tasks that do not require your specific expertise or personal touch. These might include administrative duties, routine

tasks, or even specialized projects that can be better handled by experts in those areas.

2. **Choose the Right People**: Match tasks with individuals' skills, interests, and development goals. Ensuring alignment between the task and the person's capabilities and aspirations increases the likelihood of success and engagement.

3. **Clear Communication**: When delegating, be clear about the task's objectives, expected outcomes, deadlines, and any relevant constraints or guidelines. Providing the necessary resources and support is crucial for effective task execution.

4. **Empower with Autonomy**: While it's important to set clear expectations, it's equally vital to give individuals the autonomy to determine how best to accomplish the task. This fosters innovation and ownership.

5. **Feedback and Recognition**: Provide constructive feedback and acknowledge the contributions of those to whom you've delegated tasks. Recognition reinforces positive outcomes and encourages a culture of teamwork and accountability.

Embracing Outsourcing

Outsourcing extends the principle of delegation beyond the confines of your immediate team or organization. It involves entrusting tasks or projects to external entities or specialists.

1. **Strategic Outsourcing**: Identify areas where external expertise can significantly add value or where outsourcing can lead to greater efficiency and cost savings. Common outsourcing areas include IT services, content creation, legal services, and accounting.

2. **Vendor Selection**: Choosing the right partners or service providers is critical. Consider their reputation, expertise, reliability, and the alignment of their values with your own or your organization's.

3. **Managing Relationships**: Maintain open lines of communication with your outsourcing partners. Regular check-ins, clear contracts, and mutual respect for each other's expertise are key to a fruitful relationship.

The Compound Effect

Delegation and outsourcing, when done thoughtfully, can have a compound effect on your success. They not only amplify your productivity but also contribute to a more balanced life, reducing stress and freeing up time for strategic thinking, personal growth, and leisure. Embracing these practices is a testament to your leadership and strategic acumen, marking a significant step towards achieving next-level success.

Reclaiming Your Momentum

Procrastination, the act of delaying or postponing tasks, is a common barrier that can impede progress toward success. It's often rooted in fear, perfectionism, or a lack of motivation, leading to a cycle of stress, guilt, and decreased productivity. Breaking free from the grip of procrastination is essential for regaining momentum and advancing on your path to next-level success.

Understanding Procrastination

1. **Identify the Cause**: Procrastination can stem from various sources, including fear of failure, overwhelming tasks, indecision, or lack of interest. Recognizing the underlying reason for your procrastination is the first step toward overcoming it.

2. **Acknowledge the Impact**: Reflect on how procrastination affects your goals, well-being, and stress levels. This awareness can create a sense of urgency and motivate you to take action.

Strategies to Combat Procrastination

1. **Break It Down**: Large tasks can seem daunting, leading to avoidance. Break tasks into smaller, manageable steps to make them less intimidating and easier to start.

2. **Set Clear Deadlines**: Self-imposed deadlines can create a sense of accountability. For larger projects, set mini-deadlines for each task to maintain a steady pace of progress.

3. **Use Time Management Techniques**: Techniques like working for focused intervals followed by short breaks, can help maintain concentration and reduce the urge to procrastinate.

4. **Eliminate Distractions**: Identify and remove common distractions that lead to procrastination. This might involve creating a dedicated workspace, using website blockers, or setting your phone to "Do Not Disturb" mode during work sessions.

5. **Leverage Motivation**: Connect tasks to your larger goals and values to find intrinsic motivation. Visualizing the benefits of completing a task can also provide a motivational boost.

6. **Commit Publicly**: Sharing your goals and deadlines with others can increase your sense of commitment and encourage accountability.

7. **Reward Progress**: Set up a system to reward yourself for completing tasks or making significant progress. Rewards can reinforce positive behavior and make task completion more satisfying.

Changing Your Mindset

1. **Reframe Tasks**: Alter your perspective on tasks by focusing on positive outcomes rather than the effort involved. Viewing tasks as opportunities for growth or learning can make them more appealing.

2. **Practice Self-Compassion**: Be kind to yourself when facing setbacks. Recognize that everyone procrastinates at times and that it's possible to overcome it with consistent effort.
3. **Develop a Growth Mindset**: Embrace challenges and view failures as opportunities to learn and grow. A growth mindset can reduce the fear of failure, a common cause of procrastination.

Building Momentum

Overcoming procrastination is not about achieving perfection but about making incremental progress. Each step taken towards a task builds momentum, making subsequent steps easier. Celebrate small victories and use them as a springboard to tackle more significant challenges. By applying these strategies, you can transform procrastination from a barrier into a catalyst for growth and achievement, propelling you towards your aspirations for next-level success.

Harnessing Digital Tools for Success

In today's digital age, technology offers an array of tools and resources designed to enhance productivity, creativity, and learning. From state-of-the-art Generative AI like ChatGPT to innovative image generators like Dall-E, the potential to augment your success journey is immense. However, navigating this landscape requires a mindful approach to ensure ethical use and avoid pitfalls like plagiarism.

State-of-the-Art Tools

1. **Generative AI (ChatGPT)**: ChatGPT can assist with a wide range of tasks, from generating creative writing prompts to offering explanations on complex topics. It can serve as a brainstorming partner, help draft outlines, or provide insights into various subjects.

2. **Image Generators (Dall-E):** Dall-E transforms textual descriptions into unique images, offering a new dimension to creative projects. Whether you need custom illustrations for a presentation or visual aids to enhance learning, Dall-E can bring your ideas to life.

3. **Project Management Software:** These tools can help organize tasks, track progress, and facilitate collaboration. They are invaluable for managing personal projects, group assignments, or professional workflows.

4. **Time Management Apps:** Digital tools like Todoist, Google Calendar, and Microsoft Outloook can help you prioritize tasks, schedule your day, and stay focused, turning time management into a structured and enjoyable process.

Ethical Considerations and Avoiding Plagiarism

While technology can significantly enhance productivity and creativity, it's crucial to use these tools ethically, especially concerning academic and professional integrity:

1. **Originality and Plagiarism:** When using AI tools like ChatGPT for generating content, ensure that the output is used as a starting point or inspiration rather than a final submission. It's essential to add your unique perspective and insights to maintain originality.

2. **Citing Sources:** If you incorporate ideas or direct outputs from technological tools into your work, cite them appropriately, just as you would with traditional sources. This transparency upholds academic and professional standards.

3. **Critical Evaluation:** Not all information generated by AI or found through digital tools is accurate or reliable. Apply critical thinking to evaluate the relevance and credibility of the information before using it in your work.

Maximizing the Benefits of Technology

To fully leverage technology in your success journey, consider the following strategies:

1. **Customization:** Customize digital tools to fit your needs. Many apps offer personalization options that can help you create a tailored approach to productivity and learning.

2. **Continuous Learning:** Stay updated on emerging technologies and digital tools. Regular exploration can uncover new resources that might offer innovative solutions to challenges or open up new learning opportunities.

3. **Digital Balance:** While technology can be a powerful ally, it's also important to maintain a balance. Ensure that screen time doesn't detract from essential offline activities like physical exercise, face-to-face interactions, and rest.

Leveraging technology effectively can provide a significant advantage in your pursuit of next-level success. By integrating state-of-the-art tools like ChatGPT and Dall-E into your repertoire, you can enhance your capabilities, foster creativity, and streamline your path to achievement, all while adhering to ethical standards and promoting personal integrity.

Fine-Tuning Your Path to Success

The journey to next-level success is not a straight, unchanging path but a dynamic process that requires continual reflection and adjustment. This iterative cycle of assessing your progress, learning from experiences, and making informed adjustments is crucial for sustained growth and achievement. Embracing reflection and adjustment ensures that your strategies remain aligned with your evolving goals and the ever-changing landscape of life's opportunities and challenges.

The Power of Reflection

1. **Regular Check-ins:** Establish a routine for regular self-reflection, whether daily, weekly, or monthly. Use this time to review your goals, the progress you've made, the challenges you've encountered, and the lessons learned along the way.

2. **Mindful Awareness:** Reflection involves more than a cursory review of actions and outcomes; it requires deep, reflective consideration of your experiences, your reactions to various situations, and the underlying motivations driving your choices.

3. **Journaling:** Keeping a reflective journal can be a powerful tool in this process, providing a space to document your thoughts, feelings, and insights. This practice not only aids in self-awareness but also serves as a valuable resource to revisit and assess personal growth over time.

Embracing Adjustment

1. **Agility:** Be prepared to pivot and make adjustments to your plans and goals based on your reflective insights. Agility in the face of changing circumstances or new information is a hallmark of successful individuals.

2. **Goal Reassessment:** Periodically reassess your goals to ensure they still resonate with your values and long-term vision. Life's experiences may shift your perspectives, necessitating a realignment of your objectives.

3. **Strategy Optimization:** Use the insights gained from reflection to optimize your strategies. This might involve abandoning approaches that aren't working, strengthening successful tactics, or trying new methods to overcome obstacles.

Learning from Setbacks

1. **Growth Mindset**: View setbacks and challenges as opportunities for learning and growth. Embrace the concept that every experience, especially the difficult ones, offers valuable lessons that contribute to your development.

2. **Feedback Loops**: Seek and incorporate feedback from trusted mentors, peers, or coaches. External perspectives can provide new insights and highlight areas for improvement that you might overlook.

3. **Resilience Building**: Use reflection and adjustment as tools to build resilience. By actively learning from experiences and adapting your approach, you strengthen your ability to navigate future challenges with greater confidence and flexibility.

Celebrating Progress

1. **Acknowledging Achievements**: During your reflective periods, take time to celebrate your achievements, no matter how small. Recognizing and appreciating your progress fosters a positive mindset and motivates continued effort.

2. **Gratitude Practice**: Incorporate gratitude into your reflection, acknowledging the support and opportunities that have contributed to your journey. This practice enhances well-being and reinforces a positive outlook on life.

Reflection and adjustment are integral to the continuous improvement process, enabling you to navigate the complexities of personal and professional growth effectively. By committing to regular, mindful reflection and being open to making necessary adjustments, you empower yourself to steer your journey towards next-level success with intention, resilience, and adaptability.

Embarking on Your Journey to Next-Level Success

You've now navigated through the foundational strategies and insights designed to propel you toward next-level success. From mastering your time and setting strategic boundaries to harnessing the power of habits and leveraging technology, each section has equipped you with the tools necessary for personal and professional growth. But knowledge alone isn't transformative; action is. It's time to take the leap from aspiration to actualization.

I challenge you to implement at least one strategy from each chapter in your daily life. Whether it's conducting a time audit to understand where your hours are going, setting a new boundary to protect your energy, or utilizing a new tech tool to streamline your work, each action is a step towards your goals.

Success is not a destination but a journey marked by continuous learning and growth. Embrace the mindset of a lifelong learner, always seeking new ways to enhance your skills, expand your knowledge, and refine your strategies.

You're not alone in this pursuit. Share your journey with others—friends, family, or a mentor. Discuss your goals, the strategies you're implementing, and the challenges you face. Collaboration and support can amplify your efforts and provide new perspectives.

Regularly reflect on your progress, celebrate your victories, and learn from any setbacks. Be prepared to adjust your plans and strategies as you grow and as your goals evolve. Remember, flexibility and resilience are key to overcoming obstacles and seizing new opportunities.

Don't wait for the perfect moment to start; the best time to begin is now. Choose one action you can take today, no matter how small, and commit to it. This first step is often the most challenging, but it sets the momentum for all the steps that follow.

Chapter 7

The Catalyst of Action

Welcome to the pivotal chapter of your journey towards success, "The Catalyst of Action." This is where the rubber meets the road, where dreams begin their transformation into reality. It's one thing to have a vision, to set goals, and to draft plans, but it's entirely another to breathe life into those plans through decisive action. Herein lies the heart of progress and achievement.

The journey of a thousand miles, as the ancient saying goes, begins with a single step. Yet, for many, that first step is the hardest. It's not for lack of desire or ambition but often due to the invisible chains of inertia that hold us back—fear, doubt, procrastination, and the comfort of the status quo. This chapter aims to break those chains.

Action is the lifeblood of all accomplishments. Without it, the most detailed plans and the loftiest dreams remain in the realm of potential, never realizing their full glory. But what propels us into action? What fuels that initial spark and maintains the flame, driving us forward even when the path gets steep and the nights long?

We'll explore the psychological underpinnings that either stymie our steps or spur us onwards. We'll dismantle the barriers of inertia and replace them with stepping stones of proactive habits. You'll learn to cultivate an action-oriented mindset, where taking initiative becomes as natural as breathing, and where each step, no matter how small, is celebrated as a victory.

Discipline, often misconstrued as a form of restriction, will be revealed in its true light—as the strongest ally of action. It's the discipline that ensures the consistency of our efforts, turning sporadic bursts into a steady stream of progress.

Transitioning from planning to execution is an art and a science, both of which you'll become well-versed in. We'll arm you with practical tools and techniques to turn your intentions into actions. From time management strategies to productivity hacks, you'll have a toolkit at your disposal to tackle your goals head-on.

But action is not without its trials. It's accompanied by the risk of failure, the sting of setbacks, and the weight of uncertainty. Here, you'll learn to embrace these not as stop signs but as signposts, guiding your journey and enriching your narrative with resilience and wisdom.

This chapter is not just a collection of concepts but a call to arms. It's an invitation to step into the arena, to engage with your dreams actively, and to sculpt your destiny with the clay of daily actions. So, let's embark on this journey together, from the realm of thought into the world of action, and turn the possible into the inevitable.

The Power of Taking Action

At the heart of every success story is a series of actions. It's easy to dream, to envision a future brimming with achievements and fulfillment. Yet, it's the act of stepping into the arena, of engaging with those dreams, that sets the wheels of change in motion. The power of taking action is transformative, capable of turning the intangible into the tangible, and the possible into the inevitable.

Action Breeds Clarity

One of the most potent benefits of taking action is the clarity it brings. Many await the perfect plan or the complete absence of doubt before making a move, not realizing that action itself often illuminates the path. Each step forward reveals insights that were invisible from the starting line, refining your direction and strategies as you progress.

Momentum Builds with Movement

Taking action generates momentum, much like a boulder gaining speed downhill. The initial push might require significant effort, but once in motion, each subsequent action becomes easier. This momentum not only accelerates progress but also builds confidence, as each completed task reinforces your capability and commitment.

Overcoming Fear through Action

Fear is a natural response to the unknown and a common barrier to taking action. However, action has a unique way of diminishing fear. With each step forward, the unknown becomes familiar, and what was once intimidating becomes manageable. Action transforms fear from a roadblock into a stepping stone, leading you closer to your goals.

The Compound Effect of Daily Actions

The true power of action lies in its cumulative effect. Small, consistent actions may seem inconsequential in isolation, but over time, they compound into significant results. Just as a river carves through rock not by force but by persistence, your daily actions shape the course of your life.

Action as a Catalyst for Opportunity

Taking action opens doors to opportunities that would remain closed to those who hesitate. It's through action that you meet new people, acquire new skills, and expose yourself to possibilities that can significantly alter your trajectory. In many ways, action is the key that unlocks the door to potential opportunities.

Embracing Imperfect Action

Perfectionism can be the enemy of progress. Waiting for the perfect moment or the flawless plan can result in missed opportunities and stagnation. Embracing imperfect action is about progress over perfection. It's better to move forward imperfectly than to stand still waiting for perfection.

The Ripple Effect of Taking Action

Your actions have a ripple effect, influencing not only your life but also those around you. By pursuing your goals and taking action, you inspire others to do the same. This ripple effect can transform not just individual lives but entire communities.

In conclusion, the power of taking action is undeniable. It is the bridge between potential and realization, between dreams and achievements. While the act of taking the first step can be daunting, the journey of a thousand miles truly does begin with that single step. So, let that step be forward, into the realm of action, where possibilities become realities.

Overcoming Inertia

Inertia, the tendency to do nothing or remain unchanged, is arguably one of the most formidable adversaries on the path to taking action. It's a force that keeps us tethered to our comfort zones, shackled by a blend of fear, doubt, and the allure of the familiar. Overcoming inertia isn't just about breaking out of physical inactivity; it's about shifting mental paradigms and embracing the dynamism of change.

Recognizing the Root Causes

The first step in overcoming inertia is recognizing its root causes. Often, it's fear that holds the reins—fear of failure, fear of the unknown, or even fear of success and the changes it might bring. Doubt plays its part too, sowing seeds of uncertainty about our capabilities or the worthiness of our goals. Procrastination, the art of delaying, disguises itself as a harmless respite but is, in fact, inertia's most cunning ally, leading us to perpetually postpone action.

Breaking the Cycle

Breaking the cycle of inertia begins with small, decisive actions. It's about disrupting the pattern of inactivity with intentional movements. Start with something manageable, a task or action that is undeniably doable yet signifies a break from stagnation. This could be as simple as organizing your workspace, going for a brief walk, or completing a small task that's been on your to-do list for too long. The key is to initiate motion, however minimal it may seem.

Cultivating Momentum

Every action, no matter how small, generates momentum. Like a snowball rolling down a hill, the accumulation of small actions builds up speed and size, making it easier to tackle larger, more daunting tasks. Set yourself up for early wins, and let these successes fuel your confidence and motivation to keep moving forward.

Embracing Discomfort

Stepping out of your comfort zone is inherently uncomfortable, but it's within this discomfort that growth resides. Embrace it as a sign of progress rather than a signal to retreat. Remind yourself that discomfort is temporary and that each step into the unknown strengthens your resilience and adaptability.

Establishing Routines

Routines are the antithesis of inertia. By establishing structured routines, you create a framework for consistent action. Begin with a morning routine that primes you for productivity, or an evening routine that sets the stage for the next day. Routines reduce the mental energy required to make decisions about when and how to act, making it easier to maintain momentum.

Accountability and Support

Sharing your goals and plans with someone you trust can significantly bolster your resistance to inertia. Accountability partners or support groups provide not just motivation but also a sense of obligation to follow through on your commitments. Knowing that someone else is invested in your success can be a powerful motivator to take action.

Reframing Failure

Fear of failure is a common cause of inertia, but reframing how you view failure can transform it from a deterrent to a catalyst. See failure as a learning opportunity, a necessary step in the journey to success. Every attempt, successful or not, is a victory over inertia and a testament to your courage to act.

Inertia, while daunting, is not insurmountable. It requires recognition, strategic action, and a shift in mindset from stasis to dynamism. By understanding its roots and employing these strategies, you can break free from its grasp and embark on a path of consistent, purposeful action towards your goals.

The Action-Oriented Mindset

An action-oriented mindset is the cornerstone of dynamic, fulfilling life. It's a way of thinking that prioritizes doing over deliberating, turning intentions into tangible outcomes. Cultivating this mindset involves more than just a desire to act; it requires a fundamental shift in how you perceive challenges, opportunities, and your own capabilities.

Embracing a Proactive Approach

To foster an action-oriented mindset, start by embracing proactivity. Proactive individuals don't wait for circumstances to dictate their actions; they create opportunities and address challenges head-on. This approach begins with a commitment to take responsibility for your life's direction, understanding that your decisions and actions shape your future.

Developing Decision-Making Confidence

Confidence in your decision-making abilities is crucial for an action-oriented mindset. Hesitation often stems from fear of making the wrong choice, but indecision is a decision in itself, usually one that leads to stagnation. Enhance your decision-making confidence by acknowledging that not all decisions will be perfect, but each provides valuable lessons and growth opportunities.

Cultivating Resilience

An action-oriented mindset is not deterred by setbacks. Instead, it views them as integral to the learning process. Cultivating resilience means developing the ability to bounce back from failures and disappointments, using them as fuel to propel you forward rather than reasons to retreat.

Setting and Revisiting Intentions

Regularly setting and revisiting your intentions keeps your action-oriented mindset aligned with your goals. Intentions act as reminders of what you're striving towards, helping to maintain focus and motivation. They should be clear, achievable, and revisited often to ensure your actions remain directed towards your desired outcomes.

Prioritizing and Simplifying

An overwhelmed mind is a paralyzed one. To remain action-oriented, prioritize your tasks based on their impact and urgency. Simplify your to-do list to focus on what truly matters, allowing you to dedicate your energy to tasks that significantly move you towards your goals.

The 5-Second Rule

The 5-second rule, popularized by Mel Robbins, is a simple yet powerful tool to combat procrastination and jumpstart action. When faced with a task you're hesitant to begin, count down from 5 to 1, and at 1, physically move to start the task. This method bypasses overthinking and kickstarts the process of taking action.

Embracing Imperfection

Perfectionism can be a significant barrier to an action-oriented mindset. The pursuit of perfection often leads to endless tweaking and adjustments, resulting in inaction. Embrace the concept of "good enough" and understand that imperfection is a part of growth and progress. Action, even if imperfect, always yields more results than stalled perfection.

Celebrating Action

Finally, celebrate every step you take. Recognizing and rewarding yourself for taking action, regardless of the outcome, reinforces the action-oriented mindset. It builds a positive association with taking initiative, making it more likely you'll continue to act in the face of future challenges.

An action-oriented mindset transforms potential energy into kinetic, driving progress and achievement. By adopting this mindset, you equip yourself with the tools to navigate life's challenges, seize opportunities, and turn your aspirations into achievements.

From Planning to Execution

Transitioning from planning to execution is where your aspirations begin to take shape in the real world. This critical phase is about turning your meticulously laid plans into tangible actions. It's the bridge that connects the world of ideas to the realm of results. To successfully navigate this transition, consider the following strategies:

Breaking Down Goals into Actionable Steps

Large goals can often seem overwhelming, which can hinder the transition from planning to execution. Break down your overarching goals into smaller, manageable tasks. This process, often referred to as "chunking," makes it easier to tackle complex objectives by focusing on one small step at a time. Each small task completed brings you closer to your ultimate goal and maintains your momentum.

Prioritizing Tasks

Not all tasks are created equal; some will have a more significant impact on your progress than others. Use prioritization methods, which categorizes tasks based on their urgency and importance, to focus your efforts where they are most needed. Concentrate on high-impact tasks that directly contribute to your goals, ensuring that your actions are both effective and efficient.

Setting Deadlines

Deadlines are a powerful tool for facilitating the move from planning to action. They create a sense of urgency that can motivate you to start and complete tasks. When setting deadlines, be realistic but also challenge yourself. Ensure that these time frames are specific and tied to your tasks and sub-goals, providing clear targets to aim for.

Building in Accountability

Hold yourself accountable for executing your plans. This might involve regular check-ins with a mentor, joining a mastermind group, or simply sharing your goals with friends or family who can provide support and encouragement. Accountability can also come from self-reflection through journaling or reviewing your progress at set intervals.

Embracing Flexibility

While it's important to have a plan and stick to it, be prepared to adapt as necessary. Challenges and opportunities you hadn't anticipated will arise, and your ability to pivot and adjust your actions will be crucial. Stay focused on your overall goals, but be flexible in your approach to achieving them.

Taking the First Step

Ultimately, the most important strategy is to take the first step. It can be the hardest part, but it's also the most crucial. Commit to taking one small action towards your goal today, no matter how insignificant it might seem. Action breeds more action, and before you know it, you'll have built a momentum that carries you forward.

Transitioning from planning to execution is about moving from the "what" to the "how." It's about bringing your vision to life through consistent, deliberate actions. By breaking down goals, prioritizing tasks, setting deadlines, and creating a conducive environment, you'll bridge the gap between aspiration and achievement, turning your plans into your reality.

Measuring and Adjusting Actions

Once the journey from planning to execution is underway, the next critical step is to measure the effectiveness of your actions and adjust them as needed. This iterative process ensures that your efforts are aligned with your goals and that you remain on the most efficient path to success.

Establishing Key Performance Indicators (KPIs)

To measure the impact of your actions effectively, you need to establish clear Key Performance Indicators (KPIs) that are directly tied to your goals. These indicators should be quantifiable, allowing you to track progress in a concrete way. For example, if your goal is to improve your physical health, your

KPIs might include weekly exercise duration, daily step count, or dietary intake metrics.

Regular Review and Reflection

Set aside regular intervals—be it daily, weekly, or monthly—for reviewing your progress against your KPIs. This practice of reflection allows you to assess what actions are yielding the desired results and where adjustments might be necessary. Reflective journaling can be a powerful tool in this process, providing insights into both your successes and areas for improvement.

Embracing Data-Driven Decisions

In today's world, numerous tools and apps can help you gather and analyze data related to your actions and their outcomes. Use these resources to make informed decisions about how to proceed. Data-driven adjustments are often more effective than those based on intuition alone, as they remove subjective bias from the decision-making process.

The Feedback Loop

Think of the process of measuring and adjusting actions as a feedback loop. Your actions produce outcomes, which you then measure against your KPIs. The insights gained from this measurement feed back into your planning process, informing your next set of actions. This loop ensures that your efforts are continually refined and optimized.

Adjusting for External Changes

Be mindful of external factors that may affect your progress and require adjustments to your actions. Changes in your personal life, shifts in the market (for business-related goals), or new technological advancements can all impact the effectiveness of your current approach. Stay adaptable and ready to pivot your strategies in response to these external influences.

Learning from Outcomes

Both positive and negative outcomes offer valuable learning opportunities. Celebrate your successes and analyze what contributed to these wins, so you can replicate those actions in the future. Similarly, view setbacks not as failures but as lessons that can guide your future adjustments and strategies.

Incremental Adjustments

When making adjustments, it's often more effective to implement small, incremental changes rather than overhauling your approach entirely. This allows you to isolate the impact of each adjustment and understand its specific contribution to your overall progress.

Seeking Feedback

Don't hesitate to seek feedback from mentors, peers, or even your audience (for business or creative endeavors). External perspectives can provide additional insights into the effectiveness of your actions and suggest areas for improvement you might not have considered.

Measuring and adjusting your actions is an ongoing process that plays a crucial role in achieving your goals. By setting clear KPIs, regularly reviewing your progress, and being willing to make data-driven adjustments, you ensure that your journey to success is as efficient and effective as possible. Remember, the path to achievement is rarely linear; it's the continual process of measuring, learning, and adjusting that leads to sustained success.

Celebrating Small Wins

The journey toward achieving your goals is often long and filled with challenges. It's easy to become so focused on the end result that you overlook the progress you're making along the way. Celebrating small wins is a crucial strategy in maintaining motivation, building momentum, and reinforcing the positive behaviors that drive you forward.

How to Celebrate Small Wins

1. **Make It a Habit**: Incorporate the celebration of small wins into your daily or weekly routines. This could be as simple as taking a moment at the end of the day to reflect on what you've achieved or writing down your wins in a journal.

2. **Share Your Wins**: Sharing your achievements with friends, family, or colleagues can amplify the positive feelings associated with them. It also allows others to celebrate with you, providing additional support and encouragement.

3. **Reward Yourself**: Associate small wins with small rewards. This could be anything from taking a short break, enjoying a favorite snack, watching an episode of a TV show, or anything else that feels like a treat.

4. **Visual Reminders**: Keep a visual record of your small wins. This could be a progress bar that you fill in, a jar where you add a note for each win, or a wall of sticky notes. Seeing the accumulation of wins can be incredibly motivating.

5. **Reflect on the Journey**: Regularly take time to look back on how far you've come. This reflection can provide valuable perspective, particularly during challenging times, and remind you of the cumulative impact of your small wins.

Integrating Wins into Your Growth

While celebrating, take a moment to reflect on what these small wins teach you about your strengths, strategies, and areas for improvement. This reflection can provide insights that you can apply to future challenges, further enhancing your growth and development.

Celebrating small wins is more than just a feel-good exercise; it's a powerful tool for maintaining motivation, building momentum, and reinforcing the positive habits that drive your success. By acknowledging and celebrating each step forward, you'll not only enjoy the journey more but also find yourself reaching your goals with greater ease and satisfaction.

Call to Action: Ignite Your Journey

You've journeyed through the sections, absorbed the insights, and equipped yourself with the tools needed for success. Now, it's time to step beyond the pages and into the arena of action. This is your call to action, a rallying cry to awaken your potential and catalyze your journey towards achieving your dreams.

Commit to the First Step

Every monumental journey begins with a single, decisive step. Identify one small action you can take right now that will move you closer to your goal. It doesn't have to be grand or perfect; it just needs to be a step forward. Commit to taking this step, and let it be the spark that ignites your journey.

Set Your Intentions

With clarity and conviction, set your intentions for the path ahead. Write them down, speak them aloud, or share them with someone you trust. Embed these intentions in your daily life, letting them guide your actions and decisions, keeping you aligned with your goals.

Embrace the Process

Success is as much about the journey as it is about the destination. Embrace the process of growth and discovery, celebrating each step, learning from each setback, and remaining open to the unfolding of your path. Remember, progress, not perfection, is the goal.

Build Your Support Network

You are not alone in this journey. Reach out and connect with those who can support, inspire, and challenge you. Whether it's friends, family, mentors, or peers, build a network that uplifts and propels you forward, offering encouragement and perspective along the way.

Reflect and Adjust

Regularly reflect on your progress, acknowledging your wins and learning from your experiences. Be prepared to adjust your strategies as you gain new insights and encounter unforeseen challenges. Flexibility and adaptability are your allies in navigating the path to success.

Stay Committed

The road to success is paved with persistence and dedication. Stay committed to your goals, even when the going gets tough. Remember why you started, hold fast to your vision, and trust in your ability to overcome obstacles.

Share Your Journey

Your journey can inspire and motivate others. Share your experiences, challenges, and triumphs, contributing to a community of growth and learning. Your story can be a beacon for those walking a similar path.

This is your moment, the point where intention transforms into action, where potential meets practice. Rise to the occasion, armed with knowledge, fortified by resilience, and propelled by the unwavering belief in your capacity to achieve greatness.

The journey ahead is yours to shape. Embrace it with passion, navigate it with purpose, and infuse it with the essence of your unique spirit. The world awaits the mark you will leave, the stories you will tell, and the legacy you will build. Rise, take action, and let nothing hold you back.

Conclusion

In conclusion, "The Catalyst of Action" chapter is not merely a guide but a clarion call to awaken the latent potential within you. It urges you to step beyond contemplation into the realm of tangible progress, where actions speak louder than intentions. With nearly four decades of experience, especially in the realm of artificial intelligence, I've witnessed firsthand the transformative power of taking decisive steps towards one's goals. Action is the golden key that unlocks the door to opportunities, dispels the shadows of doubt, and carves a path through the wilderness of uncertainty.

By bridging the gap between planning and execution, you not only manifest your dreams but also contribute to a larger narrative of success and fulfillment. As you embark on this journey, remember that each small step is a monumental leap in the tapestry of your life's story. Armed with the insights from this chapter, you are more than ready to ignite the engines of change, propel yourself beyond the ordinary, and etch your mark on the fabric of the world. Let the catalyst of action be your steadfast companion as you navigate the journey of achieving not just success but a legacy of meaningful impact and enduring satisfaction.

Chapter 8

Building Financial Resilience

Welcome to the "Building Financial Resilience" chapter, an essential guide designed to empower you with the knowledge and tools needed to secure your financial future. In today's ever-changing economic landscape, understanding how to manage, protect, and grow your money is not just advantageous—it's imperative.

Financial resilience is about more than just making ends meet; it's about creating a foundation that can withstand life's unexpected turns, enabling you to thrive in both prosperous and challenging times. This chapter aims to demystify the world of personal finance, making it accessible and actionable, regardless of where you're starting from.

We'll begin by laying the groundwork with financial basics, ensuring you understand the key components that shape your financial health. From there, we'll dive into practical strategies for budgeting and money management, helping you to take control of your spending and saving with confidence.

Building an emergency fund will be our next focus, emphasizing the importance of having a financial safety net in place. This will be followed by a discussion on debt management and credit health, two areas that are pivotal to your financial stability and opportunities.

Savings and investments will also take center stage, as we explore how to make your money work for you, setting the stage for long-term growth and security. Additionally, we'll cover the significance of diversifying your income streams, providing insights into how you can enhance your earning potential.

Life's major milestones bring both joy and financial implications. We'll guide you through planning for these significant events, from pursuing higher education to buying a home and planning for retirement. Understanding the role of insurance in protecting your assets and loved ones will also be a key part of our journey.

No path is without its hurdles, and financial challenges are no exception. We'll equip you with strategies to navigate these situations, ensuring you're prepared to face and overcome obstacles that may arise. Lastly, we'll discuss the importance of building a financial legacy, leaving you with a sense of purpose and direction for your financial decisions.

By the end of this chapter, you'll have a comprehensive toolkit at your disposal, ready to build a financially resilient future. Let's embark on this journey together, transforming challenges into opportunities and aspirations into achievements.

Understanding Financial Basics

Embarking on your journey toward financial resilience begins with a solid understanding of the fundamentals. This section lays the foundation of personal finance, equipping you with the essential knowledge to navigate your financial landscape effectively.

Income: Income is the cornerstone of your financial structure. It encompasses the money you receive regularly, whether from employment, business ventures, investments, or other sources. Recognizing and maximizing your income streams is crucial for financial growth and stability.

Expenses: Expenses are the costs incurred in your daily life, including necessities like housing, food, transportation, and discretionary spending such as entertainment and hobbies. Differentiating between 'needs' and 'wants' is vital for effective expense management.

Savings: Savings represent the portion of your income that is not spent on immediate expenses and is set aside for future use. Savings can serve multiple purposes: an emergency fund, a reserve for large purchases, or a nest egg for long-term goals.

Investments: Investments involve allocating money with the expectation of achieving a profitable return. This can include stocks, bonds, real estate, and other assets. Investing is a powerful tool for wealth building, leveraging the potential of compound interest over time.

Debt: Debt arises from borrowing money that must be repaid, often with interest. While some debt can be strategic, such as mortgages or some student loans, excessive or high-interest debt can undermine your financial health.

Budgeting: Budgeting is the process of creating a plan to manage your income and expenses. A well-structured budget ensures that you live within your means, save effectively, and work towards your financial goals.

Net Worth: Your net worth is the total value of your assets (what you own) minus your liabilities (what you owe). Tracking your net worth over time provides insight into your overall financial progress and health.

Key Takeaways

- **Live Within Your Means**: Ensure your expenses do not exceed your income. This fundamental principle is the bedrock of financial stability and growth.

- **Prioritize Saving**: Aim to save a portion of your income regularly. Even small amounts can accumulate over time, providing a safety net and resources for future opportunities.

- **Be Mindful of Debt**: Use debt wisely and sparingly. Understand the terms and interest rates of any borrowed money and prioritize paying off high-interest or non-strategic debt.

- **Invest for the Future**: Consider long-term investments as part of your financial strategy. Educate yourself on the risks and returns associated with different investment vehicles.

- **Budget for Success**: Develop and adhere to a budget that reflects your financial goals, adjusting as needed to stay on track.

Understanding these financial basics is the first step in building a resilient and prosperous financial future. As you grow in your financial journey, these principles will serve as your guiding lights, helping you navigate through life's financial seas with confidence and clarity.

Budgeting and Money Management

Mastering the art of budgeting and money management is the cornerstone of financial resilience. This section will guide you through the process of creating a budget, managing your money effectively, and adopting spending habits that align with your financial goals.

Creating a Personal Budget

1. **Track Your Income and Expenses**: The first step in budgeting is understanding where your money comes from and where it goes. Track all sources of income and categorize your expenses over a month. This includes fixed expenses (rent, utilities, loan payments) and variable expenses (groceries, entertainment, personal spending).

2. **Set Realistic Goals**: Based on your tracking, set realistic financial goals. These could range from saving for a vacation to paying off debt. Ensure your goals are

specific, measurable, achievable, relevant, and time-bound (SMART).

3. **Allocate Your Funds**: Divide your income among your needs, wants, savings, and debt repayment. A popular method is the 50/30/20 rule, where 50% of your income goes to needs, 30% to wants, and 20% to savings and debt repayment. Adjust these percentages to suit your personal circumstances. Of course, these amountss may vary depending on how much you must pay for housing or other basic living expenses.

4. **Prioritize Your Spending**: Always prioritize essential expenses and financial goals. This may mean cutting back on non-essential spending to ensure you can cover your basic needs and contribute to your savings or debt repayment.

5. **Use Tools and Apps**: Numerous budgeting tools and apps can help you track your spending and stick to your budget.

Effective Money Management Strategies

1. **Automate Your Finances**: Automate bill payments and savings contributions to ensure they're never overlooked. This can help avoid late fees and ensures you're consistently contributing to your financial goals.

2. **Build a Buffer**: Aim to build a small buffer in your checking account to avoid overdraft fees and provide peace of mind for unexpected expenses.

3. **Review and Adjust Regularly**: Your financial situation and goals may change over time. Regularly review and adjust your budget to reflect these changes, ensuring it always aligns with your current needs and objectives.

4. **Cut Unnecessary Expenses**: Periodically review your spending to identify areas where you can cut back. This might include subscription services you no longer use,

dining out less frequently, or finding more cost-effective alternatives for regular expenses.

5. **Focus on Value:** When spending money, especially on non-essential items, consider the value it brings to your life. This mindset can help you make more mindful spending decisions and prioritize purchases that contribute to your overall happiness and well-being.

Dealing with Irregular Income

If your income varies from month to month, such as for freelancers or commission-based workers, budgeting can be more challenging but not impossible. Base your budget on your average income or, more conservatively, on your lowest-earning months. Set aside extra income in high-earning months to cover expenses in leaner times.

By taking control of your budget and managing your money effectively, you're laying a solid foundation for financial resilience. Remember, budgeting is not about restricting yourself but about empowering yourself to make informed financial decisions that support your goals and lifestyle.

Emergency Fund and Safety Nets

An emergency fund is your financial lifeline during unexpected events. Whether it's a sudden job loss, medical emergency, or urgent home repairs, having a safety net can make all the difference. This chapter delves into the importance of an emergency fund, how to build one, and other safety nets to consider for comprehensive financial resilience.

The Importance of an Emergency Fund

An emergency fund is essentially a stash of money set aside to cover unforeseen expenses or to provide financial support during periods of income disruption. Its primary purpose is to ensure that you can handle life's surprises without resorting to high-interest debt, such as credit cards or loans, which can further strain your financial situation.

How Much to Save

The size of your emergency fund can vary based on your lifestyle, monthly costs, income stability, and dependents. A general rule of thumb is to save enough to cover 3-6 months' worth of living expenses. However, if your job is less stable or if you're the sole breadwinner in your household, aiming for a larger fund of up to 12 months' expenses may be more prudent.

Building Your Emergency Fund

1. **Start Small**: If you're starting from scratch, begin by setting a modest initial goal, such as $500 or $1,000. This can provide a psychological boost and a buffer for smaller emergencies.

2. **Set Up a Dedicated Savings Account**: Open a separate savings account for your emergency fund to avoid the temptation to dip into it for non-emergencies. Look for high-yield savings accounts to maximize your fund's growth.

3. **Automate Your Savings**: Set up automatic transfers from your checking account to your emergency fund right after payday. Treat it like a non-negotiable expense.

4. **Increase Contributions Gradually**: As you adjust to your budget, look for opportunities to increase your emergency fund contributions. Tax refunds, bonuses, and other windfalls are also excellent sources to bolster your fund.

5. **Cut Back on Non-Essentials**: Temporarily reduce discretionary spending to channel more money into your emergency fund. Even small savings can add up over time.

Other Financial Safety Nets

Beyond an emergency fund, consider these additional safety nets for a well-rounded financial security plan:

1. **Insurance**: Adequate insurance coverage, including health, life, disability, and property insurance, can protect you and your loved ones from significant financial burdens in case of accidents, illnesses, or other unforeseen events.

2. **Health Savings Account (HSA) / Flexible Spending Account (FSA)**: If eligible, utilize HSAs or FSAs to set aside pre-tax money for medical expenses, effectively creating a health-specific emergency fund.

3. **Building a Support Network**: Cultivate relationships with family, friends, and community organizations that can offer support in times of need. This network can provide not just financial assistance but also emotional and practical support during difficult times.

4. **Continued Skill Development**: Investing in your education and skills can enhance your employability, providing a safety net against job loss. Consider certifications, workshops, or new skills that can make you more versatile in the job market.

Maintaining Your Emergency Fund

Regularly review and adjust your emergency fund as your financial situation evolves. Increases in income or living expenses might necessitate a larger fund, while reaching your target amount might allow you to redirect savings towards other financial goals.

Remember, the purpose of an emergency fund is to provide peace of mind and financial stability. It's a critical component of your overall financial plan, ensuring that you're prepared to face life's uncertainties without derailing your long-term financial health.

Debt Management and Credit Health

Navigating the realm of debt and maintaining a healthy credit score are pivotal to your financial well-being. This section provides a comprehensive guide to managing your debts effectively and optimizing your credit health, laying the foundation for a financially resilient future.

Understanding Debt

Debt is not inherently negative; it can be a tool for achieving goals like education, homeownership, or starting a business. However, mismanaged debt can hinder your financial progress. Differentiating between 'good' debt (such as a mortgage or student loans) and 'high-interest' debt (like credit card debt) is crucial.

Strategies for Debt Management

1. **Assess Your Debt**: Compile a clear picture of your debts — amounts, interest rates, and monthly payments. Prioritize them based on interest rates or balances, depending on the strategy you choose to follow.

2. **The Avalanche Method**: This approach focuses on paying off debts with the highest interest rates first while maintaining minimum payments on others. It can save you money on interest over time.

3. **The Snowball Method**: Here, you start by paying off the smallest debts first, gradually working your way up to larger ones. This method can offer quick wins, boosting your motivation.

4. **Consolidation and Refinancing**: Consolidating multiple debts into a single loan with a lower interest rate or refinancing can simplify payments and reduce interest costs.

5. **Negotiate with Creditors**: If you're facing financial hardship, contact your creditors to discuss potential

adjustments to your payment terms, such as reduced interest rates or extended payment periods.

6. **Automate Payments**: Setting up automatic payments can help you stay on track and avoid late fees, further protecting your credit score.

Maintaining and Improving Credit Health

Your credit score is a crucial indicator of your financial health, influencing your ability to obtain loans, the interest rates you receive, and even your job prospects.

1. **Regularly Check Your Credit Report**: Monitor your credit report for errors or fraudulent activity. You're entitled to one free report from each major credit bureau per year.

2. **Pay Bills On Time**: Timely payments are the most significant factor in your credit score. Even small bills, like utilities or subscriptions, can impact your credit if left unpaid.

3. **Keep Credit Utilization Low**: Aim to use less than 30% of your available credit. High utilization can signal to lenders that you're over-reliant on credit, negatively affecting your score.

4. **Manage Credit Accounts Wisely**: Opening too many new accounts can lower your average account age, impacting your score. Conversely, keeping old accounts open can be beneficial, as long as they're not costing you in annual fees.

5. **Diversify Your Credit Mix**: A healthy mix of credit types (installment loans, credit cards, mortgages) can positively affect your score, demonstrating your ability to manage various credit forms responsibly.

6. **Avoid Closing Paid-Off Accounts**: Closing credit accounts can reduce your available credit and increase

your utilization ratio, negatively affecting your credit score.

7. **Seek Professional Help if Needed**: If debt becomes unmanageable, consider consulting with a reputable credit counseling service that can help you develop a debt management plan

Debt–Free Living

Aiming for a debt-free life is admirable, but it's essential to balance debt repayment with other financial goals like saving for retirement or building an emergency fund. Remember, effective debt management and maintaining a healthy credit score are continuous processes that require attention and discipline. By adopting these strategies, you can ensure that debt remains a tool for achieving your dreams rather than an obstacle.

Savings and Investment Basics

Achieving financial security and growth requires a solid understanding of savings and investment fundamentals. This section will guide you through the essentials of saving money effectively and making informed investment decisions to build wealth over time.

The Importance of Saving

1. **Start with a Purpose**: Define clear goals for your savings, whether it's for an emergency fund, a down payment on a home, retirement, or a dream vacation. Having specific targets can motivate you to save consistently.

2. **Pay Yourself First**: Treat your savings like a non-negotiable expense. Automate transfers to your savings account right after you receive your income to ensure you prioritize saving over spending.

3. **Choose the Right Savings Account:** Research and select savings accounts that offer competitive interest rates and low fees. Consider high-yield savings accounts or money market accounts for better returns on your deposits.

Introduction to Investing

Investing involves allocating money in the expectation of some benefit in the future. The primary goal of investing is to allow your money to grow, outpacing inflation and increasing your wealth over time.

1. **Understand Your Risk Tolerance:** Assess your comfort level with risk, considering factors like your investment timeline, financial goals, and emotional response to market fluctuations. Your risk tolerance will guide your investment choices.

2. **Start Small:** Begin with a manageable amount of money you're comfortable investing, especially if you're new to investing. Many platforms allow you to start with small investments and gradually increase your contributions.

3. **Diversify Your Portfolio:** Don't put all your eggs in one basket. Spread your investments across different asset classes (stocks, bonds, real estate, etc.) to reduce risk. Diversification can help protect your portfolio from significant losses.

4. **Understand the Power of Compound Interest:** Compound interest is the interest on a loan or deposit calculated based on both the initial principal and the accumulated interest from previous periods. It can significantly boost the growth of your investments over time, demonstrating the value of starting early.

5. **Regularly Review and Adjust Your Investments:** As your financial situation, goals, and risk tolerance evolve, so should your investment strategy. Regularly reviewing and adjusting your portfolio can help you stay on track to meet your financial objectives.

6. **Educate Yourself**: Continuously educate yourself about financial markets, investment strategies, and economic trends. Knowledge is power, especially when it comes to making informed investment decisions.

7. **Consider Professional Advice**: If you're unsure about where to start or how to manage your investments, consider seeking advice from a financial advisor. A professional can provide personalized guidance based on your individual financial situation and goals.

Common Investment Vehicles

- **Stocks**: Shares of ownership in a company. Stocks have the potential for high returns, but they also come with higher risk.

- **Bonds**: Loans made to corporations or governments. Bonds are generally considered safer than stocks but offer lower returns.

- **Mutual Funds**: Investment programs funded by shareholders that trade in diversified holdings and are professionally managed.

- **Exchange-Traded Funds (ETFs)**: Similar to mutual funds but traded on stock exchanges like individual stocks.

- **Retirement Accounts (401(k), IRAs)**: Tax-advantaged accounts specifically designed for retirement savings.

Investing is a journey that can lead to financial growth and security. By understanding the basics of saving and investing, you can make informed decisions that align with your financial goals and risk tolerance, paving the way for a prosperous financial future.

Income Diversification

In today's dynamic economic landscape, relying solely on a single source of income can be risky. Income diversification is about creating multiple revenue streams to enhance financial security and resilience. This chapter explores strategies for diversifying your income, reducing financial vulnerability, and paving the way for sustained financial growth.

Benefits of Diversifying Your Income

1. **Financial Stability**: Multiple income streams can provide a safety net, ensuring financial stability even if one source dwindles or disappears.

2. **Increased Earning Potential**: Diversification can significantly boost your overall income, allowing for more aggressive saving and investing.

3. **Opportunity for Growth**: Exploring different income avenues can lead to personal and professional growth, uncovering new interests and talents.

Strategies for Income Diversification

1. **Invest in the Stock Market**: Beyond traditional stock investments, consider dividend-paying stocks, which provide regular income through dividend distributions.

2. **Real Estate Investments**: Investing in real estate, whether through rental properties, real estate investment trusts (REITs), or crowdfunding platforms, can provide a steady stream of passive income.

3. **Side Hustles**: Leverage your skills and interests to create a side business. Freelancing, consulting, or starting an online business are viable options for generating additional income.

4. **Passive Income Streams**: Explore opportunities for earning passive income, such as creating digital

products, affiliate marketing, or earning royalties from creative work.

5. **Peer-to-Peer Lending**: Platforms that facilitate peer-to-peer lending allow you to lend money to individuals or small businesses in exchange for interest payments, diversifying your income sources.

6. **Participate in the Gig Economy**: Engage in gig work, such as ride-sharing, delivery services, or task-based jobs, to supplement your income.

7. **Automate Savings and Investments**: Automatically diverting a portion of your income into high-yield savings accounts or investment vehicles can help grow your wealth over time, effectively creating another "income" stream through returns.

Challenges and Considerations

While diversifying your income can offer numerous benefits, it's essential to be mindful of potential challenges:

- **Time Management**: Balancing multiple income sources can be time-consuming. It's crucial to manage your time effectively to prevent burnout.

- **Financial Management**: More income streams mean more complex financial management. Stay organized and consider consulting with a financial advisor to optimize your income and tax strategies.

- **Risk Assessment**: Not all income streams are created equal. Assess the risks associated with each and consider how they fit into your overall financial plan.

Getting Started

1. **Assess Your Skills and Interests**: Identify what you're good at and what you enjoy. These insights can reveal viable paths for income diversification.

2. **Start Small**: Begin with low-risk ventures to gain experience and confidence.

3. **Network**: Connect with others in areas you're interested in. Networking can open doors to opportunities you might not have considered.

4. **Continue Learning**: Stay informed about trends and opportunities in your chosen income streams. Continuous learning is key to adapting and growing your diversified income portfolio.

Diversifying your income is a proactive strategy to build financial resilience and independence. By exploring and implementing multiple income sources, you not only safeguard against economic uncertainties but also set the stage for sustained financial growth and opportunities. Remember, the journey to income diversification is a marathon, not a sprint. Start small, stay consistent, and gradually expand your income streams to achieve financial stability and success.

Financial Planning for Major Life Events

Life is marked by a series of significant events, each bringing its unique financial implications. Planning for these milestones is crucial to ensure they become sources of joy rather than financial stress. This section provides a roadmap for navigating the financial aspects of life's major events, from education to retirement.

Higher Education

Investing in education is investing in your future. Consider the following strategies:

1. **Start Saving Early**: Utilize education savings accounts like 529 plans to benefit from tax advantages.

2. **Explore Scholarships and Grants**: Actively seek out scholarships, grants, and work-study programs to reduce the need for student loans.

3. **Understand Student Loans**: If loans are necessary, opt for federal student loans before private ones due to their more favorable terms and repayment options.

Career and Income

Starting your career is an exciting phase with significant financial implications:

1. **Negotiate Your Salary**: Learn negotiation skills to ensure you're fairly compensated for your work.
2. **Emergency Fund**: Build an emergency fund to cover living expenses in case of job loss or transition.
3. **Retirement Savings**: Take advantage of employer-sponsored retirement plans, especially if they offer matching contributions.

Marriage

Combining lives means combining finances:

1. **Financial Transparency**: Have open discussions about debts, assets, and financial goals.
2. **Joint vs. Separate Accounts**: Decide whether to merge finances, keep them separate, or a combination of both.
3. **Budget for the Wedding**: Set a realistic budget for your wedding to avoid starting married life in debt.

Home Ownership

Buying a home is a significant milestone and a substantial financial commitment:

1. **Save for a Down Payment**: Aim to save at least 20% of the home's price to avoid private mortgage insurance (PMI).

2. **Get Pre-Approved:** Understand how much you can afford before house hunting.

3. **Consider All Costs:** Factor in property taxes, insurance, maintenance, and potential homeowners association (HOA) fees.

Starting a Family

The joy of expanding your family comes with new financial responsibilities:

1. **Plan for Increased Expenses:** Budget for the immediate and long-term costs of raising a child, including healthcare, education, and daily needs.

2. **Update Your Insurance:** Ensure your health insurance covers maternity and pediatric care and consider life insurance to protect your family's future.

3. **Estate Planning:** Draft a will and designate guardians to secure your child's future in unforeseen circumstances.

Retirement

Retirement planning is about ensuring you can enjoy your later years with financial security:

1. **Maximize Retirement Contributions:** Contribute as much as possible to retirement accounts, especially when employer matching is available.

2. **Diversify Investments:** Maintain a diversified portfolio to balance growth and risk as you approach retirement.

3. **Plan for Healthcare:** Consider healthcare costs, including Medicare and supplemental insurance, in your retirement planning.

Financial planning for major life events requires foresight, adaptability, and proactive management. By anticipating and preparing for these milestones, you can ensure that each transition not only enriches your life experience but also reinforces your financial foundation, allowing you to face the future with confidence and security.

Insurance and Protection

Insurance plays a crucial role in your overall financial plan by providing a safety net against unforeseen financial losses. This section explores various types of insurance, their importance, and how to choose the right coverage to ensure you and your assets are adequately protected.

Types of Insurance and Their Importance

1. **Health Insurance**: Covers medical expenses, including hospital stays, surgeries, prescriptions, and sometimes preventive care. Given the high cost of healthcare, health insurance is crucial to prevent medical bills from becoming overwhelming financial burdens.

2. **Life Insurance**: Provides financial support to your beneficiaries (family or dependents) in the event of your untimely death. It can help cover living expenses, debts, and future financial needs like education costs, ensuring your loved ones' financial security.

3. **Disability Insurance**: Offers income protection if you're unable to work due to illness or injury. It's essential for maintaining your lifestyle and meeting financial obligations during periods of reduced earning capacity.

4. **Homeowners/Renters Insurance**: Protects your home and personal property from damage or loss due to events like fires, theft, or natural disasters. For renters, it covers personal property within the rented premises.

5. **Auto Insurance**: Covers damages to your vehicle and liability for injuries and property damage you may cause to others in an accident. It's not only a legal requirement in many places but also critical for protecting your financial assets.

6. **Umbrella Insurance**: Provides additional liability coverage beyond the limits of your homeowners, auto, and boat insurance policies. It's beneficial for protecting against major claims and lawsuits.

Choosing the Right Insurance Coverage

1. **Assess Your Needs**: Evaluate your specific risks and financial situation to determine the types and amounts of insurance coverage you need.

2. **Shop Around**: Compare policies from multiple insurers to find the best coverage at the most reasonable price. Consider factors like premiums, deductibles, coverage limits, and exclusions.

3. **Read the Fine Print**: Understand the details of your policy, including what's covered, what's excluded, and the claims process. Knowing these details can prevent surprises when you need to use your insurance.

4. **Review and Update Regularly**: Your insurance needs can change over time due to life events like marriage, having children, buying a house, or changing jobs. Regularly review your policies and update your coverage as necessary.

5. **Consider a Trusted Advisor**: If you're unsure about your insurance needs, consider consulting with an insurance agent or financial advisor who can provide personalized advice based on your circumstances.

Insurance is an integral component of a comprehensive financial plan, offering peace of mind and protection against life's uncertainties. By carefully selecting and maintaining appropriate insurance coverage, you can protect yourself, your loved ones, and your assets, ensuring financial stability and resilience in the face of adversity.

Navigating Financial Challenges

Financial challenges are an inevitable part of life. Whether it's an unexpected job loss, a medical emergency, or economic downturns, these challenges can significantly impact your financial well-being. This section provides strategies for effectively navigating and overcoming financial hurdles, ensuring you remain resilient in the face of adversity.

Understanding Financial Challenges

Financial challenges come in various forms and can arise suddenly or accumulate over time. Recognizing the nature of these challenges is the first step toward addressing them. Common financial obstacles include:

1. **Debt Overload**: High levels of debt, especially high-interest debt, can strain your finances.
2. **Income Disruption**: Job loss or reduced income can disrupt your financial stability.
3. **Unexpected Expenses**: Emergencies like home repairs, medical bills, or car breakdowns can derail your budget.
4. **Economic Fluctuations**: Recessions or market downturns can affect your investments and overall economic security.

Strategies for Overcoming Financial Challenges

1. **Emergency Fund**: A well-funded emergency fund is your first line of defense against financial setbacks. It can provide a buffer to cover unexpected expenses or sustain you during periods of income disruption.
2. **Budget Adjustment**: Review and adjust your budget to accommodate your current financial situation. Prioritize essential expenses, and identify areas where you can cut back or eliminate spending temporarily.

3. **Debt Management:** If debt is contributing to your financial challenges, consider strategies such as debt consolidation, the debt snowball method, or negotiating with creditors for better terms.

4. **Increase Income:** Explore ways to increase your income through side hustles, freelancing, or selling unused items. Every little bit can help mitigate financial strain.

5. **Seek Financial Assistance:** Don't hesitate to seek help if you need it. Many organizations and programs offer assistance for those facing financial hardship, including government benefits, community resources, and non-profit agencies.

6. **Professional Advice:** Consulting with a financial advisor or credit counselor can provide personalized strategies for navigating your financial challenges. They can offer guidance on debt management, budgeting, and other financial planning aspects.

7. **Open Communication:** If your financial challenges involve others, such as a spouse or family members, maintain open and honest communication. Working together can make it easier to find solutions and support each other through difficult times.

8. **Stress Management:** Financial challenges can take a toll on your mental and emotional well-being. Practice stress management techniques and seek support from friends, family, or professionals if needed.

9. **Long-Term Planning:** Once you've addressed the immediate challenges, focus on long-term financial planning to prevent similar situations in the future. This might include building a more substantial emergency fund, adjusting your investment strategy, or making lifestyle changes to live within your means.

Moving Forward

Navigating financial challenges requires a proactive approach and a focus on solutions. By assessing your situation, adjusting your budget, managing debt, and seeking assistance when necessary, you can overcome financial obstacles and emerge stronger. Remember, facing financial challenges is not a failure but an opportunity to reassess, learn, and grow on your path to financial resilience.

Building a Financial Legacy

Creating a financial legacy involves more than just accumulating wealth; it's about making a lasting impact that extends beyond your lifetime. This chapter explores the concept of a financial legacy, providing strategies for establishing, nurturing, and ensuring its longevity for future generations or causes you care about.

Understanding Financial Legacy

A financial legacy encompasses the assets, values, and financial wisdom you pass on. It reflects your life's financial journey and the mark you wish to leave on your family, community, or a cause close to your heart.

Key Components of a Financial Legacy

1. **Estate Planning**: Estate planning is the foundation of a financial legacy. It involves creating a will, setting up trusts, and making other legal arrangements to ensure your assets are distributed according to your wishes.

2. **Life Insurance**: Life insurance can be a cornerstone of your financial legacy, providing financial security for your loved ones or contributing to a cause you support.

3. **Investment in Education**: Investing in the education of your children or supporting educational causes can have

a lasting impact, empowering future generations with knowledge and opportunities.

4. **Charitable Giving**: Incorporating philanthropy into your financial plan can extend your legacy's reach, making a meaningful difference in the lives of others and causes you believe in.

Strategies for Building Your Legacy

1. **Define Your Legacy Goals**: Start by reflecting on what you want your legacy to represent. Consider the values you wish to pass on and the impact you hope to make.

2. **Effective Estate Planning**: Consult with legal and financial professionals to draft a comprehensive estate plan. This should include a will, trusts (if necessary), and clear instructions for asset distribution.

3. **Life Insurance Planning**: Evaluate your life insurance needs to ensure your policy aligns with your legacy goals, providing adequate coverage for those you leave behind or supporting philanthropic endeavors.

4. **Educational Investments**: Consider setting up education funds or scholarships to support the educational aspirations of your children, grandchildren, or students in your community.

5. **Philanthropic Endeavors**: Explore options for charitable giving, such as direct donations, setting up a charitable trust, or contributing to endowments that align with your values.

6. **Impart Financial Wisdom**: Share your financial knowledge and experiences with your family or community. Educating others about financial management, investing, and responsible stewardship of wealth can be an invaluable part of your legacy.

7. **Document Your Wishes**: Ensure all your legacy plans are well-documented and accessible to your family or executors. This includes estate documents, insurance

policies, and any letters or instructions you wish to leave behind.

Ensuring Your Legacy's Longevity

1. **Regular Review and Update:** Life changes, such as marriage, birth of children, or significant financial shifts, necessitate a review and potential update of your legacy plans to ensure they remain aligned with your goals.

2. **Open Communication**: Discuss your legacy intentions with your family or beneficiaries. Transparency can prevent misunderstandings and ensure your wishes are honored.

3. **Professional Guidance**: Regularly consult with estate planning attorneys, financial advisors, and tax professionals to adapt your legacy planning to changing laws and financial landscapes.

Building a financial legacy is a deeply personal and impactful endeavor. It's about leaving a mark that reflects your values, supports your loved ones, and contributes to the greater good. By thoughtfully planning and continuously nurturing your legacy, you can create a lasting impact that resonates through generations or supports the causes dear to your heart.

Empower Your Financial Future

Congratulations on taking this significant step towards securing your financial future and building a legacy that reflects your values and aspirations. As you close this chapter and contemplate the journey ahead, remember that the path to financial resilience and legacy-building is ongoing and dynamic. It's time to put the knowledge you've gained into action and chart a course towards a future filled with promise and purpose.

Embrace Your Financial Journey

1. **Reflect on Your Goals**: Revisit the goals you've set for yourself throughout this guide. Ensure they are clear, measurable, and aligned with your values and aspirations.

2. **Create a Plan**: Armed with the strategies and insights from each chapter, draft a comprehensive financial plan that addresses your current situation, short-term objectives, and long-term goals.

3. **Take the First Step**: Identify one action you can take today, no matter how small, to move closer to your financial goals. This could be setting up a budget, opening a savings account, or scheduling a meeting with a financial advisor.

Stay Committed and Consistent

1. **Regular Reviews**: Schedule regular check-ins with yourself to assess your progress, review your financial plan, and make necessary adjustments in response to life changes or new goals.

2. **Continuous Learning**: Stay informed about financial trends, investment opportunities, and changes in tax and estate laws. Consider joining financial literacy groups or subscribing to financial education resources.

3. **Build Support Networks**: Surround yourself with a community of like-minded individuals who are also on their financial journeys. Sharing experiences and insights can provide motivation and new perspectives.

Seek Professional Guidance

1. **Consult with Experts**: Don't hesitate to seek advice from financial advisors, tax professionals, or estate planners to navigate complex financial decisions and ensure your plans are sound and effective.

2. **Leverage Resources**: Utilize available resources, tools, and services to streamline your financial management, from budgeting apps and investment platforms to educational workshops and seminars.

Give Back and Share Your Knowledge

1. **Mentor Others**: Share your financial insights and experiences with family, friends, or community members. Becoming a mentor can reinforce your own understanding and help others on their financial paths.

2. **Contribute to Your Community**: Look for opportunities to support financial literacy programs or initiatives that align with your values, enhancing the collective financial well-being of your community.

Charting Your Path Forward

1. **Document Your Plan**: Write down your financial plan, including your goals, strategies, and timelines. Having a tangible plan can serve as a roadmap and a source of motivation.

2. **Set Milestones**: Break down your goals into achievable milestones and celebrate each accomplishment along the way. This can help maintain momentum and focus.

3. **Stay Flexible**: Be prepared to adapt your plan as circumstances change. Flexibility is key to navigating life's uncertainties while staying true to your financial and legacy-building objectives.

As you move forward, remember that each step you take builds upon the last, creating a compounding effect that can lead to remarkable achievements. Your financial journey is uniquely yours, filled with opportunities to grow, learn, and leave a lasting impact. Embrace it with confidence, determination, and a vision for the future you aspire to create.

Conclusion: Financial Resilience and Legacy

As we conclude this chapter on "Building Financial Resilience," we reflect on the journey we've undertaken to empower ourselves with the knowledge and tools necessary for securing a robust financial future. In navigating the complexities of personal finance, we've explored the importance of budgeting, saving, investing, and planning for life's significant milestones. We've also delved into the intricacies of managing debt and credit, safeguarding our financial well-being through insurance, and the critical role of emergency funds.

Financial resilience is not merely about weathering economic storms but also about proactively preparing for and thriving in the face of financial challenges. It entails a comprehensive approach to managing and growing your wealth, ensuring that you can achieve your financial goals and support the aspirations of future generations.

Moreover, building a financial legacy transcends the accumulation of wealth. It's about creating a lasting impact, guided by your values and goals, that will benefit your loved ones and contribute positively to the wider community. This legacy, nurtured through strategic planning and thoughtful decision-making, becomes a testament to your life's work and dedication to financial stewardship.

As you apply the insights and strategies from this chapter, remember that financial resilience and legacy-building are ongoing processes. They require continuous learning, adaptation, and commitment to your financial principles and objectives. By taking deliberate steps towards financial empowerment, you can transform your aspirations into tangible achievements, ensuring that your financial legacy endures and inspires.

Let this chapter be a stepping stone to a future where financial resilience and a meaningful legacy are within your grasp. Embrace the journey with confidence, equipped with the knowledge and tools to create a prosperous and impactful financial path.

Chapter 9

Cultivating Meaningful Relationships

In the tapestry of life, the threads of relationships weave patterns of profound influence and meaning. As we embark on the journey of success, it's essential to recognize that our achievements are not solely the fruits of individual endeavor but are also deeply rooted in the connections we foster with those around us. "Cultivating Meaningful Relationships" is a chapter dedicated to exploring the pivotal role that relationships play in our personal and professional growth.

This chapter delves into the art and science of building, nurturing, and sustaining relationships that not only enrich our lives but also propel us toward our goals. From family and friends to mentors, colleagues, and even casual acquaintances, each interaction holds potential for impact. Here, we will uncover the principles of effective communication, empathy, and mutual support that form the foundation of meaningful connections.

We'll explore strategies for networking with purpose, maintaining balance between giving and receiving, and navigating the complexities of relationships in various spheres of life. Whether it's a deep bond with a lifelong friend or a professional rapport with a mentor, understanding the dynamics of these relationships can unlock doors to unforeseen opportunities and insights.

As we journey through this chapter, remember that the strength of your relationships often mirrors the strength of your character. In cultivating meaningful relationships, we not only enhance our capacity for success but also discover the richness of shared experiences and the joy of contributing to others' journeys. Let's embark on this exploration together, learning how to weave a network of relationships that supports, inspires, and elevates.

The Role of Relationships in Success

At the heart of every success story, there are relationships that have played a crucial role. Whether it's a mentor providing guidance, a colleague sharing a pivotal opportunity, or a friend offering support during challenging times, the influence of relationships on our journey toward success cannot be overstated. This section delves into how relationships act as catalysts for personal and professional growth, and why nurturing these connections is indispensable for achieving success.

Networking and Opportunities

Networking isn't just about exchanging business cards at social events; it's about building genuine connections with people who share similar interests and goals. These relationships can open doors to new opportunities, from career advancements to collaborations that might not have been accessible otherwise. The people you meet can introduce you to new ideas, skills, and perspectives, enriching your personal and professional development.

Emotional Support and Well-being

The journey to success is often riddled with challenges and setbacks. During these times, having a support system of friends and family can make a significant difference. Emotional support from loved ones provides a sense of security and belonging, which is crucial for maintaining mental and emotional well-being. When we feel supported, we are more resilient and better equipped to tackle obstacles that come our way.

Learning and Growth

Relationships are a rich source of learning and growth. Interacting with individuals from diverse backgrounds and experiences allows us to gain new insights, challenge our assumptions, and broaden our understanding of the world. This continuous learning is vital for personal development and can significantly enhance our problem-solving and decision-making skills, which are essential for success.

Accountability and Motivation

When we share our goals and aspirations with others, it creates a sense of accountability. Friends, family, and mentors can provide the motivation and encouragement needed to stay on track. They can celebrate our achievements, offer constructive feedback, and remind us of our commitments when we lose focus. This accountability is a powerful motivator, helping us to persevere in the face of challenges.

Collaboration and Synergy

Success is rarely a solo endeavor. Collaborating with others allows us to combine our skills, knowledge, and resources to achieve common goals. Through collaboration, we can achieve a synergy where the collective outcome is greater than the sum of individual efforts. Relationships facilitate these collaborations, leading to innovative solutions and achievements that might not have been possible alone.

In essence, relationships are not just a component of success; they are often the very foundation upon which it is built. Cultivating meaningful relationships requires intentionality, empathy, and a willingness to invest time and effort. As we navigate our paths to success, let us recognize the value of each connection and the potential it holds to enrich our journey.

Types of Relationships

In the mosaic of life, we encounter a spectrum of relationships, each serving distinct roles and purposes in our journey. Understanding the different types of relationships can help us navigate them more effectively, fostering deeper connections and leveraging their unique contributions to our success. Here are some key types of relationships that play pivotal roles in our personal and professional growth:

Familial Relationships

These are the bonds we share with our family members—parents, siblings, extended family—who often provide the foundational support system in our lives. Familial relationships offer unconditional love, security, and a sense of belonging, forming the bedrock upon which we build our identities and values. Nurturing these relationships can bring comfort and stability, essential elements for enduring the ups and downs of pursuing success.

Friendships

Friendships enrich our lives with companionship, joy, and mutual support. True friends celebrate our successes, stand by us during failures, and offer honest feedback that challenges us to grow. They are the ones we share our dreams with, and their encouragement can be a significant motivational force. Investing in deep, meaningful friendships adds a layer of richness to our lives, making the journey toward success more enjoyable and rewarding.

Romantic Relationships

Romantic partners can have a profound impact on our aspirations and the paths we choose. A supportive partner can boost our confidence and resilience, while a challenging relationship might demand compromises that affect our goals. Healthy romantic relationships are based on mutual respect, shared values, and the encouragement of each other's growth, both individually and together.

Professional Relationships

These include connections with colleagues, mentors, supervisors, and industry peers. Professional relationships can influence our career trajectories, offering opportunities for advancement, collaboration, and learning. A mentor can provide invaluable guidance and insight, helping us navigate our careers with wisdom gleaned from experience. Colleagues and peers can become collaborators or sounding boards for new ideas, broadening our professional network and opening doors to opportunities.

Acquaintances and Casual Connections

Not all relationships delve into the depths of personal connection, but even casual acquaintances can play significant roles in our success. These might be people we interact with sporadically, like neighbors, community members, or professionals we meet at networking events. Even brief interactions can lead to new opportunities, fresh perspectives, or valuable information that can aid in our pursuits.

Self-Relationship

Often overlooked, the relationship we have with ourselves is perhaps the most crucial. Self-awareness, self-compassion, and self-motivation are key components of this inner relationship. Cultivating a positive self-relationship involves recognizing our worth, nurturing our growth, and forgiving our mistakes. A healthy self-relationship sets the tone for how we engage with others and pursue our goals.

Each type of relationship offers unique benefits and challenges, and understanding how to navigate them can enhance our personal development and accelerate our journey to success. By recognizing the value of each connection and actively nurturing these relationships, we build a supportive network that propels us forward, enriches our experiences, and contributes to a fulfilling life.

Building New Relationships

Embarking on the journey of building new relationships is akin to setting sail into uncharted waters—it's an adventure filled with opportunities for growth, learning, and enrichment. Whether you're stepping into a new environment, pursuing new goals, or simply expanding your network, cultivating new connections is integral to personal and professional development. Here's how to approach the art of building new relationships with intention and openness:

Be Open to New Connections

The first step in building new relationships is to adopt an open mindset. Embrace the possibility of meeting new people and be willing to step out of your comfort zone. Attend social gatherings, networking events, and community activities where you can meet individuals with shared interests or goals. Remember, meaningful connections can arise in the most unexpected places.

Show Genuine Interest

When meeting someone new, show genuine interest in getting to know them. Ask open-ended questions that encourage dialogue and listen actively to their responses. This not only helps in understanding the person better but also demonstrates your interest in their thoughts and experiences, laying the groundwork for a meaningful relationship.

Share About Yourself

While it's important to listen, sharing about yourself is equally crucial in building a connection. Open up about your interests, experiences, and aspirations. This exchange of personal stories fosters a sense of mutual understanding and trust, which are the cornerstones of any strong relationship.

Find Common Ground

Discovering common interests, goals, or values can significantly strengthen the bond between you and a new acquaintance. Whether it's a shared hobby, professional ambition, or a similar outlook on life, finding common ground provides a solid foundation for the relationship to grow.

Follow Up and Stay Connected

After the initial meeting, take the initiative to follow up. Send a message expressing your pleasure in meeting them and suggest another meet-up if appropriate. Regular communication helps keep the relationship alive and shows your genuine interest in staying connected.

Offer Value and Support

Building relationships is not just about what you can gain from the other person but also about how you can add value to their life. Be ready to offer support, share knowledge, or lend a helping hand when needed. This reciprocal exchange of value deepens the connection and builds mutual respect.

Be Patient and Authentic

Good relationships take time to develop, so be patient. Don't rush the process; allow it to evolve naturally. Most importantly, be yourself. Authenticity attracts, and being genuine in your interactions will draw others to you who appreciate and resonate with who you truly are.

Cultivate Empathy and Kindness

Empathy and kindness are universal languages that transcend barriers and forge deep connections. Approach new relationships with a compassionate understanding and a kind heart, and you'll find that these qualities are often reciprocated, strengthening the bond between you and others.

Building new relationships requires a blend of openness, effort, and authenticity. As you navigate this process, remember that each new connection has the potential to enrich your life in unforeseen ways, contributing to your personal growth and success. By embracing the art of building relationships, you open doors to a world of opportunities, learning, and shared journeys.

Deepening Existing Relationships

While forging new connections is vital to expanding our horizons, nurturing and deepening existing relationships is equally crucial for fostering a supportive and enriching network. These relationships, whether with family, friends, or colleagues, form the bedrock of our social support system. Deepening these connections can lead to more fulfilling interactions, enhanced trust, and mutual growth. Here's how you can cultivate deeper bonds in your existing relationships:

Consistent Communication

Regular and meaningful communication is the lifeline of any strong relationship. Make an effort to stay in touch, share updates, and express interest in the other person's life. Whether through face-to-face conversations, phone calls, or messages, consistent communication keeps the relationship vibrant and shows that you value the connection.

Quality Time Together

Spending quality time together is key to deepening relationships. Engage in activities that both of you enjoy, whether it's a shared hobby, a collaborative project, or simply relaxing together. These shared experiences create lasting memories and strengthen the bond between you.

Show Appreciation and Gratitude

Expressing appreciation and gratitude for the other person's presence in your life can significantly enhance your relationship. Acknowledge their qualities, celebrate their achievements, and thank them for their support. Feeling valued and appreciated deepens emotional connections and fosters mutual respect.

Be There in Times of Need

Standing by someone during their challenging times is a powerful way to deepen your relationship. Offering your support, listening to their concerns, and being a source of comfort can strengthen the bond immeasurably. It shows that you're not just there for the good times but are a reliable pillar of support.

Open and Honest Communication

Cultivating a space where both parties feel safe to express their thoughts, feelings, and concerns without judgment is essential for deepening relationships. Encourage open dialogue, be receptive to feedback, and address conflicts constructively. Honesty and transparency build trust and understanding, which are crucial for a deeper connection.

Share Personal Goals and Dreams

Sharing your aspirations, dreams, and even fears with someone can significantly deepen your connection. It allows for a level of vulnerability and authenticity that brings people closer. Support each other's goals and celebrate achievements together to reinforce the sense of partnership in your shared journey.

Mutual Respect and Boundaries

Respecting each other's opinions, space, and boundaries is fundamental in any relationship. Understand and honor the other person's limits and preferences. Mutual respect fosters a healthy environment where the relationship can flourish.

Continuous Growth and Learning

Grow together by exploring new experiences, learning new skills, or facing challenges as a team. This not only keeps the relationship dynamic and exciting but also reinforces the bond as you both evolve.

Reciprocity

Ensure that the relationship is balanced in terms of give and take. Reciprocity doesn't necessarily mean keeping a score but ensuring that both parties feel their efforts and contributions are recognized and reciprocated in some form.

Deepening existing relationships is about building on the foundation you already have to create a more meaningful, supportive, and fulfilling connection. It requires effort, patience, and a genuine commitment to each other's well-being. By investing in these relationships, you create a network of connections that provide strength, joy, and support as you navigate the journey of life.

Conflict Resolution

Conflict is a natural part of any relationship, stemming from differences in perspectives, needs, and expectations. How we handle these conflicts can significantly impact the health and longevity of our connections. Effective conflict resolution fosters understanding, strengthens bonds, and promotes personal growth. Here are key strategies for navigating and resolving conflicts constructively:

Approach with a Calm Mindset

Entering a conflict with heightened emotions can escalate the situation. Take a step back, breathe, and approach the conversation with a calm and open mindset. This readiness to resolve the issue, rather than to win an argument, sets a positive tone for constructive dialogue.

Active Listening

One of the most crucial skills in conflict resolution is active listening. This involves fully concentrating on what the other person is saying, understanding their message, responding thoughtfully, and remembering the discussion. Active listening shows respect for the other person's perspective and helps to clarify misunderstandings.

Use "I" Statements

Communicate your feelings and perspectives without placing blame by using "I" statements. For example, instead of saying "You never consider my opinions," say "I feel overlooked when my opinions aren't considered." This approach expresses your feelings without accusing the other party, reducing the likelihood of defensive reactions.

Acknowledge Different Perspectives

Recognize that each party may have a valid perspective. Acknowledging the other person's viewpoint doesn't mean you agree with them, but it shows respect for their feelings and experiences, paving the way for a mutually acceptable resolution.

Focus on the Issue, Not the Person

Keep the discussion focused on the specific issue at hand rather than resorting to personal attacks. Addressing the problem rather than criticizing the person helps prevent the conflict from becoming a personal battle.

Seek Common Ground

Try to identify areas of agreement or common goals related to the conflict. Finding common ground can serve as a foundation for building a solution that satisfies both parties.

Explore Solutions Together

Instead of insisting on your own way of resolving the conflict, invite the other party to brainstorm potential solutions with you. This collaborative approach encourages compromise and ensures that both parties have a stake in the resolution.

Agree to Disagree When Necessary

It's important to recognize that it's not always possible to reach an agreement. In some cases, agreeing to disagree while respecting each other's perspectives can be a healthy way to resolve a conflict.

Follow Up

After reaching a resolution, follow up to ensure that the agreed-upon actions are being implemented and that the resolution is effective. This follow-up demonstrates your commitment to the relationship and to resolving issues in a lasting way.

Seek Mediation if Needed

If the conflict cannot be resolved between the parties involved, seeking mediation from a neutral third party can be helpful.

Mediators can facilitate communication, help clarify issues, and assist in finding a mutually acceptable resolution.

Effective conflict resolution is about finding a balanced solution that respects the needs and perspectives of all parties involved. By approaching conflicts with empathy, openness, and a willingness to find common ground, we can transform challenges into opportunities for strengthening our relationships and personal growth.

The Impact of Social Media

In today's interconnected world, social media plays a significant role in shaping our relationships, perceptions, and interactions. While it offers unparalleled opportunities for staying connected, sharing experiences, and accessing information, social media also presents unique challenges that can affect our well-being and the quality of our relationships. Understanding its impact is crucial for navigating social media landscapes healthily and positively.

Connectivity and Community

Social media breaks down geographical barriers, enabling us to connect with friends, family, and like-minded individuals worldwide. It fosters communities based on shared interests, causes, or experiences, providing a sense of belonging and support. This global connectivity can strengthen relationships, offering new ways to communicate and share life moments.

Comparison and Self-Esteem

One of the more challenging aspects of social media is the tendency to compare ourselves with others. Curated posts often depict an idealized version of life, leading to unrealistic benchmarks for success, beauty, and happiness. This constant comparison can adversely affect self-esteem and body image, making it important to maintain perspective and prioritize self-compassion.

Instant Communication and Misunderstandings

While social media facilitates instant communication, the lack of non-verbal cues (like tone of voice and body language) can lead to misunderstandings. Text-based communication can be misinterpreted, potentially leading to conflicts or strained relationships. Emphasizing clear communication and giving others the benefit of the doubt can mitigate these misunderstandings.

Digital Well-being and Real-life Connections

Spending excessive time on social media can impact real-life interactions and overall well-being. It's essential to find a balance, ensuring that digital connections don't replace face-to-face relationships. Setting boundaries around social media use can help maintain this balance, fostering healthier relationships both online and offline.

Privacy and Boundaries

Social media challenges traditional notions of privacy and personal boundaries. Oversharing or posting without consent can lead to discomfort and conflicts. Respecting others' privacy, thinking before sharing, and discussing boundary preferences with friends and family can help maintain respectful online interactions.

Mental Health Awareness

Social media platforms have become important spaces for discussing mental health, reducing stigma, and sharing resources. Engaging in these conversations can foster a supportive community, though it's also crucial to seek professional advice and offline support when needed.

In navigating the impact of social media on our lives and relationships, mindfulness, and intentionality are key. By using social media as a tool to enhance, not replace, real-world connections, and being aware of its potential pitfalls, we can harness its benefits while safeguarding our well-being and the quality of our relationships.

Letting Go of Toxic Relationships

Recognizing and letting go of toxic relationships is a crucial aspect of nurturing our well-being and fostering healthy connections. Toxic relationships are characterized by patterns of behavior that are consistently harmful, such as manipulation, disrespect, and a lack of support. These relationships can drain your energy, diminish your self-esteem, and distract you from your goals and personal growth. Here's how to navigate the process of identifying and letting go of toxic relationships:

Identifying Toxic Relationships

The first step is to recognize the signs of a toxic relationship. These can include feelings of constant stress or anxiety around the person, feeling belittled or devalued, one-sided efforts to maintain the relationship, and manipulative or controlling behaviors. Acknowledging these signs can be challenging but is essential for taking steps to protect your well-being.

Assessing the Impact

Reflect on how the relationship affects your mental, emotional, and physical health. Consider whether interactions with this person leave you feeling drained, upset, or demoralized. Assessing the relationship's impact can help you understand the importance of distancing yourself from harmful dynamics.

Setting Boundaries

Before ending a relationship, it may be helpful to set clear boundaries to see if the relationship can improve. Communicate your needs and limits assertively and see how the other person responds. If they respect your boundaries and the relationship improves, it may not need to end. However, if they continue to overstep or disregard your boundaries, it reinforces the need to let go.

Communicating Your Decision

If you decide to end the relationship, communicate your decision clearly and respectfully. You don't need to provide an exhaustive list of reasons, but you can express that the relationship isn't healthy for you and that you've decided to move on. It's important to remain firm in your decision, even if the other person tries to persuade you otherwise.

Seeking Support

Letting go of any relationship can be emotionally challenging. Seek support from friends, family, or a mental health professional who can provide you with the understanding and encouragement you need during this time. Sharing your feelings and experiences can alleviate the sense of isolation that often accompanies such decisions.

Focusing on Self-Care

Prioritize self-care practices that nurture your well-being, such as engaging in activities you enjoy, practicing mindfulness or meditation, and ensuring you have time for rest and relaxation. Self-care helps you rebuild your sense of self and recover from the negative effects of the toxic relationship.

Embracing Personal Growth

View the process of letting go as an opportunity for personal growth. Reflect on what you've learned from the experience and how you can use these insights to foster healthier relationships in the future. Recognizing your strength in overcoming a toxic relationship can boost your confidence and resilience.

Cultivating Positive Relationships

Focus on building and nurturing positive relationships that support your well-being and align with your values. Surrounding yourself with people who respect, encourage, and uplift you can significantly enhance your quality of life and contribute to your success.

Letting go of toxic relationships is a courageous step toward honoring your worth and nurturing a healthier, more fulfilling life. By recognizing harmful patterns, setting boundaries, and prioritizing your well-being, you open the door to more positive and supportive connections.

Mentorship and Guidance

Mentorship plays a pivotal role in personal development and the journey towards success. A mentor is someone who offers their knowledge, wisdom, and advice to less experienced individuals. This relationship can provide invaluable guidance through various stages of life and career, offering insights that only experience can teach. Here's how mentorship and guidance can significantly impact your growth and success:

The Value of Mentorship

Mentors provide more than just advice; they offer a roadmap based on their own experiences, successes, and failures. This guidance can help you navigate challenges, make informed decisions, and avoid common pitfalls. Mentors can also provide encouragement, boost your confidence, and help you stay focused on your goals.

Finding a Mentor

Identifying the right mentor involves looking for someone whose experience and values align with your personal and professional aspirations. Mentors can be found within your existing network, professional organizations, alumni associations, or online platforms dedicated to mentorship. When seeking a mentor, be clear about what you're looking for in the relationship and what you hope to achieve.

Building a Mentor–Mentee Relationship

Effective mentorship relationships are built on mutual respect, trust, and commitment. Be proactive in maintaining the relationship by setting regular meetings, coming prepared with questions or topics for discussion, and being open to feedback. Showing appreciation for your mentor's time and advice is also crucial in fostering a positive and lasting relationship.

The Role of Guidance in Personal Growth

Guidance, whether from a mentor, coach, or advisor, can provide clarity and direction, especially in times of uncertainty. It can challenge you to think differently, consider new perspectives, and take action towards your goals. Guidance can also help you refine your skills, enhance your strengths, and work on areas for improvement.

Giving Back through Mentorship

As you progress in your own journey, consider giving back by becoming a mentor to others. Sharing your experiences, knowledge, and lessons learned can be incredibly rewarding and can help others achieve their own success. Being a mentor also offers the opportunity for self-reflection and further personal growth.

The Importance of Diverse Perspectives

Seeking guidance from a diverse group of mentors and advisors can provide a wide range of perspectives and insights, enriching your understanding and approach to challenges. Diversity in mentorship can expose you to different strategies, cultural insights, and problem-solving methods, enhancing your adaptability and creativity.

Nurturing Multiple Mentoring Relationships

It's beneficial to cultivate multiple mentoring relationships, as each mentor can provide guidance on different aspects of your life and career. Some mentors may offer industry-specific advice, while others might help with personal development or leadership skills. Balancing these relationships allows you to gain a more holistic view of success and how to achieve it.

Mentorship and guidance are invaluable resources on the path to success. They provide not only the roadmap and tools needed for the journey but also the encouragement and support to persevere through challenges. By actively seeking and engaging in mentoring relationships, you open yourself up to a wealth of knowledge and experience that can significantly accelerate your growth and achievement.

Community Engagement

Community engagement represents a powerful avenue for personal growth, networking, and making a meaningful impact on the world around you. It involves actively participating in community activities, initiatives, and organizations to contribute to societal well-being and foster a sense of belonging and purpose. This section explores the importance of community engagement and how it can enrich your life and the lives of others.

Finding Your Cause

To begin your journey in community engagement, identify causes or issues that resonate with you deeply. Whether it's environmental conservation, education, public health, or social justice, aligning your efforts with your values and interests makes your involvement more meaningful and fulfilling. Explore local organizations, non-profits, and community groups that focus on these areas to see how you can contribute.

Volunteering Your Time and Skills

Volunteering is a direct and impactful way to engage with your community. Offering your time and skills can make a significant difference in various initiatives, from local clean-up projects to tutoring programs. Volunteering also allows you to apply your knowledge in real-world settings, gain practical experience, and develop new competencies.

Participating in Community Events

Attending and participating in community events, such as workshops, seminars, cultural festivals, and town hall meetings, can deepen your understanding of community dynamics and issues. These events provide platforms for networking, collaboration, and cultural exchange, enriching your personal and professional life.

Advocacy and Leadership

Community engagement can also take the form of advocacy and leadership. By raising awareness about community issues, mobilizing resources, and leading initiatives, you can drive positive change and inspire others to get involved. Developing your leadership and advocacy skills can have far-reaching effects, extending beyond your immediate community.

Building Community Networks

Engaging with your community helps you build a network of like-minded individuals who share your commitment to making a difference. These connections can support your personal and professional development, offering opportunities for collaboration, mentorship, and friendship.

Reflecting on Your Impact

Take time to reflect on the impact of your community engagement efforts. Consider the changes you've contributed to, the relationships you've built, and the personal growth you've experienced. Reflection can provide insights into how you can further your involvement and effectiveness in community initiatives.

Balancing Involvement

While community engagement is rewarding, it's important to balance your involvement with other responsibilities and commitments. Ensure that your community activities complement your personal goals and well-being, allowing you to sustain your efforts over the long term.

Community engagement enriches your life by connecting you to a larger purpose, expanding your horizons, and enabling you to contribute to societal well-being. By actively participating in your community, you not only make a tangible impact but also grow as an individual, gaining experiences and insights that shape your path to success.

Giving Back

As you progress on your journey, consider how you can give back to others. Sharing your knowledge, experiences, and resources can not only help others achieve their own success but also enrich your own life with purpose and fulfillment.

The journey to success is uniquely yours. Armed with the insights from this exploration and your personalized action plan, you're well-equipped to navigate the path ahead. Embrace the journey with openness, resilience, and a commitment to continuous growth. Here's to your next level of success!

Conclusion

In conclusion, "Cultivating Meaningful Relationships" underscores the intricate web of interactions that significantly shape our personal and professional lives. As we traverse the landscape of success, the chapter elucidates the vital role relationships play in enriching our experiences and propelling us forward. Through the lenses of communication, empathy, networking, and mutual support, we've navigated the complexities of forming and sustaining bonds that not only bring personal fulfillment but also enhance our journey towards achieving our goals.

By embracing the principles and strategies discussed, we equip ourselves with the tools necessary to build and nurture relationships that are both rewarding and influential. Whether through the enduring support of family and friends, the guidance of mentors, or the collaborative efforts with colleagues, each relationship we cultivate adds a unique strand to the fabric of our lives, enriching the tapestry of our collective existence.

As we reflect on the insights garnered, let us commit to actively fostering these connections, recognizing their transformative power in our journey of growth and success. In doing so, we not only achieve our individual aspirations but also contribute to a broader narrative of shared achievements and mutual prosperity. Thus, in the realm of meaningful relationships, we find the essence of true success – a harmonious blend of personal achievement and collective progress.

Chapter 10

Thriving: Health as Success Leverage

In the pursuit of success, we often focus on external achievements—academic accolades, career milestones, financial gains. Yet, nestled at the core of every triumph lies an indispensable ally: our health. "Thriving: Health as Success Leverage" unfolds the profound truth that our well-being is not just a part of the success equation; it is the very foundation upon which our aspirations are built and realized.

This chapter is an invitation to reframe your understanding of health, not as a mere absence of illness but as a dynamic state of complete physical, mental, and emotional well-being. It's about recognizing that the quality of your health directly influences the quality of your life and, by extension, the heights of success you can attain.

We'll delve into the critical aspects of holistic health, starting with the fuel that powers our bodies and minds: nutrition. The adage "You are what you eat" holds more truth than we often credit it with. A balanced, nutrient-rich diet is a cornerstone of good health, enabling us to perform at our peak. Conversely, the perils of poor dietary choices—reliance on junk food, overconsumption of processed goods, and indulgence in excesses—can undermine our efforts toward success by sapping our energy, clouding our minds, and impairing our physical vitality.

Physical activity, too, plays a starring role in this narrative. Regular exercise is not just about maintaining a healthy physique; it's a catalyst for mental clarity, creativity, and emotional stability. We'll explore how integrating movement into your daily routine can elevate your performance in all areas of life.

Yet, thriving extends beyond the physical realm. Mental health and mindfulness are equally critical components of a successful life. In these pages, we'll navigate the strategies for managing stress, fostering a positive outlook, and maintaining emotional equilibrium, ensuring you're as robust on the inside as you appear on the outside.

Sleep, often underrated in our fast-paced society, is another pillar of health we'll examine. Quality rest is essential for cognitive function, emotional resilience, and overall well-being. We'll provide insights into achieving restorative sleep, enabling you to wake up refreshed and ready to tackle your goals.

In our journey, we'll also confront the challenges of burnout and substance misuse, offering guidance on navigating these potential roadblocks to your success. And recognizing the importance of professional healthcare, we'll advocate for regular check-ups and proactive health management.

Through personal anecdotes and actionable advice, this chapter aims to equip you with the knowledge and tools to prioritize your health, not just as a duty to yourself but as a strategic investment in your future success. Your health is your wealth, and by nurturing it, you set the stage for a life not just of achievement, but of fulfillment and joy. Let's embark on this journey to thriving, where health and success are not just parallel paths but intertwined routes leading to your most vibrant life.

Holistic Health Overview

At the heart of a truly successful life lies the principle of holistic health—a concept that goes beyond mere physical wellness to encompass mental, emotional, and even spiritual well-being. This comprehensive approach recognizes you as a whole person, where each aspect of your health is interconnected and equally vital to your overall success and happiness.

The Pillars of Holistic Health

1. **Physical Health:** This foundational pillar involves maintaining a healthy body through nutrition, exercise, sleep, and regular healthcare. It's about nurturing your body with the right foods, keeping it active, ensuring it rests, and addressing any medical issues proactively.

2. **Mental Health:** Your cognitive functions, thoughts, and mindsets fall under this category. Mental health is about cultivating a positive outlook, managing stress effectively, and engaging in activities that stimulate and challenge your mind.

3. **Emotional Health:** This aspect pertains to understanding, expressing, and managing your feelings in a healthy manner. Emotional health is crucial for building resilience, fostering relationships, and navigating life's ups and downs with grace.

4. **Spiritual Health:** While not always associated with religion, spiritual health involves a sense of connection to something greater than oneself, which can provide a sense of purpose and meaning. This can be nurtured through meditation, mindfulness, spending time in nature, or engaging in activities that align with your personal values and beliefs.

The Interconnectedness of Health Dimensions

The beauty of holistic health lies in the synergy between its components. Your physical health can influence your mental state; your emotional well-being can impact your physical condition, and so forth. For instance, regular physical activity not only strengthens your body but also releases endorphins, which improve mood and mental clarity. Conversely, stress (an emotional and mental health aspect) can lead to physical symptoms, such as headaches or high blood pressure.

Cultivating a Holistic Approach

Embracing holistic health requires a shift in perspective—from viewing health as a series of disconnected elements to seeing it as a cohesive, interrelated system. It's about making conscious choices that benefit all aspects of your well-being. Here are a few strategies to foster holistic health:

- **Balance in Lifestyle:** Strive for a balanced lifestyle that allocates time for work, relaxation, social activities, and self-care. Avoid extremes in any area, whether it's overworking, over-exercising, or neglecting your social life.

- **Mindful Eating:** Choose foods that nourish your body and mind. Pay attention to how different foods make you feel and adjust your diet to include more of what energizes and less of what depletes you.

- **Regular Physical Activity:** Find forms of exercise that you enjoy and that suit your lifestyle. This could range from yoga and walking to more intense activities like running or weightlifting.

- **Stress Management:** Incorporate stress-reducing practices into your daily routine, such as deep breathing exercises, meditation, or spending time in nature.

- **Emotional Expression:** Cultivate healthy outlets for expressing your emotions, such as journaling, art, or talking with trusted friends or counselors.

- **Purposeful Living:** Engage in activities that bring you joy and fulfillment, contributing to a sense of purpose and well-being.

The Journey to Holistic Health

Embarking on a journey to holistic health is a personal and ongoing process. It involves tuning in to your body and mind, recognizing your needs, and making choices that support all dimensions of your health. By adopting a holistic approach, you not only enhance your ability to succeed but also enrich the quality of your life, making every achievement more meaningful and every setback more manageable.

Nutrition and Success

At the heart of peak performance, both mentally and physically, lies nutrition—a critical component often overshadowed by the bustling demands of daily life. Yet, it is the quality of the fuel we provide our bodies that ultimately dictates the quality of our output in every endeavor. This section delves into the symbiotic relationship between what we consume and how we succeed, unraveling the profound impact of dietary choices on our overall life trajectory.

The Foundation of Cognitive Function

Our brain, the command center steering the ship of our aspirations, requires a constant supply of high-quality nutrients to function optimally. Complex carbohydrates, lean proteins, healthy fats, vitamins, minerals, and water are not just components of a balanced diet; they are the building blocks of our cognitive processes. They enhance memory, concentration, and problem-solving abilities, and regulate mood, all of which are indispensable for achieving success.

Conversely, a diet laden with processed foods, excessive sugars, and unhealthy fats can lead to cognitive fog, lethargy, and mood instability. The immediate gratification these foods provide belies their long-term impact on our health and, by extension, our capacity to achieve our goals.

The Energy Equation

Sustained energy is vital for maintaining the persistence and resilience required to navigate the path to success. Nutrient-dense foods, rich in vitamins and minerals, fuel our bodies' complex energy-producing pathways, ensuring a steady supply of vigor throughout the day. Hydration also plays a crucial role in this energy equation. Even mild dehydration can lead to fatigue, diminishing our ability to focus and persevere through challenges.

The Role of Gut Health

Emerging research underscores the pivotal role of gut health in overall well-being, including mental health and cognitive function. The gut–brain axis, a bidirectional communication pathway, suggests that our intestinal flora can influence our brain's health and function. A diet rich in fiber, probiotics, and prebiotics fosters a healthy gut microbiome, which in turn supports mental clarity, emotional balance, and stress resilience—key components of a successful life.

Nutritional Balance and Personalization

Achieving nutritional balance means providing your body with the right proportions of macronutrients (carbohydrates, proteins, and fats) and micronutrients (vitamins and minerals) it needs to thrive. However, there's no one-size-fits-all solution; personalization is key. Factors such as age, gender, activity level, and individual health needs must guide dietary choices.

Incorporating a diverse range of whole foods, including fruits, vegetables, whole grains, lean proteins, and healthy fats, ensures a broad spectrum of nutrients. Mindful eating practices, such as listening to your body's hunger and fullness cues and eating without distraction, can enhance your nutritional well-being.

Moderation and Mindful Indulgence

While it's essential to focus on nutrient-rich foods, success in life also involves balance and enjoyment. Occasional indulgences, when approached mindfully, can fit into a successful lifestyle without derailing health goals. The key is moderation and making informed choices that align with your overall vision for success.

In summary, nutrition is a powerful lever for success. By making informed, intentional choices about what we eat, we fuel not just our bodies but our aspirations, paving the way for a life marked by achievement and fulfillment. As we progress through this journey, remember that each meal is an opportunity to nourish not just your body but your dreams and ambitions.

Physical Activity's Impact

The role of physical activity in paving the path to success extends far beyond the confines of physical health. It is a potent catalyst for mental clarity, emotional resilience, and overall life satisfaction. This section explores the multifaceted benefits of incorporating regular exercise into your routine, emphasizing its significance as a cornerstone of a successful, balanced life.

Enhanced Cognitive Performance

Regular physical activity boosts brain health, enhancing cognitive functions critical for success, such as memory, attention, and problem-solving skills. Exercise increases blood flow to the brain, delivering the oxygen and nutrients it needs to perform at its peak.

Stress Reduction and Emotional Well-being

The stress-relieving properties of exercise are well-documented. Engaging in physical activity triggers the release of endorphins, the body's natural mood elevators, leading to an enhanced sense of well-being. This biochemical boost can help mitigate the effects of stress, anxiety, and depression, making it easier to maintain focus and motivation toward your goals.

Regular exercise also serves as a powerful tool for emotional regulation. By providing an outlet for releasing tension and frustration, physical activity can help maintain emotional equilibrium, ensuring that temporary setbacks do not derail long-term aspirations.

Building Resilience and Discipline

The discipline and resilience developed through a consistent exercise regimen are directly transferable to other areas of life. Setting fitness goals, overcoming plateaus, and pushing through discomfort mirror the challenges encountered on the road to success. The perseverance and commitment cultivated in the gym or on the running track can inspire the same tenacity in pursuit of personal and professional objectives.

Sleep Quality and Recovery

Physical activity plays a crucial role in enhancing the quality of sleep, a critical component of recovery and overall well-being. Regular exercise can help regulate sleep patterns, making it easier to fall asleep and improving the restorative phases of sleep. This, in turn, contributes to better cognitive function, emotional resilience, and physical health, creating a virtuous cycle that supports sustained success.

Social and Community Engagement

Beyond the individual benefits, physical activity often involves social interaction, whether through team sports, group fitness classes, or community events. These interactions can foster a sense of belonging and support, providing a network that can offer encouragement, share in successes, and provide comfort in challenging times.

Finding Your Fit

Incorporating physical activity into your life doesn't necessitate hours at the gym or marathon training—unless that's your passion. Success comes from finding an activity you enjoy and can commit to regularly. Whether it's yoga, walking, hiking, dancing, cycling, or a sport, the key is consistency and enjoyment.

In essence, physical activity is not just a means to a healthier body but a cornerstone of a well-rounded, successful life. It enhances mental acuity, fortifies emotional resilience, fosters discipline, improves sleep, and provides opportunities for social connection. As you embark on or continue your journey toward success, remember that moving your body is an integral step in moving your life forward.

Mental Health and Mindfulness

In the tapestry of success, mental health and mindfulness are threads that weave through every aspect of our lives, influencing our perceptions, decisions, and interactions. This section delves into the critical importance of nurturing mental well-being and cultivating mindfulness as pivotal elements for achieving and sustaining success.

Understanding Mental Health

Mental health encompasses our emotional, psychological, and social well-being. It affects how we think, feel, act, make choices, and relate to others. In the journey toward success, mental health acts as both the foundation and the scaffold, supporting our endeavors and helping us navigate challenges with resilience and clarity.

The Role of Mindfulness

Mindfulness is the practice of being fully present and engaged in the moment, aware of our thoughts and feelings without distraction or judgment. It enhances our ability to concentrate, reduces stress, and promotes emotional equilibrium. By fostering mindfulness, we can cultivate a state of mental clarity and calm that enables us to approach our goals with focus and purpose.

Strategies for Mental Wellness

- **Regular Self-Reflection**: Dedicate time to introspection to understand your emotional states, triggers, and coping mechanisms. Journaling can be a powerful tool for self-reflection and emotional processing.

- **Stress Management Techniques:** Incorporate stress-reduction practices into your routine, such as deep breathing exercises, progressive muscle relaxation, or guided imagery. These techniques can help lower stress levels and improve your response to stressful situations.

- **Mindfulness and Meditation:** Engage in mindfulness practices or meditation to enhance your ability to remain present and reduce rumination on past or future concerns. Even a few minutes a day can have significant benefits for your mental health.

- **Healthy Social Connections:** Cultivate supportive relationships that provide emotional sustenance. Social connections can offer perspectives, advice, and comfort, contributing to a sense of belonging and well-being.

- **Seek Professional Support When Needed:** Recognize when it's time to seek help from mental health professionals. Therapy or counseling can provide valuable tools and strategies for managing mental health challenges.

Mindfulness in Daily Life

Incorporating mindfulness into daily activities can transform mundane tasks into moments of presence and awareness. Whether eating, walking, or engaging in conversation, practicing mindfulness can enhance the quality of these experiences and reduce feelings of stress or overwhelm.

The Impact of Mental Health on Success

Mental health influences our capacity to persevere, adapt, and thrive in the face of challenges. It supports our ability to maintain focus, make reasoned decisions, and interact effectively with others. By prioritizing mental wellness, we not only enhance our quality of life but also set the stage for sustained success across all areas of our lives.

Cultivating a Mindful Approach to Challenges

Approaching obstacles with mindfulness can change our relationship with challenges, allowing us to see them as opportunities for growth rather than insurmountable barriers. This mindset shift can open new pathways for problem-solving and innovation.

    Mental health and mindfulness are not just adjuncts to the pursuit of success; they are integral to it. By investing in our mental well-being and practicing mindfulness, we equip ourselves with the tools to navigate the complexities of life with grace, resilience, and unwavering focus. As we journey toward our goals, let us remember that the state of our mind is as crucial as the milestones we aspire to achieve.

Sleep's Role in Success

In the quest for success, sleep is often the first sacrifice at the altar of productivity. Yet, this overlooked cornerstone of health is pivotal in sharpening our minds, fortifying our resilience, and catalyzing our achievements. This section underscores the indispensable role of quality sleep in laying the groundwork for success, detailing its profound impacts on cognitive function, emotional well-being, and overall performance.

The Physiology of Sleep

Sleep is not merely a passive state of rest but a complex, active process crucial for our brain's functioning and our body's restoration. During sleep, our bodies undergo various processes, including muscle repair, memory consolidation, and the release of hormones regulating growth and appetite. This rejuvenation phase is essential for maintaining optimal health and functionality.

Cognitive Clarity and Decision Making

A well-rested mind is a sharp mind. Sleep enhances cognitive functions such as attention, problem-solving, creativity, and decision-making. Adequate sleep facilitates the consolidation of memories, transforming learning and experiences into long-term knowledge. Conversely, sleep deprivation can lead to impaired focus, reduced cognitive abilities, and poor judgment, directly impacting our capacity to pursue and achieve our goals.

Emotional Balance and Resilience

Sleep significantly influences our emotional and psychological well-being. Lack of sleep can heighten stress reactivity, exacerbate mood swings, and increase vulnerability to anxiety and depression. In contrast, quality sleep helps regulate our emotional responses, promoting a balanced mood and enhancing our resilience to daily stressors, enabling us to face challenges with equanimity.

Physical Health and Performance

The benefits of sleep extend to our physical health, impacting everything from immune function to weight management. Adequate rest is associated with reduced inflammation, improved heart health, and better regulation of blood sugar levels. For those engaged in physical activities or striving for fitness goals, sleep is crucial for muscle recovery and performance optimization.

Strategies for Quality Sleep

- **Consistent Sleep Schedule**: Adhering to a regular sleep schedule reinforces your body's sleep-wake cycle, improving sleep quality.
- **Optimized Sleep Environment**: Ensure your sleeping environment is conducive to rest. This includes a

comfortable mattress and pillows, minimal noise, reduced light exposure, and a cool temperature.

- **Pre-Sleep Routine**: Establish a calming pre-sleep routine to signal to your body that it's time to wind down. This might include reading, meditation, or gentle stretching

- **Mindful Consumption**: Be mindful of caffeine and heavy meals close to bedtime, as they can disrupt sleep. Limiting screen time before bed can also reduce exposure to blue light, which can interfere with your ability to fall asleep.

- **Physical Activity**: Regular physical activity can promote better sleep, helping you fall asleep faster and enjoy deeper sleep. Timing is key; engaging in vigorous exercise too close to bedtime can have the opposite effect.

The Paradox of Sleep and Success

Embracing the critical role of sleep in achieving success requires challenging the misconception that more hours awake equals more productivity. In reality, sacrificing sleep for work can lead to diminishing returns, where both the quality and efficiency of our efforts are compromised. Prioritizing sleep is, in essence, prioritizing success—it is an investment in your most valuable resource: yourself.

The path to success is not just about the hours you put into your work but also about the quality of rest you allow yourself. Sleep is the silent partner in your success story, a foundational element that supports every step you take toward your goals. By honoring your need for rest, you empower yourself to rise each day with the clarity, energy, and resilience necessary to pursue and achieve your aspirations.

Avoiding Burnout

In the high-stakes pursuit of success, burnout looms as a shadowy pitfall, capable of derailing even the most dedicated individuals. This section addresses the critical importance of recognizing, preventing, and mitigating burnout, ensuring that your journey toward success is sustainable and fulfilling.

Understanding Burnout

Burnout is a state of emotional, physical, and mental exhaustion caused by prolonged stress or frustration. It's characterized by feelings of overwhelm, emotional drain, and reduced personal accomplishment. In the context of striving for success, burnout can manifest from relentless pressure to perform, achieve, and continuously push beyond limits without adequate rest or recovery.

Recognizing the Signs

Early recognition of burnout is key to prevention. Signs include:

- **Persistent Fatigue**: Feeling tired even after rest.
- **Cynicism and Detachment**: A growing sense of disillusionment and emotional disconnection from your work or goals.
- **Feelings of Ineffectiveness**: The belief that your efforts are not yielding meaningful results.
- **Diminished Performance**: A noticeable decline in productivity and quality of work.

Strategies for Avoidance and Recovery

- **Set Realistic Goals**: Ambition is commendable, but unrealistic expectations can set you up for constant perceived failure. Set achievable goals that challenge you without pushing you to the brink.

- **Establish Boundaries**: Learn to say no and set clear boundaries between work and personal time. Protecting your off-time is crucial for mental and emotional recovery.

- **Prioritize Self-Care**: Regularly engage in activities that replenish your energy and bring you joy. Whether it's exercise, hobbies, or spending time with loved ones, these activities can counterbalance the stresses of your pursuits.

- **Practice Mindfulness and Relaxation**: Techniques such as meditation, deep breathing, and yoga can reduce stress levels and enhance your ability to cope with pressure.

- **Seek Support**: Don't shoulder the burden alone. Lean on your support network, whether it's family, friends, or professional counselors, for perspective, encouragement, and guidance.

- **Manage Time Effectively**: Refine your time management skills to ensure you're allocating your energy wisely. Distinguish between urgent and important tasks to avoid getting bogged down by inconsequential details.

- **Embrace Rest**: Recognize rest as a non-negotiable component of high performance. Regular breaks, vacations, and downtime are not signs of weakness but strategies for long-term sustainability.

Reevaluating Success

Sometimes, avoiding burnout requires reevaluating what success means to you. It's about finding fulfillment not just in the achievements but in the journey itself. Ensure that your path to success aligns with your values, passions, and well-being.

Avoiding burnout is not just about preventing collapse but about nurturing a lifestyle that supports your ambitions and well-being in equal measure. By acknowledging the signs of burnout and implementing strategies to counteract its onset, you safeguard your most valuable asset on the journey to success:

yourself. Remember, true success is not just about reaching a destination but about thriving throughout the journey.

Substance Use and Abuse

In the narrative of achieving success, the section on substance use and abuse addresses a critical aspect that can significantly influence one's journey. This section explores the impact of substance use on personal and professional growth, underscoring the importance of making informed choices to support long-term success.

The Fine Line Between Use and Abuse

Substance use becomes a concern when it shifts from casual or social use to dependency or abuse. This transition is often subtle, marked by increased reliance on substances to cope with stress, enhance performance, or escape from reality. The key to maintaining control is recognizing this fine line and understanding the potential consequences of crossing it.

Impact on Health and Well-Being

Substance abuse can have profound and lasting effects on physical and mental health. Physically, it can lead to a range of issues from short-term effects like impaired coordination and judgment to long-term health problems like liver disease, heart problems, and neurological damage. Mentally, it can exacerbate or contribute to conditions such as anxiety, depression, and psychosis, significantly hindering one's ability to function and succeed.

The Ripple Effect on Success

The repercussions of substance abuse extend beyond individual health, impacting all facets of life:

- **Professional Impact**: Substance abuse can compromise work performance, reduce productivity, and damage professional relationships, potentially derailing careers.

- **Personal Relationships**: It can strain personal relationships, leading to isolation and a lack of support, which are crucial for overcoming challenges and achieving success.

- **Financial Stability**: The financial implications of substance abuse, including the cost of substances, potential loss of employment, and medical expenses, can undermine financial security and independence.

Strategies for Prevention and Recovery

- **Awareness and Education**: Understanding the risks associated with substance use and abuse is the first step in prevention. Educate yourself about the substances, their effects, and the signs of dependency.

- **Healthy Coping Mechanisms**: Develop healthy coping strategies for stress and challenges, such as physical activity, hobbies, meditation, or seeking support from friends, family, or professionals.

- **Seeking Help**: Recognizing when you or someone you know needs help is crucial. Various resources, including counseling, support groups, and treatment programs, can provide the necessary support for recovery.

- **Creating a Supportive Environment**: Surround yourself with a positive and supportive network that encourages healthy lifestyle choices and provides a safety net during challenging times.

- **Setting Personal Boundaries**: Establish clear personal boundaries regarding substance use and stick to them, even in social situations.

Embracing Sobriety for Success

For some, sobriety becomes a powerful foundation for success. It enhances clarity, improves health, and fosters resilience, allowing individuals to pursue their goals with undivided focus and determination.

While the journey to success encompasses various challenges and pressures that might tempt one towards substance use, it's imperative to recognize the potential pitfalls and make conscious choices that support your well-being and aspirations. Remember, true success is built on a foundation of health, clarity, and well-being, and maintaining a balanced approach to substance use is crucial in safeguarding this foundation.

Regular Health Check-ups

In the pursuit of success, regular health check-ups serve as critical milestones on the journey, ensuring the vehicle driving your ambitions—your body and mind—remains in optimal condition. This section highlights the importance of preventative healthcare in maintaining peak performance and addressing potential issues before they become obstacles to your goals.

The Preventative Power of Check-ups

Regular health check-ups provide a snapshot of your current health status, offering invaluable insights into your well-being. These check-ups can detect early signs of health issues, allowing for timely intervention and treatment. Just as you wouldn't embark on a long journey without ensuring your vehicle is in top condition, regular medical screenings ensure your body is prepared to sustain the demands of your aspirations.

Components of a Comprehensive Check-up

A thorough health check-up typically includes:

- **Physical Examination**: Assessing your body for signs of potential health issues.
- **Blood Tests**: Evaluating various health indicators like cholesterol levels, blood sugar, vitamin deficiencies, and organ function.
- **Blood Pressure Measurement**: Identifying risks for heart disease and stroke.
- **Vision and Hearing Tests**: Ensuring these senses are functioning well, as they significantly impact daily functioning.
- **Mental Health Screening**: Assessing your emotional and psychological well-being.
- **Lifestyle Assessment**: Discussing your diet, exercise, alcohol, tobacco use, and other lifestyle factors that impact health.

Tailoring Check-ups to Individual Needs

Health check-up requirements can vary based on age, gender, family history, and lifestyle. For instance, women may need regular breast and cervical cancer screenings, while men might require prostate exams. Discuss with your healthcare provider which screenings are appropriate for you and at what frequency.

The Role of Check-ups in Long-term Success

- **Early Detection**: Many health conditions, when caught early, are more manageable or even curable. This proactive approach minimizes the impact on your life and goals.
- **Baseline Health Data**: Regular check-ups provide a record of your health over time, helping to identify trends or changes that might require attention.

- **Lifestyle Adjustments:** Insights gained from check-ups can inform lifestyle changes to enhance your health and performance, aligning with your success journey.

- **Peace of Mind:** Knowing you're in good health, or proactively managing health issues, reduces stress and anxiety, contributing to a more focused pursuit of your goals.

Making Health Check-ups a Priority

In the hustle of daily life and the relentless pursuit of success, it's easy to neglect health check-ups, especially when you're feeling well. However, integrating these check-ups into your routine is an investment in your most valuable asset—your health. Schedule regular appointments as non-negotiable commitments, and consider them as critical to your success as any business meeting or personal milestone.

Navigating Healthcare

Understanding your healthcare coverage and finding trusted healthcare providers are essential steps in making regular check-ups a seamless part of your life. Don't hesitate to ask questions during your appointments to fully understand your health status and any recommended actions.

Regular health check-ups are a cornerstone of a successful life strategy. They ensure that you are not only chasing success but also doing so on a foundation of robust health. By making preventative healthcare a priority, you safeguard your ability to achieve and enjoy your accomplishments, today and in the future.

Action Plan for Health

As we reach the conclusion of this chapter on leveraging health for success, it's time to translate insights and knowledge into actionable steps. Creating a personalized Action Plan for Health will empower you to integrate these health principles into your daily life, ensuring that your journey toward success is supported by a foundation of optimal well-being. Here's how to get started:

Step 1: Assess Your Current Health Status

- **Reflect on your current health**: Consider your physical, mental, and emotional well-being. Identify areas that need attention or improvement.
- **Schedule a comprehensive health check-up**: If you haven't had one recently, book an appointment for a full health assessment to establish a baseline and identify any areas that require immediate attention.

Step 2: Set Specific Health Goals

- **Define clear, achievable health goals**: Based on your health assessment, set specific and realistic goals. These could range from improving your diet, increasing physical activity, reducing stress, enhancing sleep quality, to addressing specific medical conditions.
- **Use the SMART criteria**: Ensure your goals are Specific, Measurable, Achievable, Relevant, and Time-bound.

Step 3: Develop a Strategic Plan

- **Create a step-by-step plan**: Break down each goal into smaller, manageable tasks or habits you can incorporate into your daily routine.
- **Prioritize**: Focus on one or two changes at a time to avoid feeling overwhelmed. Small, consistent changes can lead to significant health improvements.

Step 4: Integrate Mindfulness and Mental Health Practices

- **Allocate time for mindfulness:** Incorporate short mindfulness or meditation sessions into your daily routine to enhance mental and emotional well-being.//
- **Seek resources or professional support for mental health:** If you're dealing with stress, anxiety, or other mental health challenges, consider counseling or therapy as part of your action plan.

Step 5: Commit to Regular Physical Activity

- **Choose activities you enjoy:** Select forms of exercise that you look forward to, making it more likely you'll stick with them.
- **Schedule exercise into your calendar:** Treat it as a non-negotiable appointment with yourself.

Step 6: Optimize Nutrition

- **Plan healthy meals:** Focus on incorporating a variety of nutrient-dense foods into your diet. Consider consulting a nutritionist if you need personalized advice.
- **Mindful eating:** Practice being present during meals, savoring your food, and listening to your body's hunger and fullness cues.

Step 7: Prioritize Sleep

- **Establish a regular sleep schedule:** Aim for consistent sleep and wake times, even on weekends.
- **Create a restful environment:** Ensure your bedroom is conducive to sleep, focusing on comfort, temperature, and minimal light and noise.

Step 8: Monitor Progress and Adjust as Needed

- **Keep a health journal**: Track your progress, challenges, and how you feel physically and mentally as you implement your plan.
- **Be flexible**: Be willing to adjust your plan as you go along. What works well for others may not work for you, and that's okay.

Step 9: Celebrate Successes

- **Acknowledge your achievements**: Celebrate milestones and improvements in your health, no matter how small. Recognizing your progress can provide motivation to continue.

Step 10: Continual Re-evaluation

- **Regularly review and update your plan**: As your health improves and your goals evolve, update your action plan to reflect new objectives and challenges.

In creating your Action Plan for Health, remember that the journey to success is a marathon, not a sprint. Your health is the fuel that will power you through the ups and downs of this marathon. By committing to this plan, you are not just investing in your health; you are investing in your future success, happiness, and fulfillment.

Conclusion

In conclusion, "Thriving: Health as Success Leverage" underscores the indispensable role of health in achieving and sustaining success. We have journeyed through the multifaceted aspects of holistic health, highlighting the interplay between physical, mental, emotional, and spiritual well-being. This chapter has not only illuminated the critical impact of nutrition, physical activity, mental health, and sleep on our performance but also offered practical strategies to integrate these elements into our daily lives.

Embracing the principles of holistic health is a transformative process that requires mindfulness, commitment, and consistency. It's about making intentional choices that nurture our well-being and, in turn, empower us to reach our fullest potential. As we close this chapter, let us carry forward the understanding that health is not merely a component of success but the very foundation upon which our aspirations are built. By prioritizing our health, we pave the way for a life of achievement, fulfillment, and sustained well-being, ensuring that we can not only reach our goals but also enjoy the journey along the way.

Chapter 11

Beyond Obstacles: Turning Setbacks into Success

In the journey of life, the path to success is rarely a straight line. Along the way, we inevitably encounter obstacles that test our resolve, challenge our abilities, and sometimes even make us question our goals. It's easy to perceive these setbacks as failures, moments where we fall short of our expectations and perhaps even contemplate giving up. However, what if we were to tell you that these very obstacles hold the secret keys to unlocking levels of success you've never imagined?

Welcome to "Beyond Obstacles: Turning Setbacks Into Success," a chapter dedicated to transforming your perspective on challenges and failures. Here, we're not just going to talk about overcoming obstacles; we're going to delve into how you can harness them as powerful catalysts for growth, learning, and unparalleled achievement.

This chapter is an invitation to shift your mindset, to see the hurdles not as dead ends but as detours on the road to success, each with its own lessons and opportunities. We'll explore the art of reframing failure, the resilience required to rise above challenges, and the actionable steps you can take to turn every setback into a stepping stone towards your goals.

Through inspiring stories of perseverance, practical strategies for resilience, and a fresh perspective on failure, this chapter aims to equip you with the tools and mindset to navigate life's inevitable challenges with grace and determination. So, as we embark on this transformative journey together, remember that every obstacle faced is not a stop sign but a guideline, steering you towards greater heights of success. Let's turn those setbacks into comebacks and rise beyond the obstacles that lie in our path.

Historical Successes Born from Failure

History is replete with luminaries and trailblazers whose journeys to success were punctuated by setbacks, failures, and outright rejections. These stories serve as powerful reminders that the road to achievement is often paved with the stones of perseverance and resilience.

Thomas Edison, the prolific inventor behind the electric light bulb, is a quintessential example. Edison's journey to inventing the light bulb was fraught with over 10,000 unsuccessful attempts. Yet, he famously reframed these not as failures but as 10,000 ways that didn't work, each one bringing him closer to the ultimate solution. Edison's persistence in the face of repeated setbacks not only revolutionized the world but also stands as a testament to the power of resilience.

J.K. Rowling, the author of the beloved Harry Potter series, faced numerous rejections before her work captured the imagination of a global audience. Rowling submitted her manuscript to twelve different publishers, each turning her down, before a publisher finally took a chance on her magical world. Her story underscores the importance of believing in one's vision, even when faced with discouragement and disbelief from others.

Steve Jobs, co-founder of Apple, experienced his own significant setbacks, including being ousted from the very company he helped create. Yet, this period of exile led him to other ventures, including the significant success of Pixar, and eventually a triumphant return to Apple. Jobs' journey is a compelling narrative about the necessity of adaptability and the unseen opportunities that setbacks can present.

Walt Disney was once fired from a newspaper because he "lacked imagination and had no good ideas." This early career setback didn't deter him; instead, it propelled him towards creating one of the most iconic entertainment companies in the world. Disney's legacy is a vivid illustration of how early failures can't predict future success and how creativity often thrives in the face of adversity.

These narratives illuminate a common thread: setbacks, failures, and rejections are not the end but rather critical chapters in the larger story of success. Each of these individuals faced obstacles that could have halted their progress, yet they chose to persevere, to learn from their experiences, and to rise above the challenges. Their stories are not just tales of personal triumph but also blueprints for turning our own setbacks into stepping stones towards achieving next-level success.

Analyzing Setbacks

The ability to analyze setbacks critically is a cornerstone of turning challenges into opportunities for growth and success. This section delves into a structured approach to dissecting setbacks, enabling you to extract valuable insights and actionable steps from each experience.

Step 1: Objective Assessment

Begin by recounting the setback without attaching emotions or judgments. Describe the situation as if you were an outside observer, focusing on the facts. This detachment helps to prevent emotions from clouding your analysis and allows for a clearer understanding of what transpired.

Step 2: Identify Contributing Factors

Break down the event into its constituent elements to identify potential contributing factors. These could range from personal oversights, external circumstances, lack of resources, or unforeseen complications. Recognizing these elements provides a comprehensive view of the various dimensions of the setback.

Step 3: Acknowledge Your Role

Take ownership of your part in the setback. Acknowledging your role is not about self-blame but about empowering yourself to recognize areas for personal growth and improvement. This step is crucial for fostering a sense of control and agency over your journey.

Step 4: Gather External Perspectives

Sometimes, our own biases can obscure the complete picture. Seeking feedback from trusted mentors, peers, or colleagues can provide new insights and help you see aspects of the situation you might have missed. This external input can be invaluable in broadening your understanding.

Step 5: Extract Lessons

With a comprehensive understanding of the setback, identify the key lessons it offers. These could be about specific skills that need development, insights into decision-making processes, or revelations about personal resilience. Each setback teaches a unique lesson that contributes to your growth.

Step 6: Formulate Actionable Steps

Transform the lessons learned into actionable steps. These could involve acquiring new skills, adjusting your strategies, enhancing your decision-making processes, or implementing safeguards against similar setbacks in the future. Actionable steps convert the theoretical lessons into practical applications, closing the loop on the learning process.

Step 7: Document and Reflect

Maintain a journal or a record of setbacks, analyses, and the ensuing action plans. This documentation serves as a reference for future challenges and a testament to your growth over time. Periodic reflection on past setbacks and the journey since then can be a powerful motivator and a source of valuable insights.

Step 8: Release and Move Forward

Finally, having analyzed the setback and extracted the lessons, release any lingering emotions associated with the event. Embracing a forward-looking mindset is essential for applying the lessons learned and approaching new opportunities with confidence and clarity.

Analyzing setbacks in this structured manner transforms them from mere obstacles into rich sources of insight and learning. By dissecting and understanding each setback, you equip yourself with the knowledge and skills to navigate future challenges more adeptly, turning potential stumbling blocks into stepping stones towards success.

The Role of Resilience

Resilience is the bedrock upon which the ability to transform setbacks into success is built. It is not just about bouncing back from challenges; it's about growing stronger and more adept in the face of adversity. This section explores the pivotal role of resilience in navigating life's inevitable obstacles and how to cultivate it within yourself.

Cultivating a Resilient Mindset

1. **Embrace a Growth Mindset**: Resilient individuals see challenges as opportunities to grow and learn. Cultivating a growth mindset involves shifting from a perspective that views abilities as fixed, to one that sees skills and intelligence as qualities that can be developed.

2. **Acceptance**: Accepting that setbacks are a part of life helps in reducing the resistance and negative emotions associated with them. Acceptance allows you to focus on moving forward rather than dwelling on the unchangeable past.

3. **Maintain Perspective**: Keep setbacks in perspective by not allowing them to overshadow your achievements and strengths. This involves recognizing that a setback in one area does not define your worth or predict your future successes.

4. **Build a Support Network**: A robust support network of friends, family, and mentors can provide emotional support, advice, and encouragement. Knowing you're not alone in your journey can bolster your resilience.

5. **Self–Care**: Regular physical activity, adequate rest, healthy eating, and mindfulness practices like meditation can enhance your physical and mental resilience. Taking care of your body and mind equips you better to handle stress and bounce back from setbacks.

Resilience in Action

Resilience is not just about enduring; it's about how you respond to and grow from adversity. It involves:

- **Problem–Solving**: Facing challenges head-on and seeking solutions rather than avoiding problems.

- **Adaptability**: Being flexible in your approaches and willing to adjust your strategies in the face of new information or changing circumstances.

- **Optimism**: Maintaining a positive outlook, focusing on the possibilities and opportunities that lie ahead.

Strengthening Resilience

Building resilience is an ongoing process that involves:

1. **Setting and Achieving Small Goals**: Accomplishing small tasks can boost your confidence and provide a sense of progress, reinforcing your belief in your ability to overcome challenges.

2. **Learning from Past Setbacks**: Reflect on past challenges and the strategies that helped you overcome them. This reflection can provide valuable insights and reinforce your resilience.

3. **Practicing Gratitude**: Focusing on the positive aspects of your life can shift your perspective from what's lacking to what's abundant, fostering resilience.

Resilience is more than just a buffer against adversity; it's a dynamic force that propels you forward, transforming setbacks into stepping stones. By understanding and cultivating resilience, you equip yourself with the inner strength to navigate life's challenges and emerge not just unscathed but enhanced, ready to face the next challenge with confidence and grace.

Learning and Growing from Challenges

Every challenge we face holds the potential for growth and learning. Rather than viewing obstacles as mere hurdles, recognizing them as opportunities can transform our approach to setbacks, leading to personal and professional development. This section delves into how to extract valuable lessons from challenges and use them as catalysts for growth.

Embracing Challenges as Opportunities

The first step in learning from challenges is to shift your perspective. Instead of seeing obstacles as impediments, view them as integral parts of your success journey, each with something valuable to teach. This mindset encourages a proactive approach to learning and growth.

Identifying Learning Opportunities

When faced with a challenge, ask yourself:

- What can this situation teach me?
- Are there skills I need to develop to overcome similar challenges in the future?
- What insights can I gain about my decision-making process or problem-solving approach?

Answering these questions can help pinpoint specific areas for growth and development.

Reflective Practice

Reflection is a powerful tool for learning from challenges. Take time to reflect on both the challenge and your response to it:

- What were the key factors that led to the situation?
- How did I respond, and what was the outcome?
- What would I do differently next time?

Writing down these reflections can enhance learning and provide a reference for future challenges.

Seeking Feedback

Feedback from others can provide new perspectives and insights into how you handle challenges. Seek constructive feedback from mentors, peers, or colleagues who are familiar with the situation. Their observations can offer valuable lessons and alternative strategies.

Applying Lessons to Future Situations

Learning from challenges involves not just identifying lessons but also applying them to future situations. Use what you've learned to inform your actions and decisions moving forward. This application solidifies the learning and turns theoretical insights into practical skills.

Cultivating Resilience

Overcoming challenges and learning from them builds resilience. Each challenge you navigate successfully strengthens your confidence and ability to handle future obstacles, creating a positive feedback loop of learning and growth.

Expanding Your Comfort Zone

Challenges often push us beyond our comfort zones, prompting growth. Embrace these opportunities to expand your boundaries and discover new capabilities. This expansion not only enhances personal development but also opens up new opportunities.

The Role of Mindset

Adopting a growth mindset is crucial for learning from challenges. Believe in your ability to grow and improve through effort and persistence. This mindset fosters a love for learning and a resilience that is essential for great accomplishment.

Learning and growing from challenges is an essential component of the journey to success. By embracing obstacles as opportunities for growth, reflecting on experiences, seeking feedback, and applying lessons learned, you can turn every challenge into a stepping stone towards achieving your goals. Remember, it's not the obstacles we face that define us, but how we grow from them.

Action Plans for Recovery

After analyzing setbacks and extracting valuable lessons, the next crucial step is to create actionable plans for recovery. This section focuses on developing structured, strategic plans to bounce back from challenges, ensuring that every setback becomes a setup for a future comeback.

Setting Clear Recovery Goals

Begin by defining clear, specific goals for your recovery. These goals should address both the immediate steps needed to overcome the setback and the longer-term objectives for personal or professional growth. Ensure these goals are realistic, achievable, and aligned with your broader vision of success.

Developing a Step-by-Step Plan

Break down your recovery goals into manageable, actionable steps. Each step should be clear and concrete, with defined timelines and success criteria. This breakdown transforms the daunting task of recovery into a series of achievable actions, making the process more manageable and less overwhelming.

Identifying Resources and Support

Determine what resources, tools, and support you'll need for your recovery plan. This might include seeking advice from mentors, leveraging educational resources to build skills, or utilizing tools and technologies that facilitate your goals. Additionally, identify individuals in your support network who can provide encouragement and accountability.

Prioritizing Actions Based on Impact

Prioritize your recovery steps based on their potential impact and urgency. Focus first on actions that will have the most significant positive effect on your recovery and contribute to your momentum. This prioritization ensures that your efforts are directed most effectively towards your recovery goals.

Incorporating Flexibility

While it's important to have a structured plan, flexibility is key. Be prepared to adjust your plan as you progress, incorporating new insights and adapting to changing circumstances. This adaptability ensures that your plan remains relevant and effective, even as situations evolve.

Maintaining a Positive Outlook

Throughout the recovery process, maintain a positive, forward-looking attitude. Focus on the opportunities for growth and learning that the setback has provided, and remain confident in your ability to overcome challenges.

Documenting the Journey

Keep a detailed record of your recovery journey, including the challenges faced, actions taken, lessons learned, and progress made. This documentation can serve as a valuable resource for future challenges, providing insights and strategies that have proven effective.

Developing and implementing an action plan for recovery is a proactive step towards turning setbacks into successes. By setting clear goals, prioritizing actions, and maintaining flexibility and a positive outlook, you can navigate the path to recovery with confidence and resilience. Remember, the goal of recovery is not just to return to where you were before the setback but to emerge stronger, wiser, and better equipped for the challenges ahead.

Maintaining Motivation

Navigating through setbacks and working towards recovery can be a long and challenging process. Keeping your motivation high is crucial for sustaining effort and ensuring progress. This section offers strategies to help maintain motivation, even when the going gets tough.

Reconnect with Your Why

Remind yourself of the reasons behind your goals. Reconnecting with your core motivations can reignite your passion and drive. Whether it's personal fulfillment, the desire to make a difference, or a specific achievement you're aiming for, keeping your "why" at the forefront can provide the necessary push to keep moving forward.

Set Small, Achievable Goals

Breaking down larger objectives into smaller, manageable goals can prevent feelings of overwhelm and provide a clear path forward. Each small achievement builds momentum and reinforces your belief in your ability to succeed, keeping motivation levels high.

Visualize Success

Regularly visualize your success, imagining the fulfillment and satisfaction of achieving your goals. Visualization can be a powerful motivator, creating a mental image of the future you're working towards and making it feel more tangible and achievable.

Celebrate Progress

Recognize and celebrate every step of progress, no matter how small. Acknowledging your achievements reinforces positive behavior and keeps motivation levels high. Celebrations can be simple, such as taking a moment to reflect on what you've accomplished or treating yourself to something you enjoy.

Seek Inspiration

Look for inspiration in the stories of others who have overcome similar challenges or achieved goals similar to yours. Books, podcasts, documentaries, and even conversations with mentors or peers can provide motivational boosts and valuable insights.

Stay Connected to Your Support Network

Lean on your support network of friends, family, and mentors during challenging times. Sharing your struggles and successes with others can provide emotional support, encouragement, and practical advice to keep you motivated.

Maintain Balance

Ensure you're not burning out by maintaining a balance between work towards your goals and activities that rejuvenate you. Hobbies, exercise, social activities, and relaxation are all important for keeping stress levels manageable and maintaining overall motivation.

Adjust Your Approach as Needed

Be open to adjusting your strategies if you find your motivation waning. Sometimes, a change in approach can renew your energy and enthusiasm for your goals. This could mean setting new goals, trying different tactics, or even taking a step back to reassess your plans.

Use Affirmations and Positive Self-Talk

Positive affirmations and self-talk can counteract doubts and negative thoughts that may dampen motivation. Reinforce your self-belief and resilience with positive statements about your capabilities and your commitment to your goals.

Keep the End in Sight

Finally, always keep the end goal in sight. Remind yourself of what you're working towards and why it's important to you.

Keeping the end in mind can help you push through the tough times and stay motivated on your journey to success.

Maintaining motivation is a dynamic and ongoing process that requires attention and intention. By employing these strategies, you can sustain your drive and enthusiasm, even in the face of challenges, propelling you towards achieving your goals and turning setbacks into success.

Harnessing Setbacks for Greater Success

In concluding our journey through "Beyond Obstacles: Turning Setbacks into Success," we recognize that setbacks are not just barriers but essential elements in the fabric of our success stories. They test our resilience, challenge our resolve, and ultimately, refine our character and capabilities. Embracing the lessons learned from each obstacle, we can transform these experiences into powerful catalysts for growth and achievement.

The stories of Edison, Rowling, Jobs, and Disney remind us that the path to extraordinary success is often littered with obstacles. Yet, it is our response to these challenges that defines our trajectory. By critically analyzing setbacks, cultivating resilience, and learning from each challenge, we can not only overcome these obstacles but also use them as stepping stones to reach new heights of personal and professional fulfillment.

As we move forward, let us carry the insights and strategies outlined in this chapter as tools in our arsenal. Let's commit to viewing setbacks not as final verdicts but as opportunities for growth, innovation, and transformation. By doing so, we empower ourselves to navigate the complexities of life and career with agility and grace, continually evolving and advancing towards our most ambitious goals.

Remember, every setback is a setup for a comeback. With the right mindset and actions, we can turn our obstacles into avenues of success, charting a course that goes beyond mere recovery to achieving greatness. Herein lies the true essence of turning setbacks into success.

Chapter 12

Your Next Level – Reflecting and Moving Forward

As we reach the conclusion of our journey together through the pages of this book, it's time to pause and reflect on the ground we've covered, the insights gained, and the challenges overcome. The Epilogue, "Your Next Level – Reflecting and Moving Forward," is not merely a closing note but a launching pad into your future—a future you are now better equipped to shape with intention, wisdom, and an empowered sense of purpose.

This chapter is an invitation to take a moment to appreciate your growth, to acknowledge the shifts in your mindset, and to set your sights on the horizons yet to be explored. It's about recognizing that while this book might end, your journey of personal and professional development is an ongoing adventure, one that continually asks you to rise to your next level of success.

As you stand at this pivotal point, ready to turn the page to the next chapter of your life, let's reflect on the essential lessons that have prepared you for what lies ahead and contemplate the endless possibilities that your future holds.

Reflection on the Journey

As you find yourself at this reflective juncture, take a moment to look back on the path you've traversed since beginning this book. Each chapter was designed as a stepping stone, not just to impart knowledge, but to provoke thought, inspire action, and foster a deeper understanding of what it means to live a life aligned with your definitions of success.

Reflect on the initial exercises in defining success and setting goals. How have your definitions evolved? Have your goals shifted as you delved deeper into understanding what truly matters to you? It's natural for our visions of success to morph as we grow and gain new insights. Embrace these changes as signs of your evolving perspective and personal growth.

Consider the strategies and habits you've adopted along the way. Which ones have become integral to your daily routine, and how have they impacted your progress towards your goals? Acknowledge the discipline it took to integrate these new habits into your life and the strength you found in yourself to stick with them, even when it was challenging.

Think back to the moments of discovery and realization, the times when something clicked, and you saw your situation, a problem, or even yourself in a new light. These moments of clarity are invaluable, illuminating the path forward and empowering you to make informed decisions.

Reflect, too, on the challenges and setbacks you encountered. These, as much as the victories, are integral to your journey. Each obstacle was an opportunity to learn resilience, to practice adaptability, and to reaffirm your commitment to your goals. How did you navigate these challenges, and what did they teach you about your resourcefulness and determination?

As you ponder your journey, also consider the relationships and connections you've nurtured or strengthened along the way. Success is seldom a solo endeavor; it's enriched and supported by the people we share our journey with. How have these relationships impacted your journey, and how have you contributed to the growth and success of others?

This reflection is not just a look back but a grounding exercise, connecting you with the depth of your experiences and the breadth of your growth. It's a celebration of where you've been and an acknowledgment of the foundation you've built for where you're going next.

Celebrating Achievements

In the pursuit of success, it's easy to keep our eyes fixed on the horizon, always focusing on the next goal or challenge. However, taking the time to celebrate your achievements, both big and small, is crucial for maintaining motivation and acknowledging your hard work and progress.

Celebration is an act of gratitude and recognition. It's a way to honor the effort you've invested, the obstacles you've overcome, and the milestones you've reached. These moments of celebration create memories and markers along your journey, infusing your path with joy and a sense of accomplishment.

Begin by acknowledging the steps you've taken since embarking on this journey. Whether it's a newfound understanding of your financial landscape, a healthier lifestyle, improved time management, or deeper, more meaningful relationships, each achievement deserves recognition. Celebrate the shifts in your mindset that have led to these tangible outcomes, for they are indicative of your internal growth.

Don't overlook the small victories. The daily discipline of adhering to your habits, the courage to take action even when faced with uncertainty, and the resilience to bounce back from setbacks are all achievements worthy of celebration. These are the building blocks of your larger successes and recognizing them reinforces their value.

Share your achievements with those who have supported you along the way. Celebrating with friends, family, or mentors not only allows you to express gratitude for their support but also strengthens your communal bonds and shared joy in your success.

Find meaningful ways to celebrate that resonate with you personally. It might be something as simple as taking a moment of quiet reflection to savor the achievement, or it could involve a more tangible reward or celebration. The key is to make the act of celebration a deliberate and conscious part of your success journey.

Lastly, let each celebration be a springboard for future aspirations. With every achievement, consider what's next on your path. Use the momentum of your success to propel you forward, setting your sights on new goals with the confidence and wisdom gained from your accomplishments.

Celebrating your achievements keeps the flame of your ambition alive, reminding you of how far you've come and fueling your drive to continue reaching for your next level of success.

Assessing Unmet Goals: Pathways to Progress

In the pursuit of success, it's inevitable that some goals will remain beyond our reach within the expected timeframe, or perhaps elude us altogether. It's crucial to view these unmet goals not as failures, but as rich opportunities for deep learning and strategic realignment. This section is dedicated to navigating the assessment of unrealized goals, offering a structured approach to extract valuable lessons and recalibrate your path forward.

Reflective Analysis

1. **List Unmet Goals:** Start by listing the goals you haven't yet achieved. Approach this task with neutrality, recognizing that every ambitious journey includes some uncharted territories.
2. **Individual Reflection:** Reflect on each goal separately. Consider the efforts you've put forth, the strategies you've employed, and the circumstances surrounding these efforts. It's important to conduct this reflection without self-criticism, understanding that growth often stems from unexpected outcomes.

Deconstructing Barriers

1. **Identify Contributing Factors:** For each goal, identify the factors that played a role in the current outcome. Distinguish between external influences (like changing

market conditions or unforeseen events) and internal factors (such as skill gaps or motivational challenges).
2. **Tools for Insight**: Utilize tools like SWOT analysis (Strengths, Weaknesses, Opportunities, Threats) to systematically evaluate both internal and external elements that impacted your progress.

Contextualizing Challenges

1. **Assess the Environment**: Acknowledge the broader context of your efforts. Were there significant life events or shifts in priority that influenced your journey? Understanding the impact of these changes can provide a more forgiving and realistic perspective on your progress.
2. **Journaling for Perspective**: Maintain a journal to document the ebb and flow of your journey, offering a tangible record that can help contextualize the challenges faced along the way.

Strategic Adjustments

1. **Revise Approaches**: Armed with insights from your reflection and analysis, consider how you might adjust your strategies. This could involve redefining timelines, segmenting goals into more attainable tasks, or acquiring new resources and skills.
2. **Mind Mapping for Planning**: Employ mind mapping to visually reorganize your goals and the revised strategies for achieving them, allowing for a clear, holistic view of your adjusted path.

Recommitment and Release

1. **Evaluate Relevance**: Critically assess whether each unmet goal still aligns with your current values, priorities, and long-term vision. It's okay to let go of goals that no longer serve your path, making space for

objectives that better resonate with your evolving journey.
2. **Renewed Commitment:** For goals that remain pertinent, formally recommit to them. Define a renewed action plan, incorporating the lessons learned and strategies refined through this introspective process.

Building Support Systems

1. **Establish Accountability:** Set up mechanisms for accountability, such as check-ins with a mentor or peer group, to maintain momentum and focus.
2. **Seek Mentorship:** Consider engaging a mentor who can offer guidance, support, and an external perspective on your revised goals and strategies.
3. **Optimize Your Environment:** Make adjustments to your environment to minimize distractions and barriers, creating a conducive space for focused effort towards your goals.

In reassessing unmet goals, the aim is to transform these moments into springboards for further growth, equipped with deeper insights and a refined strategy. This process celebrates your resilience, acknowledges the complexity of the journey, and equips you for continued advancement towards your vision of success. Remember, the journey of success is as much about the landscapes you navigate and the lessons you gather as it is about the destinations you reach.

Growth and Transformation

Embarking on this journey of self-discovery and goal achievement isn't just about checking boxes or reaching a finish line; it's a profound process of personal evolution and transformation. This section is designed to guide you through reflecting on the significant internal shifts you've experienced and how they've sculpted your pathway to success.

Reflecting on Personal Evolution

Your concept of success has likely undergone a remarkable transformation since the start of this journey. Take a moment to consider the following:

- **Mindset Shifts**. Identify specific changes in your mindset, attitudes, and beliefs regarding success. How have these shifts moved you closer to your authentic self and your true aspirations?
- **Resilience and Adaptability**: Reflect on the challenges you've faced and the resilience you've developed in overcoming them. How have these experiences fortified your ability to adapt and grow?

Exploring Expanded Horizons

Growth often leads to the discovery of new paths and opportunities. Consider:

- **New Interests and Avenues**: What new interests or career paths have you explored? How have these contributed to a more comprehensive view of success?
- **Opening of Opportunities**: Acknowledge how your personal growth has led to new opportunities, and use vision boards to visualize and continue attracting these opportunities into your life.

Deepening Connections

The evolution you've undergone has undoubtedly impacted your relationships. Reflect on:

- **Enhanced Relationships**: How has your growth led to deeper, more meaningful connections? Utilize reflective listening and empathy exercises to continue strengthening these relationships.

Embracing Clarity of Purpose

With growth comes a sharper clarity of purpose. Delve into:

- **Purpose-Driven Decisions**: How has a clearer purpose influenced your choices? Employ goal-setting workshops or seminars to align your future goals with this refined purpose.

Stepping into Leadership

Your journey has prepared you to lead and inspire. Reflect on:

- **Leadership Roles**: In what ways have you taken on leadership roles, however big or small? Consider leadership training or mentorship programs to hone these skills further.

Committing to Continuous Growth

Recognize that your journey of transformation doesn't end here. It's a lifelong commitment to learning and evolving. To stay on this path:

- **Lifelong Learning**: Engage in continuous education, whether through formal courses, self-study, or experiential learning, to keep expanding your knowledge and skills.
- **Adaptability Practices**: Regularly challenge yourself to step out of your comfort zone. This could be through travel, learning new skills, or taking on new challenges that broaden your perspective and adaptability.

Your Next Steps

As you reflect on your growth and transformation, consider what your next steps might be. What new goals, dreams, or areas of personal development are calling to you? How can you continue to build on the foundation you've laid through this journey?

This chapter is not just a pause for reflection; it's a launchpad for your continued journey of growth and success. It's an invitation to embrace the ever-evolving nature of your aspirations and to celebrate the person you are becoming with each step forward. Remember, the journey to success is as much about the transformation within as it is about the milestones achieved. Keep charting your course with curiosity, resilience, and an open heart, and there's no limit to the heights you can reach.

Setting New Horizons: Charting Your Ascent

As you reach this significant milestone in your journey, having navigated the terrain of personal and professional growth, the horizon of your future stretches infinitely before you. This moment, rich with achievement and learning, is not an end but a vantage point—the base camp for your next ascent. "Setting New Horizons" invites you to elevate your ambitions, forge new goals, and embrace the boundless opportunities that lie ahead, much like a mountaineer who, upon reaching one peak, sets their sights on the next, higher one.

Envisioning Beyond Success

1. **Expand Your Vision**: Dare to dream beyond your current achievements. Reflect on the aspirations that ignite your passion and resonate with the person you've evolved into. Like identifying a new peak to conquer, envisioning beyond your current success sets the groundwork for future achievements.
2. **Imagine the Possibilities**: Use visualization techniques to imagine your future achievements vividly. Picture yourself conquering these new challenges, celebrating these successes, and the impact they have on your life and others.

Identifying New Goals

1. **Set Elevated Goals:** With a refined understanding of success, articulate new goals that push you to extend your limits. These goals should be ambitious yet anchored in the reality of your newfound capabilities and insights.
2. **Utilize the SMARTER Framework:** Building on the SMART criteria, add 'E' for Exciting and 'R' for Rewarding. Your new goals should not only be specific, measurable, achievable, relevant, and time-bound but also thrilling and fulfilling.

Leveraging Lessons Learned

1. **Apply Past Strategies:** Reflect on the strategies and mindsets that have propelled you thus far. Adapt and scale these approaches to align with your new, loftier goals, ensuring your past successes lay the foundation for future triumphs.
2. **Create a Lessons-Learned Log:** Regularly update a log of key lessons from past experiences. This log will serve as a valuable resource as you encounter new challenges and opportunities.

Navigating Uncertainty with Confidence

1. **Build Resilience:** Strengthen your resilience through continued practice of stress management techniques and a consistent reflection routine, preparing you to face future uncertainties with grace.
2. **Develop Contingency Plans:** For each new goal, brainstorm potential challenges and devise multiple strategies to overcome them. This preparation ensures you can pivot and adapt as needed.

Cultivating a Supportive Network

1. **Network Intentionally**: Seek out and nurture relationships with individuals who align with your new aspirations. Engage with communities, both online and offline, that share your interests and goals.
2. **Establish a Mastermind Group**: Form or join a mastermind group of like-minded individuals focused on growth and achievement. This collective can offer diverse perspectives, accountability, and support.

Embracing Lifelong Learning

1. **Curate a Learning Agenda**: Identify new skills and knowledge areas crucial for your next goals. Design a personal learning agenda with courses, books, and other resources to continuously evolve.
2. **Practice Reflective Learning**: After each new learning experience, take time to reflect on how it applies to your goals and how you can integrate this new knowledge into your actions.

Crafting an Action Plan for New Horizons

1. **Breakdown Goals into Actionable Steps**: Delineate clear, manageable steps for each new goal, assigning deadlines and resources to each task. This breakdown transforms your lofty goals into a navigable pathway.

Maintaining Flexibility Through Reflection

1. **Regular Reflection Sessions**: Dedicate time weekly or monthly to assess your progress towards these new horizons. Adjust your strategies in response to reflections and any new circumstances you encounter.
2. **Celebrate Adaptability**: Recognize and celebrate instances where flexibility and adaptability have led to unexpected successes. These celebrations reinforce the value of being open to change.

Setting new horizons is an affirmation of your commitment to continuous growth, a declaration that the summits you've reached are merely platforms for reaching even greater heights. By thoughtfully planning your next steps, embracing continuous learning, and cultivating resilience and adaptability, you prepare yourself for the endless journey of success. Each new peak attained offers not just a view but a vision of higher peaks to conquer, each more challenging and rewarding than the last.

Building a Support System: Your Success Network

Embarking on your journey to next-level success is not a solo expedition. The strength of your support system—comprising mentors, peers, family, and community—plays a pivotal role in navigating the complexities of your path. This section offers concrete steps and considerations for cultivating a network that not only supports but also enriches your journey.

Recognizing the Value of Community

Understand that the journey to success is a collective effort. The diversity within your support system brings a wealth of perspectives, advice, and encouragement essential for overcoming obstacles and celebrating milestones.

- **Identify Key Roles**: Reflect on what kind of support you need most—be it guidance, motivation, accountability, or emotional backing. This clarity will help you seek out individuals who can best fulfill these roles.

Seeking Mentors and Role Models

Mentors and role models are beacons of inspiration and knowledge, guiding you through their experiences and insights.

- **Research Potential Mentors**: Look for individuals whose career paths, skills, or achievements align with

your aspirations. Use platforms like LinkedIn to connect and learn more about their journeys.
- **Craft a Genuine Outreach Strategy**: When reaching out, be specific about why you admire them and what you hope to learn. Offer something in return, even if it's just fresh perspectives or enthusiasm.
- **Foster a Reciprocal Relationship**: Engage in regular, meaningful exchanges. Share your progress, ask insightful questions, and be open to providing assistance in return, fostering a mutually beneficial relationship.

Cultivating Peer Networks

Peers walking a similar path can become collaborators, motivators, and close confidantes.

- **Engage in Communities**: Join professional groups, online forums, or local clubs that align with your interests and goals. Platforms like Meetup or industry-specific associations are great places to start.
- **Initiate Peer Accountability Groups**: Form or join small groups with shared goals for regular check-ins. These groups can provide motivation, exchange of ideas, and constructive feedback.

Leveraging Family and Close Relationships

The support from family and friends is unmatched, providing a foundation of emotional and practical support.

- **Communicate Your Vision**: Share your aspirations and the significance of their support clearly and openly. This helps set expectations and fosters understanding.
- **Establish Boundaries and Needs**: Clearly define how they can best support you, whether it's through space, time, or encouragement, and be respectful of their boundaries as well.

Creating a Supportive Environment

Your physical and emotional environment should be conducive to growth and productivity.

- **Optimize Your Spaces**: Ensure your living and workspaces are organized and inspire productivity. Small changes like decluttering or adding motivational elements can make a big difference.
- **Set Healthy Boundaries**: Learn to say no to commitments that detract from your goals. Prioritize activities and relationships that align with your vision.

Giving Back to Your Support System

A thriving support system is reciprocal. Look for opportunities to support the growth and success of others within your network.

- **Offer Your Skills and Time**: Share your expertise, provide feedback, or volunteer your time in ways that benefit your network.
- **Celebrate Others' Successes**: Actively celebrate the achievements of your peers, mentors, and supporters, fostering a positive and encouraging community.

Nurturing Your Support System

Invest time and effort in maintaining and deepening the connections within your support network.

- **Regular Check-ins**: Schedule periodic updates or catch-ups with your mentors, peers, and supporters to share progress and solicit feedback.
- **Express Gratitude**: Regularly acknowledge and thank your network for their support. Personal notes, messages, or gestures of appreciation can strengthen these bonds.

Building and nurturing a robust support system is a dynamic process that evolves alongside your journey. By actively engaging with, contributing to, and appreciating your network, you create a shared path to success, marked by collective growth, resilience, and achievement.

Giving Back: Extending Your Success

Achieving personal and professional success opens up a world of opportunities not just for further self-advancement but for contributing to the broader community. The act of giving back is a powerful way to use your success for a greater purpose, enriching both your own life and the lives of others. Here's how to integrate altruism into your journey, creating a cycle of generosity that fosters growth, fulfillment, and lasting impact.

Understanding the Ripple Effect of Generosity

Every act of kindness, no matter how small, has the potential to create waves of positive change. Whether you're mentoring a young professional, volunteering your time, or contributing resources to a cause, your actions can inspire others to pay it forward, creating a ripple effect of generosity. Reflect on the unique gifts you have—skills, knowledge, resources—and how they can serve as tools for positive change in your community and beyond.

Practical Steps to Weaving Altruism into Your Life

1. **Identify Your Passions**: Start by pinpointing causes or issues that resonate deeply with you. Your efforts will be most impactful and fulfilling when aligned with your personal values and interests.
2. **Assess Your Resources**: Consider what you can offer. This might be your time, expertise, financial support, or even your network. Recognize that giving back doesn't always require grand gestures; even small contributions can make a significant difference.

3. **Find Your Avenue for Impact**: Research organizations, initiatives, and community projects where your contributions could be most beneficial. Look for opportunities that match your skills and interests, ensuring a meaningful and rewarding experience.
4. **Set Altruistic Goals**: Just as you set personal and professional goals, define clear, achievable objectives for your philanthropic efforts. These could range from volunteering a certain number of hours each month to launching a community project.
5. **Incorporate Giving into Your Routine**: Make altruism a regular part of your life by scheduling time for volunteer work, mentorship sessions, or other giving activities, just as you would for any other important commitment.

The Personal Growth Benefits of Giving

Altruism not only impacts the lives of recipients but also fosters your own personal development. Engaging in acts of generosity can enhance your well-being, expand your worldview, and imbue your life with a deeper sense of purpose. It challenges you to grow in empathy, understanding, and compassion, enriching your character and life experience.

Building a Legacy Through Generosity

Consider the legacy you aim to build and how acts of giving fit within that vision. Your legacy is defined not only by your achievements but by the positive influence you've had on the world around you. Envision the long-term impact you hope to create and how your current actions can lay the groundwork for a legacy of generosity and positive change.

Encouraging a Giving Mindset in Others

Lead by example and foster a culture of giving within your circles. Share your experiences, organize group volunteer opportunities, and highlight the joy and fulfillment that come from giving back. By demonstrating the value of altruism, you can inspire others to embark on their own journeys of giving, amplifying the collective impact of your efforts.

Remember, you don't need to wait until you've reached the pinnacle of success to start giving back. Regardless of where you are on your journey, there's always something valuable you can offer. Embrace the power of giving to not only enrich the lives of others but to add depth and meaning to your own path to success.

Final Words of Encouragement

As we conclude this journey together through the pages of this book, I extend these final words not as a farewell, but as a vibrant rally cry to propel you into the boundless realms of your potential. The path to next-level success is both a map and a compass, uniquely yours, guiding you towards horizons only you can envision.

Your path to success is as individual as your fingerprint, a bespoke voyage through the landscapes of your aspirations. Trust in this journey, even when the path veers or the peaks seem shrouded in mist. Within every twist lies a lesson; within every ascent, a victory awaiting your claim.

Acknowledge the distance traversed from where you first set foot on this path. You've blossomed in knowledge, skill, wisdom, and character. This growth, your most authentic success, lays the groundwork for all future endeavors.

Your vision is the beacon that illuminates your way. Hold it close, yet allow its evolution as you grow. Flexibility and adaptability in your aspirations are marks of wisdom, not compromise.

Let the fire of your passion fuel your journey through challenges. Remember the spark that set you on this path and let that unwavering 'why' drive you through any storm.

May kindness and integrity be the twin stars guiding your leadership. Success at the expense of others rings hollow. True fulfillment flows from a life that uplifts and inspires, anchored in respect and compassion.

As you step beyond the confines of this book into the next chapter of your life, move forward with the confidence that you are more than ready to meet the world, to mold it, and to marvel at it. Your journey of success continues, ever more thrilling and fulfilling.

* * *

Here's to your unwavering success, boundless growth, and enduring happiness. To the future—may it be ever bright, ever yours. Onward and upward, to the next level and beyond!

Chapter 13

Voices of Experience

This chapter unfolds as a tapestry woven with the wisdom, guidance, and insights of those who have journeyed ahead of you on life's winding path. These individuals, once at the starting line much like yourself, have navigated the vast expanse of their careers, through peaks of success and valleys of challenge, to offer you the essence of their lived experiences.

Contained within these pages are diverse voices—each sharing their unique slices of wisdom, heartfelt stories, and actionable strategies they wish to impart to you, the emerging force ready to make your mark. From the nuanced realities of achieving success to the resilience required in the pursuit of your passions, their narratives aim to illuminate your path forward.

Envision this chapter as a fireside chat with a trusted advisor, a compendium of lessons from those who have artfully steered their ships through both still and stormy waters, eager to equip you with the knowledge to navigate your own course. So, settle in, perhaps with a warm beverage in hand, and let these voices of experience be your guide.

* * *

ALONSO SARAVIA
Actor/Performer

"My personal definition of success is doing what makes you happy. Do what puts a smile on your face at the end of the day because no one else is going to live your life. If your job doesn't feel like work, then I consider that success."

My advice and guidance are: "Ask questions. Don't be afraid to fail. When you fail you succeed because now you know what not to do. Don't stop becoming teachable, always humble yourself because there will always be opportunities for you to grow & gain knowledge. Another keep factor is don't be afraid to put yourself out. Network as much as you can. Being shy will get you nowhere in life. Step out of your comfort zone & watch how much more you can do & how much more confidence you will have."

What I wish I had known when I was younger is to "love yourself above all else. When I got older, I realized that some of the biggest opportunities I got were simply because I was being myself. I used to be bullied in High School for the way I dressed & because of my freckles. Now I get paid because of my look & some of my biggest opportunities have come to me because of my personality & because of my character."

* * *

AMI MOLINELLI
Musician, percussionist, Founder and Executive Director
Music Is First!
MFA California Institute of the Arts, BS, UC Berkeley

"The path I ended up taking was not a path typical for my family, background or gender. Do not deny yourself the aspirations and interests that genuinely motivate you and take time to explore what those are. My path has had as many failures as successes and what has always been the best path is to gravitate to those who support and encourage me. It took me a long time to find a mentorship. And I believe if you find a true mentor, honor that connection as it's not as easy to find as you may think."

* * *

ANDY LIN
Chief Executive Officer
Provoke Solutions
BA in Biochemistry, UC Berkeley

"Success is a collection of habits that provide you the lifelong experience of learning and achieving milestones that continuously enhance your ability to positively impact yourself, your family, your team and the wider community."

My advice and guidance include: "1) Be impatient with taking action to learn but be extra patient with seeing or feeling the results; 2) Talent determines where you start, but discipline and commitment gets you to success; 3) Be humble and learn from those who have traveled the road that you are about to embark on; a good coach or mentor will help you accelerate towards success; 4) There are no shortcuts or workarounds to hard work; those who truly "work smart" learned from and never stop "working hard"; and 5) Lead with "how can I add value" and success will come finding you."

What I wish I had known when I was younger is to: "1) Focus on what you have control over and shut out the noise; 2) Success treats every win and loss as a lesson; failure is when you stop trying or become complacent/rest on your laurels; and 3) Every successful person was underpaid and overworked when they started to level up."

* * *

CARL ILG
Son, Brother, Friend, Husband, Father, Grandfather
Financial Advisor
BS in Business and Psychology, UC Santa Barbara

"When I turned 17 years old, my dad gave me a square plaque which had a silhouette of a person sitting on a big rock, overlooking the ocean as the orange sunset filled the sky and a few seagulls flew by. On the plaque were the printed inspirational words: "Trust in God, Believe in Yourself, Dare to Dream". I hung the plaque on my bedroom wall and each morning as I rose from bed, I read the plaque to inspire me each day. That plaque still hangs on the wall above my home office desk. I still read it, and live it, every single day.

When I began my professional career, I was part of a group of young men and women who were called "The Leaders of Tomorrow Today". We were all very motivated to do our very best for the company we worked for, for the people we worked with, for the people we served, and for the world we lived in. Together, we committed ourselves to "Work Hard, Do Good, Have Fun" and we did. We worked very hard at our jobs; we gave our time and money to charities; we shared meals, baseball games, and good and bad times with each other as friends do.

And lastly, I say The Serenity Prayer each morning and night: *God grant me the serenity to accept the things I cannot change, the courage to change the things I can, and the wisdom to know the difference."*

* * *

CHRIS LEWIS
Fintech Investor and Adviser
BA in English and American Literature, UC San Diego

"Regardless of what industry you end up working in or what area of professional expertise you develop, it is almost a given that you will be working with people. This may seem like stating the obvious, but an absolute key to your success will be how you get along with others, how you work within a team, and how you instill confidence in colleagues, the boss, industry peers, business partners and clients alike that you are reliable and trustworthy. People naturally gravitate to other people who they believe they can trust. This has been true, in my experience, in both my professional as well as personal life.

Also, whatever you end up doing, establish good relationships early on and do not be afraid to connect with people who you think you would not normally get along with. You will need all the help you can get during your professional journey, so don't limit yourself to only those who you are comfortable with.

Finally, always be truthful but also always be sure before you say anything, before you release that email, or before you text someone, that you are sure that that's the message you want to deliver. Once the arrow is released, as they say, you cannot control where it lands or what impact it may have. Take that pause, whether you are in the office or at home, before you share any of your thoughts with anyone to ensure it represents who you really are, and not just the emotion of the moment."

* * *

DEBORAH WATSON
Transportation and Distribution Manager
MBA and BA in Business Administration

"For me, success is all about living a life grounded in integrity and love, inspired by the teachings and wisdom of my Lord and Savior, Jesus Christ. I always advocate for following your heart and staying true to yourself. Think about the legacy you want to leave behind and the lessons you want others to learn from your journey.

If I could go back and chat with my younger self, I'd emphasize the importance of trusting the process. Nothing worthwhile comes easy, but it's the journey that truly shapes us and provides invaluable and meaningful experiences."

* * *

LATONYA PYE
Career and Community Leadership Coordinator
Leadership Public Schools
MA and BA in Psychology

"Success is something that looks different for everyone, so enjoy the journey and know that hard work and strong relationships go a long way. My hope is that you all find something that you are passionate and excited about! Working at Leadership Public Schools has brought so much joy in my life because I am able to work with students from a community that means a lot to me. Having that intrinsic motivation and love for what I do carries me through when things feel hard. Stay the course, keep working hard, and know that being the first one to do break barriers is tough, but so worth it!"

* * *

JEFF SKINNER
Chief Executive Officer
LFG Security Consulting
MBA and BS Business Administration

My personal definition or formula for success

"Success is personal. Success is earned. Success is something realized and is a byproduct of ambition, awareness, commitment, accountability, and resilience. In some cases, it's not immediately obvious, in others it's a fleeting moment. From whichever aspect of life, you're measuring success; its meaning comes from your fulfillment.

It's ok to be selfish with your definition of success because you'll realize that, by doing so, you'll be bringing those around you along for the ride. This does not mean that your individual performance, outcome, or result is more important than that of the team. In fact, it's the exact opposite.

Consistently showing up and doing the hard work, while necessary, are table stakes to becoming above average. Most people with a sense of pride or accountability can pull that off. What separates the elite performers is their ability to fight through failure, fatigue, and discomfort.

There's not an elite athlete in any sport that got to that level by solely showing up for scheduled practice sessions. Talent alone isn't enough. It's those that are up before the sun, the first to arrive at practice and the last to leave, putting in the time when no one else is around to see it. They're on a journey to see how far they take it and if they're fortunate enough to get to the top, they're selfish enough to want to do it again.

While it's not possible for all of us to be elite athletes, we can all be elite in whatever journey we take. It starts with expecting great things from yourself, finding the right influences, and remaining forward-looking."

What would I tell my younger self?

"You're in control. You own your future. Stop worrying about what others may think. Stop doing things that you don't want to do. Eliminate toxic people from your world. Figure out what matters to you and pursue it with passion. Don't you dare let anyone tell you can't. Don't take advice (or criticism) from someone you don't respect. Don't wait until they say (or you think) you're ready. It's ok to be afraid. It's ok to ask for help. It's ok to feel like an idiot. Everyone does something stupid, try not to do it again. Excuses are lame, no one cares. The right people notice the right things, your initiative will show itself without self-promotion. You define yourself when no one is watching. The world is full of people who don't follow-up, don't be one of them. Where you came from does not determine where you end up. Listen more than you talk. Protect and maintain the relationships that matter most. Cynicism is a disease, fight hard to fend it off. People will remember how respectful you are and how well you treated them. Accumulating success and achievement is meaningless if you don't share it."

* * *

JULIE BRYANT
Teacher
MA and BA in Education, University of San Francisco

"Success, in my eyes, is a harmonious blend of passion, purpose, and perseverance. It's about setting realistic goals, fostering resilience, and turning setbacks into learning opportunities. Beyond personal achievements, true success encompasses forging deep connections and making a positive impact on those around us."

"To carve your path to success, commit to lifelong learning, embrace adaptability, and surround yourself with supportive and uplifting influences. Take calculated risks, remain humble, and craft your own definition of success. Practice patience, recognize and celebrate your progress, and remember, success is more about the journey you undertake than the final destination you reach."

* * *

KEVIN MOOS
Business Executive and former CEO
BS, Sanford University

"As you embark on the next chapter of your life, remember that true success is not measured solely by personal achievements, but by the impact you have on others. My formula for success is rooted in empowering those around me to reach their full potential. I've learned that by providing opportunities and guidance, we can create pathways to success for others, fostering a community where everyone thrives.

My advice is to never underestimate the power of human connection. While technology may evolve and systems may change, it is the relationships we build and the empathy we show that truly make a difference. Take the time to listen to others, understand their perspectives, and support them in their endeavors. In doing so, you'll not only create a positive environment for collaboration but also cultivate a network of advocates who will champion your own growth and success.

Reflecting on my own journey, I wish I had known earlier the importance of embracing every opportunity and approaching life with an open mind. Your path to success may not always be linear, but each experience—whether big or small—has the potential to shape your future in unexpected ways. Don't be afraid to step outside of your comfort zone, learn new skills, and adapt to changing circumstances. Remember, success is not a destination but a continuous journey of growth and discovery.

Remember that success is not measured by what you accomplish for yourself, but by how you uplift and empower those around you. May you continue to inspire and be inspired on your path to greatness."

* * *

KYONDA TRASS
Business Onwer / Lead Esthetician
Sweet Almond Esthetician

"Stay focused and limit distractions. I'd only take advice from people that I'd solicited it from. I'd stick to my morals and beliefs and not associate with anyone that doesn't respect me and my lifestyle choices. Keep a strong watch on the care and keeping of your mind. Your mind is what creates your reality and as with any imagination, there are no limits. If you can visualize it, you can attain it. Embrace failure as a great teacher, learn your lessons and try again is appropriate."

* * *

SUSAN GONZALES
Founder & Chief Executive Officer
AIandYou

"'Get comfortable with being uncomfortable' was sage advice many years ago. As women of color in tech, we are often the only ones in the room, and it can be very uncomfortable. Yet, our seat at the table can make all the difference in the world. My best advice is to create your own opportunities, whether it is convincing a company to create a position for you or starting your own nonprofit as a labor of love – chart your own path. Most of my work experience in corporate America in tech and telecom came from my own action of reaching out to senior people in the company or asking my network for an introduction. I reached out and asked for 30 minutes of their time and convinced them I would add value to the organization. It worked every time. Chart your own path! It is possible."

* * *

SUZANNE BORUSHOK
Sales Executive
BA in Social Ecology, UC Irvine

"Success, to me, is the harmonious blend of passion, perseverance, and continuous learning. It involves setting clear goals, staying adaptable to change, and cultivating resilience in the face of challenges. My formula for success revolves around embracing failures as opportunities to learn, maintaining a positive mindset, and fostering meaningful connections. To achieve success, one must define their values, consistently work towards their objectives, and prioritize self-care to sustain long-term growth. Looking back, I wish I had known the importance of balance and the significance of enjoying the journey rather than fixating solely on the destination. My advice to my younger self would be to trust the process, be patient, and appreciate the lessons embedded in every experience."

* * *

TAYLOR MOXON
Career and Community Leadership Coordinator
Leadership Public Schools
BA, UC Santa Cruz

"Success is not based solely on achievements but also on how your work and accomplishments make you feel. No one enjoys their work all the time, but I encourage you to find work that you enjoy doing most of the time. Often, we have an idea in our head of what a job will be like, and the reality of the job is much different. You won't know until you experience it so try to gain a variety of work experiences in the career fields that interest you. This is particularly important while you're young because it becomes much harder to try out different jobs as you get older. This means try out different internships, classes, summer programs, and other opportunities with the goal of finding a career field where you enjoy the work you do daily."

* * *

www.ingramcontent.com/pod-product-compliance
Lightning Source LLC
Chambersburg PA
CBHW070757020526
44118CB00036B/1825